SUPERWRITE

Alphabetic Writing System

Office Professional

1

Second Edition

A. James Lemaster, Ed. D.
Professor Emeritus
Rider University
Lawrenceville, New Jersey

John Baer, Ph. D.
Associate Professor of
Education
Rider University
Lawrenceville, New Jersey

VISIT US ON THE INTERNET
www.swep.com

South-Western Educational Publishing
an International Thomson Publishing company I(T)P®
www.thomson.com

Cincinnati • Albany, NY • Belmont, CA • Bonn • Boston • Detroit • Johannesburg • London • Madrid
Melbourne • Mexico City • New York • Paris • Singapore • Tokyo • Toronto • Washington

Credits:
Team Leader: Karen Schmohe
Project Manager: Dr. Inell Bolls
Production Coordinator: Jane Congdon
Editor: Carol Spencer
Marketing Manager: Tim Gleim
Art & Design Coordinator: Darren Wright
Cover Design: Creech Creative
Script Artist: Anna Durham
Production Services: Cover to Cover Publishing

Copyright © 1999
by SOUTH-WESTERN EDUCATIONAL PUBLISHING
Cincinnati, Ohio

I(T)P®
International Thomson Publishing
South-Western Educational Publishing is a division of International Thomson Publishing, Inc.
The ITP logo is a registered trademark used herein under license.

ISBN: 0-538-72160-X

2 3 4 5 6 7 8 9 D 03 02 01 00 99
Printed in the United States of America

Library of Congress Cataloging-in-Publication Data

Lemaster, A. James,
    SuperWrite : alphabetic writing system : office professional / A.
James Lemaster, John Baer. -- 2nd ed.
        p.   cm.
    ISBN 0-538-72160-X (v. 1), -- ISBN 0-538-72163-4 (v. 2)
    1. Shorthand--SuperWrite. I. Baer, John, 1948-   . II. Title.
Z56.2.S94L45   1998
653'.42--dc21
                                          98-34130
                                            CIP

PREFACE

SUPERWRITE, VOLUME ONE, SECOND EDITION

The second edition retains the theory principles and theory lessons from the first edition. A number of changes have been made in the Keyboarding Style exercises to bring the material up to date and to make it compatible with the newest word processing programs. Eight new lessons entitled Toward Personal Success have been added to the text.

THE SYSTEM

SuperWrite is an abbreviated writing system based primarily on longhand and secondarily on phonetics. It is a quick, easy-to-learn writing system that is easy to write and read. *Webster's Ninth New Collegiate Dictionary* was the reference source for pronunciations.

SuperWrite does not require memorizing a new alphabet or changing one's normal writing style. There are no special symbols. To make learning easy, all 26 longhand letters are used.

SuperWrite is not designed for extremely high writing speeds. However, students should be able to increase their writing speed significantly. Many will be able to double their writing speed, and others will be able to do even better.

SuperWrite follows the principle of abbreviating from the longhand spelling. Long vowels are written to aid in legibility. Short vowels within words are not written. Initial and final vowels are written. If a letter or letters are pronounced as an unrelated sound, the phonetic letter is written. For example, *phone* is written *f-o-n* and *few* is written *f-u.*

There are 75 special abbreviations standing for 98 words in *SuperWrite.* These are short and highly suggestive forms for frequently used words. For example, the abbreviation for the word *for* is *f.*

There are 14 word beginnings and 9 word endings. For example, the word beginning *be-* is written *b,* and the word ending *-ment* is written *m.*

PURPOSES

SuperWrite is designed for three purposes:

1. To assist business executives and students to increase their speed in making legible notes.

2. To supply a fast and legible note-taking system than can be learned quickly for use in the office by information-processing personnel.

3. To give the entering, prospective, or returning administrative assistant the ability to take notes from dictation and transcribe them in a usable form.

TEXT DESIGN

Volume One is designed to be used at the secondary, college, and adult levels. It begins with simple abbreviating principles and builds lesson by lesson to more advanced principles. The text presents the principles in the easiest form possible.

Volume One contains 40 *SuperWrite* lessons and 8 lessons on personal success. Part 1, Lessons 1 through 20, covers Principles of Construction. Part 2, Lessons 21 through 40, covers Beginning Transcription. A lesson may be presented in one class period, or it may be divided and presented in two class periods. For classes that meet for several hours once or twice per week, two or three lessons may be taught in one extended class period. Students should spend a comparable amount of time out of class reading and writing the lesson.

PART 1

PRINCIPLES OF CONSTRUCTION

A typical theory lesson in Part 1 contains several abbreviating principles and a number of words for which there are special abbreviations. Abbreviating principles are introduced through a "read, spell, write" exercise in which a word is shown first in type, then as it is spelled in *SuperWrite*, and finally as it is written in *SuperWrite*. The students are then asked to copy the words in *SuperWrite* in their notebooks. Words for which there are special abbreviations are shown in type and then in *SuperWrite*. The students are asked to copy the *SuperWrite* for each word in their notebooks.

Each numbered lesson in Part 1 contains an Application section consisting of sentences, letters, or memorandums that apply the principles. A key to give the students immediate reinforcement follows the Application. The students are asked to read and copy the Application of each lesson.

Beginning with Lesson 6, each numbered lesson contains a supplemental document entitled, "A Word to the Wise." These documents may be used for individual reading in or out of class, for extra writing practice, or for testing.

PART 2

BEGINNING TRANSCRIPTION

Part 2 is designed to teach beginning transcription skills as well as to continue speed development. Various lessons contain exercises on keyboarding style, punctuation, spelling, and vocabulary development.

Each numbered lesson in Part 2 begins with a *SuperWrite* review. Abbreviations, word beginnings, word endings, and various other principles are covered. The students are asked to read the review words, referring to the key if necessary. They are then asked to copy the words in their notebooks.

Keyboarding style exercises begin with Lesson 21. There are 14 lessons containing these exercises. They include such items as the format for letters, memorandums, and reports as well as the correct way to key dates, times of day, and amounts of money. The Application emphasizes the keyboarding style element introduced in the current lesson.

Punctuation rules begin in Lesson 21 and are included in 10 lessons. Some of the rules include the use of commas in compound sentences, with items in a series, and with introductory elements. The Application emphasizes the punctuation rule covered in the current lesson.

Beginning with Lesson 22, spelling words are included in each lesson. Many commonly used but often misspelled words are included, 10 in each lesson. The Application consists of business documents that contain the spelling words from the lesson.

Vocabulary development begins with Lesson 26, where 5 vocabulary words are presented. Each lesson thereafter has 5 additional vocabulary words for the students to learn. The vocabulary words are included in the Application.

The Application section of Lessons 21–35 includes four business documents. These documents contain illustrations of the *SuperWrite* principles, the punctuation rules, the spelling words, and the vocabulary terms. Document 1 is a Timed Reading. The students may time their individual reading rate and compare the rate with a suggested goal. Document 2 is a Speed Builder. The instructor may dictate the document on a speed-building plan. Document 4 is a Punctuation Check designed to check student ability to use the punctuation marks taught to that point in the text.

The punctuation marks are included in the first three *SuperWrite* documents in each lesson. Internal punctuation marks are not included in the fourth document, the Punctuation Check. The key to the four documents follows the *SuperWrite*. The fourth key includes the punctuation marks that were omitted from the *SuperWrite* documents, and the reasons for using the punctuation marks are also noted. The students are asked to read and copy all four documents and insert the necessary punctuation in the last document before typing it in the correct format.

Business letters make up the content of the Application of Lessons 21–30. Memorandums are introduced and included along with business letters in Lessons 31–35. Extended business reports make up the content of the Applications of Lessons 36–40.

TOWARD PERSONAL SUCCESS

Volume One contains eight new lessons entitled Toward Personal Success. They are lettered Lesson A through Lesson H; a new lesson is included after each five lessons of *SuperWrite*. The lessons include information on vital topics related to personal success, such as setting goals and improving one's memory. Each lesson also includes discussion questions, activities, and case studies.

WORD COUNTS

The words in the Application exercises are counted in groups of 20. In the sets of sentences in Lessons 1 and 2, the words are quite short, and actual word counts are used. In everyday writing, however, an average word is somewhat longer and contains more than one syllable. Over the years, the 1.4-syllable word has been accepted in business education. Beginning with Lesson 3, the 1.4-syllable count is used. Beginning with Lesson 4, names are included, and salutations are introduced in Lesson 5. Word counts always begin with the first paragraph rather than with the name or salutation.

SUPPLEMENTAL MATERIALS

A comprehensive instructor's manual is available for use with Volume One. The manual contains suggested teaching procedures, supplemental dictation documents, and a key.

A workbook is also available for supplementary practice with Volume One. It includes exercises on the *SuperWrite* lessons as well as the new lessons on personal success. The key to the workbook is included in the instructor's manual. The workbook lessons may be completed in class, or they may be part of the homework assignment.

A dictionary containing over 5,000 words written in *SuperWrite* is also available.

Two sets of tapes containing material from the text and the instructor's manual are available for writing and transcription practice.

A FINAL WORD

SuperWrite is designed to give the administrative assistant, the student, and the executive a way to write quickly with a minimum of learning time. It should be quite beneficial to every person who studies it.

THE AUTHORS

Dr. A. James Lemaster. Dr. Lemaster is professor emeritus of education at Rider University in Lawrenceville, New Jersey. He is the co-author of 25 textbooks, numerous teaching aids, and journal articles. He has served as a speaker and business education consultant throughout the world.

Dr. Lemaster has taught at every secondary and postsecondary level from middle school through graduate school.

Dr. John Baer. Dr. Baer is associate professor of education at Rider University in Lawrenceville, New Jersey. He is the author of two books and more than 20 journal articles and book chapters. He has won national awards both for his research and his teaching.

Dr. Baer has taught at every secondary and postsecondary level from middle school through graduate school.

CONTENTS

LESSON 5

LESSON A

LESSON 6

LESSON 7

LESSON 8

PART 1

PRINCIPLES
OF
CONSTRUCTION

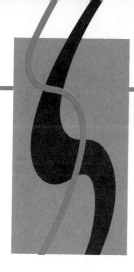

only write long vowels

LESSON 1

PRINCIPLES OF CONSTRUCTION

Silent Letters

● In order to write faster, in *SuperWrite* you will not write silent letters.

In the following words, what letters are silent?

day *da*	see *se*	aid *ad*
save	dough *do*	easy

In the word <u>day</u>, the **y** is silent.

In <u>see</u>, one **e** is silent.

In <u>aid</u>, the **i** is silent.

In <u>save</u>, the **e** is silent.

In <u>dough</u>, the **u**, the **g**, and the **h** are silent.

In <u>easy</u>, the **a** is silent.

The letters that should be written are:

day, **d-a**	see, **s-e**	aid, **a-d**
save, **s-a-v**	dough, **d-o**	easy, **e-s-y**

Read, spell, and then write in your own notebook the following words, omitting any silent letters. Do not use capital letters; capitals will be used later.

Read	Spell	*SuperWrite*
fee	**f-e**	*fe*
say	**s-a**	*sa*

(continued)

3

Read	Spell	SuperWrite
feed	f-e-d	*fed*
pay	p-a	*pa*
prize	p-r-i-z	*priz*
rice	r-i-c	*ric*
daisy	d-a-s-y	*dasy*
phone	f-o-n	*fon*

Notice that in <u>phone</u>, **ph** has the sound of **f** and is written **f**.

Punctuation

● Marks of punctuation are the same as those in longhand.

Abbreviations

There are a number of words in the English language for which there are special abbreviations. In *SuperWrite* you will also use a number of special abbreviations. They are marked with an **A** in the lists. Here is your first group. Practice writing them in your own notebook until you can do so without hesitation.

Words	Abbreviations
you, your (A)	*u*
will (A)	*l*
as, is (A)	*s*

APPLICATION

A number of sentences follow using the principles you have learned. Practice the exercises in the following way.

1. Spell and read each sentence in Set 1. If you have trouble with any word, refer to the key immediately.

2. Write each sentence in Set 1 in your own notebook.

3. Continue the above steps for the remaining sets.

Set 1-1

1. u fe s lo. 2. l u pa u fe? 3. u fe s zero. 4. s u no, my fe s zero. 5. u gam s esy.

Set 1-2

1. s u pony old? 2. my nic pony s old. 3. he s fin. 4. l u se me? 5. s u no, he s lazy.

Set 1-3

1. s u sa, u pa s lo. 2. sav u pa. 3. l u sav u pa? 4. he l sav u pa. 5. s my nam esy? 6. u nam s esy.

Set 1-1

1. /Your fee is low.   **2.** Will you pay your fee?   **3.** Your fee is zero.   **4.** As you know, my fee is zero./   **5.** Your game is easy. (24)

Set 1-2

1. /Is your pony old?   **2.** My nice pony is old.   **3.** He is fine.   **4.** Will you see me?   **5.** As you know, he/is lazy. (22)

Set 1-3

1. /As you say, your pay is low.   **2.** Save your pay.   **3.** Will you save your pay?   **4.** He will save your pay./   **5.** Is my name easy?   **6.** Your name is easy. (28)

LESSON 2

PRINCIPLES OF CONSTRUCTION

The Letter T

● In order to speed your writing, do not cross **t's.**

t $\mathcal{l}$ tea $\mathcal{le}$ eat $\mathcal{el}$

Read	Spell	SuperWrite
tea	**t-e**	$\mathcal{le}$
eat	**e-t**	$\mathcal{el}$
feet	**f-e-t**	$\mathcal{fel}$
treat	**t-r-e-t**	$\mathcal{lrel}$
try	**t-r-y**	$\mathcal{lry}$

Long Vowels

● In *SuperWrite* we will consider a long vowel one that is pronounced in a word similar to how it is pronounced alone. For example:

a as in <u>ate</u>   **e** as in <u>eat</u> and <u>near</u>   **i** as in <u>light</u>

o as in <u>vote</u>   **u** as in <u>hue</u>

In addition, we will consider the **u** in <u>rule</u>, the **y** in <u>try</u>, and the **y** in <u>easy</u> to be long.

ate	near	light	easy
vote	hue	try	

● Write long vowel sounds.

Read, spell, and then write the following words in your own notebook.

Read	Spell	SuperWrite
date	d-a-t	*dat*
feed	f-e-d	*fed*
here	h-e-r	*her*
die	d-i	*di*
roll	r-o-l	*rol*
true	t-r-u	*tru*
fly	f-l-y	*fly*
lazy	l-a-z-y	*lazy*

Abbreviations

Here is the next set of abbreviations. Write them in your own notebook.

Words	Abbreviations
are, or, our (A)	*r*
can (A)	*c*
for (A)	*f*

APPLICATION

Here are several more sets of sentences. Practice as you did in Lesson 1. Read the sentences, referring to the key if you have trouble. Then copy the *SuperWrite* in your notebook.

1. s I tol d u, r lir s lo.   2. c u gag r lir?   3. l u try?   4. I c gag u lir f u, r u c gag u on lir.   5. r u ril?   6. u r lazy.

1. I c pla r, nic lun f u.   2. r lun s esy.   3. l u sta, r l u go?   4. I mil fly hom.   5. my ag s 21; r u 21?   6. s I tol d u, he s 22.

1. r u fin? I fel fin.   2. c u sta f le, r l u lev?   3. I mil lev.   4. s u no, I c sta.   5. r le s ic cold.   6. s u le ic cold?   7. c u pla my esy gam?   8. I c try.

1. r u her f r pla?   2. c u sta, r l u lev?   3. I c sta f u pla; I c sta s lat s u c   4. u rol a nic pla.   5. my pla s esy.

Set 2-1

1. /As I told you, our tire is low.   **2.** Can you gauge our tire?   **3.** Will you try?   **4.** I can gauge your/tire for you, or you can gauge your own tire.   **5.** Are you right? **6.** You are lazy. (36)

Set 2-2

1. /I can play our nice tune for you.   **2.** Our tune is easy.   **3.** Will you stay, or will you go?   **4.** I/might fly home.   **5.** My age is 21; are you 21?   **6.** As I told you, he is 22. (37)

Set 2-3

1. /Are you fine? I feel fine.   **2.** Can you stay for tea, or will you leave?   **3.** I might leave.   **4.** As you/know, I can stay.   **5.** Our tea is ice cold.   **6.** Is your tea ice cold?   **7.** Can you play my easy game?/   **8.** I can try. (43)

Set 2-4

1. /Are you here for our play?   **2.** Can you stay, or will you leave?   **3.** I can stay for your play; I/can stay as late as you can.   **4.** You wrote a nice play.   **5.** My play is easy. (36)

LESSON 3

PRINCIPLES OF CONSTRUCTION

Different Long Vowel

● When a letter or letters is pronounced as a different long vowel, write that long vowel. For example, in the word <u>freight</u>, the **e-i** combination is pronounced **a**; therefore, we will write **f-r-a-t.**

Read, spell, and then write the following words.

Read	Spell	SuperWrite
freight	**f-r-a-t**	*fral*
pool	**p-u-l**	*pul*
move	**m-u-v**	*muv*
few	**f-u**	*fu*

Short Vowels
Short Vowel in the Body of a Word

We will consider most other vowel sounds to be short.

● Do not write short vowels in the body of a word.

For example, in the word <u>even</u>, we would write **e-v-n,** omitting the **e** in the body of the word. Read, spell, and then write the following words.

Read	Spell	SuperWrite
even	**e-v-n**	*evn*
lesson	**l-s-n**	*lsn*

(continued)

Read	Spell	SuperWrite
center	c-n-t-r	*cntr*
softball	s-f-t-b-l	*sftbl*
correct	c-r-c-t	*crct*
written	r-t-n	*rtn*
cough	c-f	*cf*

Initial Short Vowel

● Write the vowel if the word begins with a short vowel sound.
For example, in the word <u>add</u>, the beginning short vowel **a** is written.
Read, spell, and then write the following words.

Read	Spell	SuperWrite
add	a-d	*ad*
earn	e-r-n	*ern*
if	i-f	*if*
object	o-b-j-c-t	*objct*
ought	o-t	*ot*
us	u-s	*us*
oven	o-v-n	*ovn*
honor	o-n-r	*onr*

Final Short Vowel

● Write the vowel if a word ends in a short vowel sound.
For example, in the word <u>data</u>, the final short vowel **a** is written.

Read, spell, and then write the following words.

Read	Spell	SuperWrite
data	d-a-t-a	*data*
era	e-r-a	*era*
saw	s-a	*sa*
law	l-a	*la*

Abbreviations

Here is the next set of abbreviations. Write them in your notebook.

Words	Abbreviations
at, it, to (A)	*l*
has, have (A)	*h*
very (A)	*v*
do (A)	*d*

APPLICATION

Read the following sets, referring immediately to the key if you have any trouble. Then write them in your own notebook.

h u gn l vol yt? he h gn. s u no,
he l vol l r ofc. if u r l lest 18, u c
vol. u ag s 18; u ol l vol. d u wnl
me l driv u l vol, r d u wnl l driv?
u vol s ncsry. l s v lal, bl u c sll
vol. l u vol f me?

d u pln l alnd clg? u ol l h a pln
mad. my pln s mad.

he h a pln f clg. he l alnd cls l
r locl clg. he l sldy la. s u no, l s
v gd l sldy la.

u idea s ril. if u r gd l la, u c
ern gd pa. he l ern v gd pa.

I c lev r ofc l 5, bl I mil sta ll 6 r 7.

l s v lal. r u rdy l lev u ofc? I sa hm l hs la ofc. he s rdy l lev f hom. he l try l mel us lalr.

d u wnl l h dnr l 7 r l 8? s u no, I pln l h dnr l 8.

l u clcl dala f my srva?
I l oblan dala f u if l s ncsry. I c clcl dala l r ofc, r u c clcl l.
d u h enf dala l d u jb?
no, bl he h enf dala l d l. he l cl u l u hom l 7 lnil.
s I told u, he h dn a v gd jb.

Set 3-1

(Counted in Words of 1.4 Syllables)

/Have you gone to vote yet? He has gone. As you know, he will vote at our office. If you are at least 18, you can/vote. Your age is 18; you ought to vote. Do you want me to drive you to vote, or do you want to drive? Your vote is/necessary. It is very late, but you can still vote. Will you vote for me? (54)

Set 3-2

/Do you plan to attend college? You ought to have a plan made. My plan is made.

He has a plan for college. He will/attend class at our local college. He will study law. As you know, it is very good to study law.

Your/idea is right. If you are good at law, you can earn good pay. He will earn very good pay. (56)

Set 3-3

/I can leave our office at five, but I might stay till six or seven.

It is very late. Are you ready to leave/your office? I saw him at his law office. He is ready to leave for home. He will try to meet us later.

Do/you want to have dinner at seven or at eight? As you know, I plan to have dinner at eight. (56)

Set 3-4

/Will you collect data for my survey?

I will obtain data for you if it is necessary. I can/collect data at our office, or you can collect it.

Do you have enough data to do your job?

No, but he/has enough data to do it. He will call you at your home at seven tonight.

As I told you, he has done a/very good job. (62)

LESSON 4

PRINCIPLES OF CONSTRUCTION

Sh

● The sound of **sh** is spelled many ways in longhand. In *SuperWrite* it is written <u>capital</u> **S.**

Read, spell, and then write the following words.

Read	Spell	SuperWrite
shoe	**sh-u**	*Su*
issue	**i-sh-u**	*iSu*
sugar	**sh-g-r**	*Sgr*
cash	**c-sh**	*cS*
official	**o-f-sh-l**	*ofSl*
special	**s-p-sh-l**	*spSl*

Ch

● **Ch** as in <u>chief</u> is written <u>capital</u> **C.**

Read, spell, and then write the following words.

Read	Spell	SuperWrite
chief	**ch-e-f**	*Cef*
reach	**r-e-ch**	*reC*
teacher	**t-e-ch-r**	*teCr*
bleacher	**b-l-e-ch-r**	*bleCr*

Word Ending -Ing

● The word ending **-ing** as in <u>growing</u> is written as a <u>disjoined</u> **g.**

grow *gro*   growing *gro g*

Read, spell, and then write the following words.

Read	Spell	SuperWrite
growing	g-r-o- g	*gro g*
keeping	k-e-p- g	*kep g*
writing	r-i-t- g	*rit g*
agreeing	a-g-r-e- g	*agre g*
knowing	n-o- g	*no g*

Adding S to a Word

● To add **s** to a word, write **s.**

For example, <u>plays</u> is written **p-l-a-s;** <u>feels</u>, **f-e-l-s;** <u>laws</u>, **l-a-s.**

Write the following words in *SuperWrite,* including the final **s.**

Word	Add *s*	SuperWrite
play	plays	*plas*
fee	fees	*fes*
price	prices	*prics*
feel	feels	*fels*
drama	dramas	*drmas*
law	laws	*las*

Abbreviations

Write the abbreviations for the following words.

Words	Abbreviations
we (A)	*e*
which (A)	*C*
soon (A)	*sn*

Personal Titles

● Personal titles such as Mr. or Mrs. are written in *SuperWrite* the same as they are in longhand, but the period is omitted.

Write the personal titles in your notebook.

Title	SuperWrite
Mr.	*Mr*
Mrs.	*Mrs*
Miss	*Miss*
Ms.	*Ms*
Dr.	*Dr*

Names

● A name is written in full in longhand the first time it is used. Only the first letter is written when the name occurs again in the same document.

Mr. Jones spoke to our club.

Mr Jones spok l r clb.

Did you meet Mr. Jones?

dd u met Mr J?

APPLICATION

Read the following documents and then write them in your notebook.

Mr Davis:

wn I wnl Sp g, I sa a v nic Cr C
s slg f a lo pric. l s on spSl sal f
a da r so l r locl ofc sply stor.

d u fel prCs g a nu Cr f r ofcs s a
gd pln, Mr D? if u r Sr e Sd d l, l u
go l se l wn u h a Cnc?

I h an idea prCs g l sn l sav us
mny.
                                        Bill Jones

Mrs Dalton:

s u no, Miss Mary Green, r dslrcl
Cef, vsld r Sp f a fu das. durg hr
vsl Se rol sm nols, C I l alC, cncrn g
r Sp.

Miss G fels e r opral g v wl, bl
e mil d an evn blr jb if e lry. Se
h mny ideas C r v gd. I fel Sr e
c us hr ideas. c e lk l u ofc sn?
                                        Carl Lee

DOCUMENT 4-3

Dr Carter:

I jsl lkd l an old frnd, Ms Sara Cates, hu h sm lnd C I fel e Sd prCs f r nu stor.

hr ask g pric s hi, bl I h an idea Se s l g l accpl a lll ls mny. d u fel e Sd mak hr an ofSl ofr f hr lnd? I hop u l cl me l my ofc sn.

Ken Gray

DOCUMENT 4-4

Ms Clay:

s u no, e Sd sn Cus nu crpl g f r ofcs. f r man ofc, e msl lry l gl a v strng crpl C l sta clen. f r Sp g rum, e Sd Cus an evn strngr crpl. l h l slnd up l v hvy us.

l u go Sp g f nu crpl sn, r d u wnl me l d r Sp g?

Ann Morris

DOCUMENT 4-1

(Word Counts Begin with First Paragraph)

Mr. Davis:

/When I went shopping, I saw a very nice chair which is selling for a low price. It is on special sale for a/day or so at our local office supply store.

Do you feel purchasing a new chair for our offices is a good/plan, Mr. Davis? If you are sure we should do it, will you go to see it when you have a chance?

I have an/idea purchasing it soon will save us money. Bill Jones (71)

DOCUMENT 4-2

Mrs. Dalton:

/As you know, Miss Mary Green, our district chief, visited our shop for a few days. During her visit she wrote some/notes, which I will attach, concerning our shop.

Miss Green feels we are operating very well, but we might do an/even better job if we try. She has many ideas which are very good. I feel sure we can use her/ideas. Can we talk at your office soon? Carl Lee (69)

DOCUMENT 4-3

Dr. Carter:

/I just talked to an old friend, Ms. Sara Cates, who has some land which I feel we should purchase for our new store.

Her/asking price is high, but I have an idea she is willing to accept a little less money. Do you feel/we should make her an official offer for her land? I hope you will call me at my office soon. Ken Gray (59)

DOCUMENT 4-4

Ms. Clay:

/As you know, we should soon choose new carpeting for our offices. For our main office, we must try to get a/very strong carpet which will stay clean. For our shipping room, we should choose an even stronger carpet. It has to stand/up to very heavy use.

Will you go shopping for new carpet soon, or do you want me to do our shopping? Ann/ Morris (61)

LESSON 5

PRINCIPLES OF CONSTRUCTION

Th

● **Th** as in these is written as a crossed **t**.

Read	Spell	*SuperWrite*
these	**th-e-s**	*tes*
them	**th-m**	*tm*
both	**b-o-th**	*bot*
bathe	**b-a-th**	*bat*
bother	**b-th-r**	*btr*
tooth	**t-u-th**	*lut*

Abbreviations

Words	Abbreviations
the (A)	*t*
and, in (A)	*n*

Salutations and Closings

● Write the first letter or abbreviation in lower case for salutations and closings.

Words	SuperWrite
Dear	*d*
Ladies and Gentlemen	*l n g*
Yours truly	*u l*
Very sincerely yours	*v s u*

Geographic Names

● The names of cities are written in full in longhand the first time they are used. Only the first letter is written if the word occurs again in the same document.

● The names of states should be abbreviated using the United States Postal Service abbreviations shown on page 431.

he plas f t Cincinnati tem n C, OH.

He plays for the Cincinnati team in Cincinnati, Ohio.

APPLICATION

Read the following documents and then write them in your own note-book.

DOCUMENT 5-1

Miss Janet James   d Miss J:
wn I vsld Mr n Mrs Lane n tr hom n Portland, OR, a da r so ago, I lkd l tr dlr, Ann. Se told me tl Se

---

wnld l vsl u n u hom sn.

s u no, A s 18 n h jsl fnSd hi scul. evn to Se dd v wl n hi scul n P, I h an idea tl Se neds sm hlp n Cus g t ril clg.

d u fel u c gv hr t hlp Se neds, Miss J? if u d, l u cl hr l hr hom?

v s u,

l n g:

e r v hpy l ll u tl Miss Mary Key l hd r nu stor n Chicago, IL. e r v sry tl Se s lev g r man stor, bl e no Se l d s wl l t nu stor s Se h dn her. Se s t ril prsn f t jb.

e r hop g f gd sals n r nu C stor n wS M t v bsl n hr nu jb.

Carl Bates

Dr William Shaw   d Dr S:

Miss Lane vsld me n my hom ts mrng, n e lkd a wil. l s gd tl Se s plng f t futr.

Se hops l vsl bot locl clgs n Reno, NV, sn l se C 1 Se liks blr.

Se l ril u n a da r so s sn s Se h mad up hr mind cncrng hr plns.   u l

Mr n Mrs R L Key   d Mr n Mrs K:

s u no, I spok l u sn n my hom a da r 2 ago. e r v hpy tl he vsld r clg her n Milwaukee, WI, evn to e lkd f jsl a fu mnls. I l mal hm t paprs he ma ned n a da r so.

l s a gd idea f hm l vsl otr sculs. wn he h hd a Cnc l se bot area clgs, e hop tl he l Cus rs.
                    v c u

DOCUMENT 5-1

Miss Janet James
Dear Miss James:

/When I visited Mr. and Mrs. Lane in their home in Portland, Oregon, a day or so ago, I talked/to their daughter, Ann. She told me that she wanted to visit you in your home soon.

As you know, Ann is 18 and/has just finished high school. Even though she did very well in high school in Portland, I have an idea that she/needs some help in choosing the right college.

Do you feel you can give her the help she needs, Miss James? If you do, will you/call her at her home? Very sincerely yours, (88)

DOCUMENT 5-2

Ladies and Gentlemen:

/We are very happy to tell you that Miss Mary Key will head our new store in Chicago, Illinois. We are/very sorry that she is leaving our main store, but we know she will do as well at the new store as she has done/here. She is the right person for the job.

We are hoping for good sales in our new Chicago store and wish/Mary the very best in her new job. Carl Bates (69)

DOCUMENT 5-3

Dr. William Shaw
Dear Dr. Shaw:

/Miss Lane visited me in my home this morning, and we talked a while. It is good that she is planning for the/future.

She hopes to visit both local colleges in Reno, Nevada, soon to see which one she likes/better.

She will write you in a day or so as soon as she has made up her mind concerning her plans. Yours truly, (58)

DOCUMENT 5-4

Mr. and Mrs. R. L. Key
Dear Mr. and Mrs. Key:

/As you know, I spoke to your son in my home a day or two ago. We are very happy that he visited/our college here in Milwaukee, Wisconsin, even though we talked for just a few minutes. I will mail him the/papers he may need in a day or so.

It is a good idea for him to visit other schools. When he has had/a chance to see both area colleges, we hope that he will choose ours. Very cordially yours, (77)

LESSON A

TOWARD PERSONAL SUCCESS

After each five lessons of *SuperWrite* theory in Volume One, there is a lesson designed to help you on your way to personal success. Each lesson contains information about a subject that should be of vital concern to you. Read the material and then complete the exercises that follow.

The lesson today concerns a very important topic, setting goals.

SETTING GOALS

Most of us do not spend much time thinking about the things that will affect us in the years ahead. It is easier just to concentrate on more immediate things, such as the activities we have planned for the day. If we want to control our futures, however, we must set definite goals for ourselves and implement specific plans to meet these goals. Each of us should have personal, educational, and professional goals, as well as a plan to meet those goals.

Some Questions to Think About

What do you want to accomplish in one year, five years, or twenty years? What do you want to study? What type of work do you want to do? Where do you want to live? How much money do you want to make? These questions are not easy to answer, but they are of vital importance to your future. If you can answer them and others like them, you will be well on your way to a life of accomplishment.

Set Your Own Goals

To set your goals, you should sit quietly and think about your future. You should determine what you want to do and when you plan to do it. When you know exactly what you want to accomplish, you can begin to make a specific list of things you should do to meet these goals. You need not fear that making plans now will limit your future. It is always possible to modify your plans. However, if you do not set goals for yourself, you will never be able to accomplish them.

Your goals should not be the same as those of your friends or classmates. Your goals must fit you individually, and they should lead to a fulfilling future.

Start Now

There is no better time than right now to begin planning for the years ahead. Begin to make plans now concerning your personal life, your education, and your work. It is your future you are planning.

Discussion

Here are your first discussion questions. Think about the questions carefully and discuss them with your family or with members of the class.

1. Why do you believe that most people give little time to planning their future?

2. Do you think you should give some time to planning how much money you will need in the future? Why?

3. Do you believe that if you make plans for your future too early, it will be difficult to change them? Why?

4. What will be the outcome if you do not plan for your future?

Case Studies

Here are two case studies concerning setting goals. Read the cases carefully and answer the questions that follow. Determine if there are things in the cases that might apply to you.

Case Study 1—Joe Martin's Goals

Joe Martin always dreamed of being a business executive in Chicago. He could see himself managing a large company in a luxurious office overlooking Lake Michigan.

However, Joe took no action to make his dream come true. Although he could have gone to college, he did not do so. He graduated from high school ten years ago, and he has worked at the same job since then.

Discussion Questions

1. What did Joe do wrong?

2. What should he have done in order to make his dream come true?

3. Was there a relation between Joe's failure to make his dream come true and his failure to set goals?

Case Study 2—Mary's Decision

Mary Stevens is a student in Central Business College in Detroit. She is planning to be a medical secretary and has enrolled in a one-year program. After the first course in medical terminology, Mary decided that she probably would not enjoy this field. The words were unfamiliar to her, and she did not seem to have the time to spend to learn them all.

Mary talked with her counselor at the school and decided to change to the executive assistant program, even though it will take her an extra three months to complete. She feels better about the situation, but she wonders if she made the right decision.

Discussion Questions

1. What did Mary do right in this situation? What did she do wrong?

2. Do you think Mary made the right decision to change majors in school?

3. Did Mary plan properly before she entered business college?

4. What would you suggest that Mary do now?

Activities

Here are several suggested activities for you to do. In today's lesson, you are asked to set personal, educational, and professional goals and list things that will help you to meet each goal.

1. List two major personal goals that you wish to achieve during your lifetime and two specific things you can do to help in meeting each goal.

2. List two major education goals that you wish to achieve and two specific things you can do to help in meeting each goal.

3. List two major professional goals that you wish to achieve and two specific things you can do to help in meeting each goal.

LESSON 6

PRINCIPLES OF CONSTRUCTION

Abbreviations

Words	Abbreviations
am, more (A)	*m*
be, been, by (A)	*b*
month (A)	*mo*

Word Beginning Be-

● The word beginning **be-** as in <u>became</u> is written **b**.

Read	Spell	SuperWrite
became	**b-c-a-m**	*bcam*
believe	**b-l-e-v**	*blev*
begin	**b-g-n**	*bgn*
because	**b-c-s**	*bcs*
beyond	**b-y-n-d**	*bynd*

Word Beginnings In-, En-

● The word beginnings **in-** as in <u>inside</u> and **en-** as in <u>endanger</u> are written **n,** <u>before a consonant</u>.

Read	Spell	SuperWrite
in-		
inside	**n-s-i-d**	*nsid*
invite	**n-v-i-t**	*nvit*
indeed	**n-d-e-d**	*nded*
instead	**n-s-t-d**	*nstd*
en-		
endanger	**n-d-a-n-g-r**	*ndangr*
encourage	**n-c-r-g**	*ncrg*
endeavor	**n-d-v-r**	*ndvr*
entire	**n-t-i-r**	*ntir*

Word Beginning Re-

● The word beginning **re-** as in <u>repair</u> is written **r.**

Read	Spell	SuperWrite
repair	**r-p-r**	*rpr*
receipt	**r-c-e-t**	*rcet*
reply	**r-p-l-y**	*rply*
result	**r-s-l-t**	*rslt*
retire	**r-t-i-r**	*rtir*
regroup	**r-g-r-u-p**	*rgrup*

Word Beginning De-

● The word beginning **de-** as in <u>decide</u> is written **d.**

Read	Spell	SuperWrite
decide	d-c-i-d	*dcid*
delay	d-l-a	*dla*
delight	d-l-i-t	*dlil*
depend	d-p-n-d	*dpnd*
defuse	d-f-u-s	*dfus*

APPLICATION

Read and write the following documents.

DOCUMENT 6-1

Mr Keith Case: d Mr C:

I m sry nded l ll u tl Mrs Smith n I l nl b l t dnr C u h plnd l onr Ann Sanders wn Se rlirs.

e l nl alnd bcs e r nl plng l rlrn l Dallas b t dal u h plnd t dnr. s u no, e h b n Vail, CO, f an nlir mo.

if t dnr c b dlad a da r so, e l b m tn hpy l b tr.

u v s

DOCUMENT 6-2

Mr n Mrs Ben C Smith   d Mr n Mrs S:

I m v sry u l nl b bk n Dallas, TX, b t dal e pln l h t dnr l onr Ms Sanders.

e h b pln g t dnr f m tn 3 mos. l msl nl b dlad bcs e h nvild m tn 20 gsts, n eC h accpld.

ma I ncrg u l lak Ms S l lnC wn u rlrn l D.

u c

DOCUMENT 6-3

l n g:

I m v hpy l ll u tl Mr James Blake l b rlrn g l t ofc sn. s u no, Mr B h b il f m tn 3 mos. f t psl mo, he h b rsl g l hs sn's hom n Phoenix, AZ.

evn to Mr B fels wl, Dr Gray blevs he Sd nl sla n t ofc v lng eC da ll he rgans hs hlt.

(continued)

b sla g l t ofc a Srl wil eC da,
he c rsum mny dules. l s nded
ncrg g l no tl Mr B l b rlrn g sn,
n e l b dlild l h hm bk.

A B Tate

Miles Jenkins:

I m dlild l ll u tl dur g t psl
6 mos sals n eC rgn h b go g up
wil csls h nl ncresd. sals n t
Los Angeles, CA, rgn n t Santa Fe,
NM, rgn h ncresd m tn 20%.

e r Sr tl ts l b v ncrg g nus
f u n u slf, M.

I blev tl b ncres g r sals bgl
jsl a lll, e c ncres r ncm evn m
n t mos ahd. d u agre?

A C Moore

DOCUMENT 6-1

Mr. Keith Case
Dear Mr. Case:

/I am sorry indeed to tell you that Mrs. Smith and I will not be at the dinner which you have planned to/honor Ann Sanders when she retires.

We will not attend because we are not planning to return to Dallas by the/date you have planned the dinner. As you know, we have been in Vail, Colorado, for an entire month.

If the dinner/can be delayed a day or so, we will be more than happy to be there. Yours very sincerely, (77)

DOCUMENT 6-2

Mr. and Mrs. Ben C. Smith
Dear Mr. and Mrs. Smith:

/I am very sorry you will not be back in Dallas, Texas, by the date we plan to have the dinner to/honor Ms. Sanders.

We have been planning the dinner for more than three months. It must not be delayed because we have/invited more than 20 guests, and each has accepted.

May I encourage you to take Ms. Sanders to lunch when/you return to Dallas. Yours cordially, (67)

DOCUMENT 6-3

Ladies and Gentlemen:

/I am very happy to tell you that Mr. James Blake will be returning to the office soon. As you know,/Mr. Blake has been ill for more than three months. For the past month, he has been resting at his son's home in Phoenix, Arizona./

Even though Mr. Blake feels well, Dr. Gray believes he should not stay in the office very long each/day till he regains his health.

By staying at the office a short while each day, he can resume many duties. It/is indeed encouraging to know that Mr. Blake will be returning soon, and we will be delighted to have/him back. A. B. Tate (104)

DOCUMENT 6-4

Miles Jenkins:

/I am delighted to tell you that during the past six months sales in each region have been going up while costs have/not increased. Sales in the Los Angeles, California, region and the Santa Fe, New Mexico, region have/increased more than 20 percent.

We are sure that this will be very encouraging news for you and your staff, Miles./

I believe that by increasing our sales budget just a little, we can increase our income even more in the/months ahead. Do you agree? A. C. Moore (87)

SUPPLEMENTARY ACTIVITY

A Word to the Wise

Beginning with Lesson 6, a supplementary activity is included in each lesson. The documents are entitled "A Word to the Wise," and they appear in type. Using the type as a guide, write the documents in *SuperWrite* in your own notebook, or follow any special instructions given by your teacher.

Self-Confidence

/If you have been discouraged by failures in the past, here are some ideas to increase your self-confidence.

If/you believe you are going to fail, the battle is lost at the beginning. If you believe you can do a job,/the battle is half won.

Say the words "I am going to do this job very well" and the job will be easy.

When/you have finished, review what you have done. You may well find that you have done much more than you had planned. This will delight/and encourage you.

Set goals that you can meet. Then you must strive to finish each job. Day by day, month by month, you will increase/your self-confidence. (104)

LESSON 7

PRINCIPLES OF CONSTRUCTION

Word Ending -Tion

● The word ending **-tion** is spelled many ways in longhand. In *SuperWrite* it is written <u>capital</u> **S.**

Read	Spell	SuperWrite
location	**l-o-c-a-shun**	*locaS*
relation	**r-l-a-shun**	*rlaS*
vocation	**v-o-c-a-shun**	*vocaS*
suspension	**s-s-p-n-shun**	*sspnS*
sufficient	**s-f-shun-t**	*sfSt*
efficiency	**e-f-shun-c-y**	*efScy*
physician	**f-s-shun**	*fsS*

Ou, Ow

● The sound of **ou** as in <u>house</u> is written in full, **ou**.

Read	Spell	SuperWrite
ou		
house	**h-o-u-s**	*hous*
proud	**p-r-o-u-d**	*proud*
ounce	**o-u-n-c**	*ounc*

● The sound of **ow** as in <u>now</u> is written in full, **o-w**.

Read	Spell	SuperWrite
ow		
now	**n-o-w**	*now*
flower	**f-l-o-w-r**	*flowr*
brown	**b-r-o-w-n**	*brown*

Word Ending -Ly

● The word ending **-ly** as in <u>lately</u> is written **l**.

Read	Spell	SuperWrite
lately	**l-a-t-l**	*latl*
briefly	**b-r-e-f-l**	*brefl*
highly	**h-i-l**	*hil*
only	**o-n-l**	*onl*
nationally	**n-shun-l-l**	*nSll*
annually	**a-n-u-l-l**	*anull*
family	**f-m-l**	*fml*
steadily	**s-t-d-l**	*sldl*
easily	**e-s-l**	*esl*

Abbreviations

Words	Abbreviations
from (A)	*fm*
of (A)	*o*

Words	Abbreviations
year (A)	*yr*
let (A)	*le*

APPLICATION

DOCUMENT 7-1

Mrs Chay:

sals n mosl o r rtal stors h b ncres g slol bl sldl dur g t psl 3 yrs. e r v proud o ts, bl r csls h ncresd s wl.

n fcl, fm t frsl o t yr tru t end o lsl mo, e aclull lsl mny n r 2 loca$s n Atlanta, GA. alto sals r up slill, nl ncm s down.

t bord o drclrs rcnll vold l le tes slors rman n opra$ f a fu m mos l se if sals c b ncresd n csls hld down.

(continued)

I m Sr, Mrs C, tt u l d u bsl l hlp tes slors ncres tr efScy l rman n opraS. e l mak a finl dcS b t end o t yr.

RC Key

Miss Jane Hall   d Miss H:

smr s jsl around t crnr, n u l likl bqn makg u vacaS plns sn.

makg qnrl vacaS plns s usull fn, bl aclull makg rsrvaSs n prCsg tkls c b v lirg.

ts yr, wy nl le r lrvl agncy hndl t dlals f u? e h b hndlg vacaS dlals f lrvlrs sC s u f m tn 20 yrs. e c pln a vacaS f u l NY, CA, r FL. jsl nam t plac u wnl l go, n e l d t rsl.

e c mak u hotl rsrvas. e c prCs
u plan tkts. e c evn arang l lak u
fm u hous l t ar trmnl.

tes r onl a fu o t mny dtals e c
hndl esl n efSl f u. e ncrg u l cl
us now l ll us wr u wnl l go n won
u wS l lev. e l lak l fm tr.

v s u

Dr Sam Chase   d Dr C:

r u spnd g m tn u Sd l kep u
hous cul n t smr mos? if u ar
cndSr s m tn 10 yrs old, u ma actull
b wasl g powr s wl s mny.

dpnd g on t locaS o u hous, a nu
ar cndSr c esl cl u powr csls nerl n
hf.

cl us now, n le 1 o t slf fm r man
ofc slp b u hom l gv u an eslml o t

(continued)

csl o rplac g u old sslm. l l lak onl
a fu mnls. tr l nl b a Crg, n u l h
no oblgaS.

 u l

Mr Carlos Lopez   d Mr L:

 I m dlild l anounc tl fm now ll
t end o t yr, e l h a spSl sal on mny
ilms f u hous n u fml.

 ilms C usull sl l mC hir prics l b
on spSl sal f t lsl 2 mos o t yr onl. u
c slcl ilms fm r spSl clcS f onl a
frcS o t pric u wd nrmll pa.

 d nl wal; b t end o t yr, r slk l
h b dpleld. cm n now n le us So u
r fin slcS. e l b walg f u.

 v l u

DOCUMENT 7-1

Mrs. Chay:

/Sales in most of our retail stores have been increasing slowly but steadily during the past three years. We are/very proud of this, but our costs have increased as well.

In fact, from the first of the year through the end of last month, we/actually lost money in our two locations in Atlanta, Georgia. Although sales are up slightly, net income/is down.

The board of directors recently voted to let these stores remain in operation for a few more/months to see if sales can be increased and costs held down.

I am sure, Mrs. Chay, that you will do your best to help these/stores increase their efficiency to remain in operation. We will make a final decision by the end/of the year. R. C. Key (124)

DOCUMENT 7-2

Miss Jane Hall
Dear Miss Hall:

/Summer is just around the corner, and you will likely begin making your vacation plans soon.

Making general/vacation plans is usually fun, but actually making reservations and purchasing tickets/can be very tiring.

This year, why not let our travel agency handle the details for you? We have been/handling vacation details for travelers such as you for more than twenty years. We can plan a vacation for you/to New York, California, or Florida. Just name the place you want to go, and we will do the rest.

We/can make your hotel reservations. We can purchase your plane tickets. We can even arrange to take you from your/house to the air terminal.

These are only a few of the many details we can handle easily and/efficiently for you. We encourage you to call us now to tell us where you want to go and when you wish to leave./We will take it from there. Very sincerely yours, (169)

DOCUMENT 7-3

Dr. Sam Chase
Dear Dr. Chase:

/Are you spending more than you should to keep your house cool in the summer months? If your air conditioner is more than/ten years old, you may actually be wasting power as well as money.

Depending on the location of/your house, a new air conditioner can easily cut your power costs nearly in half.

(continued)

Call us now, and let one/of the staff from our main office stop by your home to give you an estimate of the cost of replacing your old/system. It will take only a few minutes. There will not be a charge, and you will have no obligation. Yours/truly, (101)

DOCUMENT 7-4

Mr. Carlos Lopez
Dear Mr. Lopez:

/I am delighted to announce that from now till the end of the year, we will have a special sale on many/items for your house and your family.

Items which usually sell at much higher prices will be on special/sale for the last two months of the year only. You can select items from our special collection for only a/fraction of the price you would normally pay.

Do not wait; by the end of the year, our stock will have been depleted./Come in now and let us show you our fine selection. We will be waiting for you. Very truly yours, (98)

SUPPLEMENTARY ACTIVITY

A Word to the Wise

Using a Dictionary

/It never pays to let a word go if you have a doubt concerning its spelling.

Why? A person reading your/paper could actually be misled. Or worse still, the reader may concentrate on the error and pay no attention/to your main ideas. The person may even look down on you for not checking your paper.

It is a good/idea to have a small dictionary in your briefcase. It will always be handy, and there will be no/reason for not using it.

Don't take a chance concerning the spelling of a word; it is not worth the risk. Let this be/the year you resolve: "I will use a dictionary regularly from now on."

A good dictionary can be/your best friend. (122)

LESSON 8

PRINCIPLES OF CONSTRUCTION

Word Ending -Ment

● The word ending **-ment** as in <u>payment</u> is written **m**.

Read	Spell	*SuperWrite*
payment	**p-a-m**	*pam*
treatment	**t-r-e-t-m**	*tretm*
engagement	**n-g-a-g-m**	*ngagm*
settlement	**s-t-l-m**	*stlm*
attachments	**a-t-ch-m-s**	*atChms*
elementary	**e-l-m-r-y**	*elmry*

Word Ending -Ble

● The word ending **-ble** as in <u>capable</u> is written **b**.

Read	Spell	*SuperWrite*
-ble		
capable	**c-a-p-b**	*capb*
trouble	**t-r-b**	*trb*
possible	**p-s-b**	*psb*
able	**a-b**	*ab*
table	**t-a-b**	*tab*

Abbreviations

Words	Abbreviations
after (A)	*afl*
business (A)	*bus*
company (A)	*co*
responsible (A)	*rsp*

Quantities

The quantity hundred is written **h**; thousand is written as a <u>crossed</u> **t**.

hundred   *h*   thousand   *t*

Quantity	SuperWrite
300	*3 h*
$500	*$5 h*
$2,000	*$2 t*
$300,000	*$3 h t*

APPLICATION

DOCUMENT 8-1

Mr C R Brown   d Mr B:

f m tn a yr, u h b prLs g gds fm r co l sl n u rlal bus eslblSm n Wichita, KS. u orgnll agred l pa f t itms C u prCsd on a mol bass, n u pam rcrd hd b v gd f nerl a yr.

bt afl 90 das, u h nl snt us u pams f t lsl 2 Spms. u l rcl tl u bl $2 t wrt o gds fm us 3 mos ago n $5 h wrt o gds fm r co 2 mos ago.

l frsl e tl t bls hd slpd u mind. bl bcs u h nl rspndd l r rmindrs, e now blev tl l s psb u bus s h g fnnSl lrbs.

e c mak arangms l gv u an adSl mo r so l mak u pams, bl u msl lak rsp acS now b le g us no wt t lrb s. won'l u cl us lda. u crdl ral g cd psbl b dmgd if u d nl.

u l

l n g:

r rvisd co bgl f t cmg yr s

(continued)

alCd. s u c esl se, e r now pln g
f an ncres n bus.

afl onl 3 yrs n bus, e blev e c
aclull aCev gros sals o $8 h t r $9 h t
nxl yr.

s u no, u aCevms h gvn us a
gral del o ncrgm, n I m v proud
o u rcrd. eC o u h b prsnll rsp
f an ncres n sals o m tn $10 t
dur g t psl yr.

l u le me h u ideas on t bgl s
sn s psb. I hop l fnS r rvu b t
end o t mo.

Ann Wright

Dr M W Casey   d Dr C:

u nol ask g f a rfrnc f Mr Slade arivd lda. Mr S hd b on t slf o r co nerl 3 yrs wn he lfl. he srvd n t acounls pab dvS f 1 yr n n t Cef acounlnl's ofc nerl 2 yrs. he ernd a bgn g slry o $20 t, n he gl a ras o $2 h a mo afl onl 1 yr. he lfl r co afl b g her nerl 3 yrs l opn hs on bus n Des Moines, IA.

Mr S s a dpndb prsn hu h v gd jgm. he hndls hs bus n a capb n rsp wa, n he h my hisl rcmndaS.

v s u

Miss Kim Lacy:

l l b psb f u l mak arangms l acl s my rplacm l t bus cnvnS n Charlotte, NC, nxl mo?

I m rsp f co labr rlaSs, n I l b awa on co bus n VA, wr e r hq labr lrbs. if e d nl reC an erl sllm, l s psb I l nl b rlrng ll afl t frsl o t yr.

e now eslmal tr l b 9 h r prhps l t l t cnvnS, n I blev r co Sd dfnll h a prsn tr. l u le me h u ansr sn.

Lee Downs

DOCUMENT 8-1

Mr. C. R. Brown

Dear Mr. Brown:

/For more than a year, you have been purchasing goods from our company to sell in your retail business establishment/in Wichita, Kansas. You originally agreed to pay for the items which you purchased on a/monthly basis, and your payment record had been very good for nearly a year.

But after ninety days, you have not/sent us your payments for the last two shipments. You will recall that you bought $2,000 worth of goods from us/three months ago and $500 worth of goods from our company two months ago.

At first we thought the bills/had slipped your mind. But because you have not responded to our reminders, we now believe that it is possible/your business is having financial troubles.

We can make arrangements to give you an additional month or so/to make your payments, but you must take responsible action now by letting us know what the trouble is. Won't you/call us today. Your credit rating could possibly be damaged if you do not. Yours truly, (176)

DOCUMENT 8-2

Ladies and Gentlemen:

/Our revised company budget for the coming year is attached. As you can easily see, we are now planning/for an increase in business.

After only three years in business, we believe we can actually achieve gross/sales of $800,000 or $900,000 next year.

As you know, your achievements have/given us a great deal of encouragement, and I am very proud of your record. Each of you has been personally/responsible for an increase in sales of more than $10,000 during the past year.

Will you let me/have your ideas on the budget as soon as possible. I hope to finish our review by the end of the/month. Ann Wright (122)

DOCUMENT 8-3

Dr. M. W. Casey
Dear Dr. Casey:

/Your note asking for a reference for Mr. Slade arrived today. Mr. Slade had been on the staff of our/company nearly three years when he left. He served in the accounts payable division for one year and in the chief/accountant's office nearly two years. He earned a beginning salary of $20,000 and he got/a raise of $200 a month after only one year. He left our company after being here/nearly three years to open his own business in Des Moines, Iowa.

Mr. Slade is a dependable person/who has very good judgment. He handles his business in a capable and responsible way, and he has my/highest recommendation. Very sincerely yours, (129)

DOCUMENT 8-4

Miss Kim Lacy:

/Will it be possible for you to make arrangements to act as my replacement at the business convention in/Charlotte, North Carolina, next month?

I am responsible for company labor relations, and I will be/away on company business in Virginia, where we are having labor troubles. If we do not reach an/early settlement, it is possible I will not be returning till after the first of the year.

We now estimate/there will be 900 or perhaps 1,000 at the convention, and I believe our company should/definitely have a person there. Will you let me have your answer soon. Lee Downs (114)

SUPPLEMENTARY ACTIVITY

A Word to the Wise

Planning—the Road to Success

/Would you start on a company business trip of 500 or 1,000 miles and have no road map? No/responsible person would.

But many students begin each school year and have no real plan. If you have no plan, after a/while you will realize you do not know where you are going or when you should get there.

If you plan well, it is/possible that you will accomplish a great deal. If you do not make good plans, your accomplishments will be small indeed. In/addition, you will waste energy and lose months or even years. You may even arrive at a destination/where you did not intend to go!

There is no substitute for good planning. Plan your school year and the rest of your life/ as well. (121)

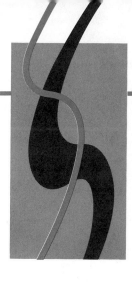

LESSON 9

PRINCIPLES OF CONSTRUCTION

Oi, Oy

● The sound of **oi** as <u>oil</u> is written in full, **o-i**.

Read	Spell	*SuperWrite*
oi		
oil	**o-i-l**	*oil*
toil	**t-o-i-l**	*toil*
choice	**ch-o-i-c**	*coic*
poise	**p-o-i-s**	*pois*

● The sound of **oy** as in <u>boy</u> is written in full, **o-y**.

oy		
boy	**b-o-y**	*boy*
destroy	**d-s-t-r-o-y**	*dstroy*
royal	**r-o-y-l**	*royl*

Word Beginnings Im-, Em-

● The word beginnings **im-** as in <u>impress</u> and **em-** as in <u>emphasize</u> are written **m**.

Read	Spell	*SuperWrite*
im-		
impress	**m-p-r-s**	*mprs*

(continued)

Read	Spell	SuperWrite
impossible	m-p-s-b	*mpsb*
import	m-p-o-r-t	*mport*

em-

emphasize	m-f-s-i-z	*mfsiz*
emphasis	m-f-s-s	*mfss*
embassy	m-b-s-y	*mbsy*

Quantities

● The quantity million is written **m**; billion is written **b**.

million *m*　　　　billion *b*

Quantity	SuperWrite
5 million	*5 m*
8 billion	*8 b*

Abbreviations

Words	Abbreviations
was, were, with (A)	*w*
importance, important (A)	*imp*
department (A)	*dept*
week, work (A)	*wk*
employ (A)	*mpl*

Capitalization

● When a word is to be capitalized and it is not written in full, write two short lines under the first letter. Note: If the word to be capitalized begins a sentence, do not write cap marks under the word.

National   *nSl*

If several words in a series are to be capitalized, write the cap marks under the first word only.

National Oil Company   *nSl oil co*

Terms	SuperWrite
the West	*t wsl*
the East Coast	*t esl cosl*
Southern Supply Company	*strn sply co*
Central Gas Company is closed.	*cnlrl gs co s closd.*

APPLICATION

DOCUMENT 9-1

Mrs Rodriguez:

c u psbl join us f a v imp bus mel g o depl hds o t strn co n r LA ofc t frsl o nxl mo? s u no, t mel g w orgnll scduld ts mo. l w Cangd l ncres alndnc.

I msl mfsiz t imp o ts mel g; e l b wkg on an imp co pln C dels w t

(continued)

Coic o nvstm frms n C e l plac blwen $9 h m n $1 b fm t mple rlirm fnd. bcs u w hd o t bgt cmte lst yr, u npt l b nvlub l us.

e ned u ansr sn. if l s mpsb f u l b w us, le Mr Miller no aft t frst o t wk.

May White

l dept hds:

l s w plSr tt I mak an anouncm o grat imp l eC mple. lst wk t onrs o r co w ab l reC an agrem l prCs cntrol g stk n t nSt oil co o Ogden, UT. t stk C w prCsd s wrt m tn $5 h m n l brng r totl nvstm n t oil ndstry l nerl $3 b.

I wnt l mfsiz tt t mrgr l rstt n no rdcS o wk stf n l actull brng mpruvd bnfts l mples o bot cos.

m dlals cncrn g ts imp prCs l
b mald l eC wkr n a wk r so.

                              Bill Meadows

Miss Simms:

   t speC C u gav lsl wk l t bus
mel g o t depl hds o r co w v
mprsv. u mfss on lng-lrm nvslms
hd a gral mpcl. n fcl, u w rsp f r
b g ab l mak l lesl 1 v imp dcS
cncrn g r mple bnfl fnd.

   afl u lk, e dcidd l nvsl $1 b w t
estrn co o Philadelphia, PA. e l likl
plac t rman g $20 m w 3 r 4 otr cos
nxl yr.

   u plad a rol o gral imp n hlp g
us Cus gd nvslm cos, Miss S. s a rsll
o u gd wk, I m Sr e w ab l mak
sound Coics.

                              L C Trent

l t slf:

lsl wk w 1 o majr imp l t Essex co.
dur g t wk r nvoics w m tn $6 m,
C w $1 h t hir tn dur g t sam wk
lsl yr. 8 o r 10 depts aclull sl nu
1-wk sals rcrds.

r loyl mples w drcll rsp f ts
mprsv rcrd. I m v proud o eC wkr
n r co. I wS l w psb f me l lk w
eC o u prsnll, bl l s nl psb f me
l d so. l s v imp, to, tl eC o u nos
e vlu u loylly n ddcaS.

w u cnlnud hrd wk, e l sl evn
hir rcrds n t yrs ahd.

R D Babb

DOCUMENT 9-1

Mrs. Rodriguez:

/Can you possibly join us for a very important business meeting of department heads of the Southern/Company in our Louisiana office the first of next month? As you know, the meeting was originally/scheduled this month. It was changed to increase attendance.

I must emphasize the importance of this meeting; we will/be working on an important company plan which deals with the choice of investment firms in which we will place/ between $900 million and $1 billion from the employee retirement fund. Because you were head/of the budget committee last year, your input will be invaluable to us.

We need your answer soon. If/it is impossible for you to be with us, let Mr. Miller know after the first of the week. May White (139)

DOCUMENT 9-2

To Department Heads:

/It is with pleasure that I make an announcement of great importance to each employee. Last week the owners of/our company were able to reach an agreement to purchase controlling stock in the National Oil Company/of Ogden, Utah. The stock which was purchased is worth more than $500 million and will bring our/total investment in the oil industry to nearly $3 billion.

I want to emphasize that the merger/will result in no reduction of work staff and will actually bring improved benefits to employees of/both companies.

More details concerning this important purchase will be mailed to each worker in a week or so./Bill Meadows (122)

DOCUMENT 9-3

Miss Simms:

/The speech which you gave last week at the business meeting of the department heads of our company was very/impressive. Your emphasis on long-term investments had a great impact. In fact, you were responsible for our/being able to make at least one very important decision concerning our employee benefit fund./

After your talk, we decided to invest $1 billion with the Eastern Company of Philadelphia,/ Pennsylvania. We will likely place the remaining $20 million with three or four other companies/next year.

You played a role of great importance in helping us choose good investment companies, Miss Simms. As a/result of your good work, I am sure we were able to make sound choices. L. C. Trent (134)

DOCUMENT 9-4

To the Staff:

/Last week was one of major importance to the Essex Company. During the week our invoices were more than/$6 million, which was $100,000 higher than during the same week last year. Eight of our ten/departments actually set new one-week sales records.

Our loyal employees were directly responsible/for this impressive record. I am very proud of each worker in our company. I wish it were possible/for me to talk with each of you personally, but it is not possible for me to do so. It is very/important, though, that each of you knows we value your loyalty and dedication.

With your continued hard work,/we will set even higher records in the years ahead.
R. D. Babb (132)

SUPPLEMENTARY ACTIVITY

A Word to the Wise

Loyalty to Your Employer

/As a worker, you must be loyal to your employer. It is impossible to emphasize this enough./Whether your employer grosses $100,000, $1 million, or even $1 billion a/year, loyalty is necessary. It was important in the past, and it will be of great importance in the/ future.

An employee who wishes to remain with a company must be loyal. A disloyal employee/ will soon be looking for a job with a different company. If you were able to take back a disloyal/remark, you would likely do so. But once a remark is made, it is impossible to retract. You can avoid/a great deal of trouble by thinking first and speaking later.

Whether you are a weekly worker or a monthly/worker—whether you work in the sales department or the finance department—whether you work in the front office/or the back, company loyalty is essential. (169)

LESSON 10

PRINCIPLES OF CONSTRUCTION

Qu

● **Qu** as in quite is written **q**.

Read	Spell	SuperWrite
quite	**q-i-t**	*qil*
quail	**q-a-l**	*qal*
quit	**q-t**	*ql*
request	**r-q-s-t**	*rqsl*

Word Ending -Ity

● The word ending **-ity** as in locality is written as a disjoined **t**.

Read	Spell	SuperWrite
locality	**l-o-c-l- t**	*locl l*
quality	**q-l- t**	*ql l*
charity	**ch-r- t**	*Cr l*
sincerity	**s-n-c-r- t**	*sncr l*
quantities	**q-n-t- ts**	*qnl ls*

Abbreviations

Words	Abbreviations
how (A)	*hw*
out (A)	*ol*
require (A)	*rqr*
they (A)	*ty*

APPLICATION

DOCUMENT 10-1

Mrs Jane Ford   d Mrs F:

if u r cncrnd w t qll o lif n r locl l, u l ws l gv u sporl l t wk bg dn b a grup o loyl clzns. s u ma no, t clzns w apoinld l t cmle b <u>mar</u> Carson.

ts wk e r makg an imp srva l dlrmn hw t rsdnls o t area fel cncrn g nvirnml iSus n if ty wnl a la psd l mpruv t qll o t wlr n ar n r vcn l.

if sC a la s psd, l l, qil nlrll, afcl mny mplrs bot n n ol o t cly.

ty mil b rqrd l adpl nu, strngnl opral g plns l mel t nu rqrms.

e wnl l no hw u fel, s an mplr, cncrn g ts iSu, C l b o sC gral imp l t m tn 2 m clzns hu l lv n wk n ts area n t yrs ahd.

ma l ncrg u l fl ol n rlrn t alCd srva l r pblc rlaSs depl sn le me mfsiz tl u rspns l b kpl cnfdnSl.

                                        c u

Miss Abbott:

l u accpl t rspl o hd g a cmle l wk on a nu rcrds rlnS sslm f t nSl co?

r fil g sslm w dsind m tn 20 yrs ago, n e no tl l s now qil ol o dal. e blev e ma h b kep g mny paprs tl r lu old l b o vlu, n n

(continued)

al liklhd ty Sd b dslroyd. bl if e w l tro ol paprs e r rqrd b la l rlan, l wd b qil bd.

e msl apoinl a prsn o atr l l wk w t mples n eC depl. tl prsn msl no al t legl rqrms n hw ty afcl buss sC s rs, so tl e d nl tro ol imp dcums.

ma l mfsiz t imp o ts psS. u h t capbl l hndl t jb v wl, Miss A. if u c accpl ts apoinlm, le me no afl t frsl o t wk wn n hw u wd lik l mplm u plns.

R G Baird

Mr Charles Trent   d Mr T:

l s a plSr l srv s a rfrnc f Mr Tom Carr, hu wkd f me l my co, t Yates oil co o Denver, CO, a fu yrs ago.

t prsnl rfrnc Sel C u askd me l fl ol s alCd.

I m hpy l ll u hw I fel cncrn g Mr C n hs abl s a wkr. Mr C h b a frnd o my fml f m tn 10 yrs. he w an mple o my co f nerl 5 yrs. he gls alng wl w otrs, n ty lik hm prsnll.

Mr C s a prsn o nlgr l n rlib l. he s loyl l hs mplr, n he ds hs wk qkl. he s dpndb n ds nl rqr clos suprvS. I blev he cd hndl a psS o atr l n rspl w u co, if he w gvn l.

ts Sd gv u an idea o hw wl Mr C dd wn he w mpld b my co n hw mprsd e w w hm. I l b hpy l fl ol adSl paprs f Mr C if ty r rqrd.

v s u

l t slf:

s u no, t Warren co h wkd sldl f t psl 2 yrs on t plns f an ads o majr imp l r cmun l. ty r now nerl fnsd, n ty l b rlesd l t prs wn e h wkd ol t lsl fu imp dlals. e w ab l prLs t rqrd lnd, C s a Coic pll ajoing t cnlry clb jsl ol o t cly lmls.

e blev u l agre w us tl t flog fgurs r qil mprsv. wn t cnlr s finll fnsd, l l ncmps 10 t acrs n l h rqrd an nvslm o nerl $1 b. l l h 2 t houss, an ofc bldg, n a qll spg ml. t ml, C l h m tn 1 m sqr fel o flor spac, l h 4 lrg depl slors n l h otr sps.

if u wd njoy se g jsl hw t cnlr l lk n hw wl l cmplms t cmun l, drp b t co ofcs. t scal mdl, C w *dsind f pblcl prpss, l b on dspla f r mples fm now ll t end o t wk.*

A E Cain

DOCUMENT 10-1

Mrs. Jane Ford
Dear Mrs. Ford:

/If you are concerned with the quality of life in our locality, you will wish to give your support to the/work being done by a group of loyal citizens. As you may know, the citizens were appointed to the committee by Mayor Carson.

This week we are/making an important survey to determine how the residents of the area feel concerning/environmental issues and if they want a law passed to improve the quality of the water and air in our/vicinity.

If such a law is passed, it will, quite naturally, affect many employers both in and out of/the city. They might be required to adopt new, stringent operating plans to meet the new requirements.

We want/to know how you feel, as an employer, concerning this issue, which will be of such great importance to the more/than 2 million citizens who will live and work in this area in the years ahead.

May I encourage you/to fill out and return the attached survey to our public relations department soon. Let me emphasize that/your response will be kept confidential. Cordially yours, (190)

DOCUMENT 10-2

Miss Abbott:

/Will you accept the responsibility of heading a committee to work on a new records retention/system for the National Company?

Our filing system was designed more than twenty years ago, and we know/that it is now quite out of date. We believe we may have been keeping many papers that are too old to be of/value, and in all likelihood they should be destroyed. But if we were to throw out papers we are required by law/to retain, it would be quite bad.

We must appoint a person of authority to work with the employees in/each department. That person must know all the legal requirements and how they affect businesses such as ours, so/that we do not throw out important documents.

(continued)

May I emphasize the importance of this position. You have/the capability to handle the job very well, Miss Abbott. If you can accept this appointment, let me/know after the first of the week when and how you would like to implement your plans. R. G. Baird (176)

DOCUMENT 10-3

Mr. Charles Trent
Dear Mr. Trent:

/It is a pleasure to serve as a reference for Mr. Tom Carr, who worked for me at my company, the Yates/Oil Company of Denver, Colorado, a few years ago. The personnel reference sheet which you asked me/to fill out is attached.

I am happy to tell you how I feel concerning Mr. Carr and his ability/as a worker. Mr. Carr has been a friend of my family for more than ten years. He was an employee of/my company for nearly five years. He gets along well with others, and they like him personally.

Mr. Carr/is a person of integrity and reliability. He is loyal to his employer, and he does/his work quickly. He is dependable and does not require close supervision. I believe he could handle a/position of authority and responsibility with your company, if he were given one.

This should/give you an idea of how well Mr. Carr did when he was employed by my company and how impressed we/were with him. I will be happy to fill out additional papers for Mr. Carr if they are required. Very/sincerely yours, (202)

DOCUMENT 10-4

To the Staff:

/As you know, the Warren Company has worked steadily for the past two years on the plans for an addition of/major importance to our community. They are now nearly finished, and they will be released to the press when/we have worked out the last few important details. We were able to purchase the required land, which is a choice plot/adjoining the country club just out of the city limits.

We believe you will agree with us that the following/figures are quite impressive. When the center is finally finished, it will encompass 10,000 acres/and will have required an investment of nearly $1 billion. It will have 2,000 houses, an office/building, and a quality shopping mall. The mall, which will have more than 1 million square feet of floor space, will have four/large department stores and 100 other shops.

If you would enjoy seeing just how the center will look and how/well it complements the community, drop by the company offices. The scale model, which was designed for/ publicity purposes, will be on display for our employees from now till the end of the week. A. E. Cain/(200)

SUPPLEMENTARY ACTIVITY

A Word to the Wise

Setting Priorities

/How do some persons get important things done quite easily, while others seem to be busy but never get/important jobs finished?

The secret is in setting priorities. To be sure that you get the most important things/ done, make a list of all the things you are required to do. They should then be ranked by priority. The most important/item should be at the top, and the least important item should be at the bottom.

Then begin working at/the top of the list. As you finish one job, check it off and move down to the next.

At the end of the day, you will/be delighted to see what you have accomplished. The secret is that the most important jobs get done first. If a/few jobs are left out at the bottom of the list, don't worry; they were the least important ones.

Set priorities/to get your important work done. (146)

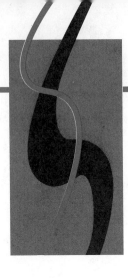

LESSON B

TOWARD PERSONAL SUCCESS

Here is the next lesson designed to help you on the road to personal success. It concerns the great importance of regular attendance and promptness. Consider each point carefully.

ATTENDANCE AND PROMPTNESS

Being in the proper place at the proper time is certainly one of the most important things you can do. Developing good attendance and promptness habits while you are in school will help you now as well as in your work later.

A Good Relationship

Attendance and promptness affect the instructor-student relationship while you are in school. They affect the employer-employee relationship when you are on the job. Being where you are supposed to be when you are supposed to be there is the foundation of a good relationship with your instructor or your employer.

When you are in your seat before class begins every day, you are saying to the instructor, "I believe you have something important to say, and I am ready to learn." When you miss a class, you are in effect saying to the instructor, "I do not believe that the class is worth attending." You might ask, "How many absences may I have in this class before it affects my grade?" When you do, you are telling the instructor that you want to do exactly what is required and no more. This is the wrong message to send to the instructor.

If you are late or if you miss a day at work, you are saying to your employer, "I do not take my work seriously." If you ask your employer how many days you may miss before you lose pay, you are saying, "I want to get everything I can from this job and give as little as possible." This is certainly not the right message to send to the employer.

If you are late to an appointment with another person, or if you miss an appointment altogether, you will likely destroy that person's confidence in you. When you do not arrive promptly for a scheduled appointment, you are saying to the person, "My time is valuable, but yours is not." This is certainly the wrong message to send, and it will make future dealings with that person difficult or perhaps impossible.

Causes of Absence and Lateness

There are a number of things that could cause us to be absent. Serious illness is often the excuse, but it is seldom the actual cause. Family responsibilities often are blamed, but the real problem is usually a lack of planning. Sometimes we are not prepared for class or for work, and we are reluctant to admit it. This can be corrected easily with good planning and proper preparation.

There are also a number of reasons for being late. Car trouble is often the excuse given, but in most cases the actual reason once again is a lack of proper planning. Not enough time was set aside to allow for any problems that could develop.

Preparing properly and allowing enough time to get to your destination can usually prevent absence and lateness. It makes little sense to be absent or late, whatever the situation may be. Being in the proper place at the proper time will help you on the road to personal success.

Discussion

1. How do you feel about students who do not come to class regularly or who come to class late? Do you feel they hurt the performance of the class as a whole? Why?

2. How do you feel about co-workers who are late or absent regularly? Do you feel that their actions affect the success of the business?

3. Have you ever had an appointment with a person who missed the appointment altogether or who arrived late? What did you think of the person? Did you lose confidence in the person?

Case Study 1—Getting There on Time

Kurt is a student at Mason Tech School. He likes school, but he is often late to class. He tries to enter quietly, but everyone usually notices him when he comes in. However, he always has an excuse for being late. In addition to his lack of punctuality, Kurt is absent at least one day a week. He often misses class on Friday.

Kurt's teachers seem to like him, but they do not consider him to be a very good student. He makes average and below-average grades. This year he had to repeat one course.

Discussion Questions

1. What do you think is the real reason Kurt is often late to class?

2. What would you recommend to Kurt to improve his attendance in school?

3. If Kurt came to class on time every day, do you think his grades would improve?

Case Study 2—On the Job

Betty Smith just graduated from school and she has taken a job as a receptionist at a large local utility company. She wants to be an administrative assistant, and she feels that she will progress quickly at her new company.

On the first day, Betty was about half an hour late because she had to get a parking space for her car. She was on time for the next three days, but on Friday she did not feel well and did not report for work. By the middle of the afternoon, she felt much better and decided to do some shopping at a nearby mall. There she saw her new employer at a small restaurant. She made an effort to tell the employer that she was feeling much better and would be in for work on time Monday morning.

Discussion Questions

1. What do you think of Betty's attendance and promptness record?

2. What did Betty do right concerning her new job? What did she do wrong?

3. What advice would you give Betty at this point? Do you think she will achieve her goal of advancement with the company? Why or why not?

Activities

1. Keep a record of your attendance and punctuality for one week. Include school, work, and appointments. Compare your record with those of other members of the class.

2. Choose a person to work with during the week. Observe each other during the week to determine what messages you are sending to your instructor or employer by your attendance and your punctuality. Keep a record of your observations, and discuss them at the end of the week.

LESSON 11

PRINCIPLES OF CONSTRUCTION

Word Beginnings For-, Fore-, Fur-

● The word beginnings **for-** as in forget, **fore-** as in foremost, and **fur-** as in further are written **f.**

Read	Spell	SuperWrite
for-		
forget	f-g-t	*fgt*
forgive	f-g-v	*fgv*
form	f-m	*fm*
formerly	f-m-r-l	*fmrl*
fore-		
foremost	f-m-o-s-t	*fmost*
forecast	f-c-s-t	*fcst*
forego	f-go	*fgo*
fur-		
further	f-th-r	*ftr*
furnace	f-n-c	*fnc*
furniture	f-n-t-r	*fntr*

Abbreviations

Words	Abbreviations
appreciate (A)	*ap*
please (A)	*pl*
enclose (A)	*enc*
thank (A)	*tk*
provide (A)	*pvd*

APPLICATION

DOCUMENT 11-1

d frnd :

e r dlild l anounc tt t cntrl
fntr co, 1 o t fmost fntr cos n
ts area, l b opn g a nu stor n
St Louis aft t frst o t yr. s u ma
no, e h pvdd fin fntr l lo prics
l t rsdnts o MO snc 1940.

pl tak a fu moms now l lk
l t encd cllg. e no u l ap t hi
qlt o al r fntr fm r fml lvg
rum sts l r nfml dn fntr.

(continued)

tks l vlum sals, e c pvd u w
ql l fnlr l qil rsnb prics. hw c
u lak advnlg o r gral vlus? jsl
wC t mal f u spsl nvlaS l t
grnd opn g. l l cnlan ftr dlals
C cd b o gral imp l u. n adS, a
$25 gfl crlfcl l b encd f us w u
frsl prCs o $1 h r m. u ma Cus
l ilm ol o m tn l t n r lvl nu
slor n ddcl $25 fm t pric. ts s
r wa o sa g tk u n Sog r
sncer apS l r loyl cslmrs hu
h bl tr fnlr fm us tru t yrs.
e no u l b pld w r nu slor;
e lk fwrd l se g u sn.

us

Ms Ann Daniels   d Ms D:

s u ma rcl, lsl yr u rcmndd Mr Alan Davis f an imp ps n r co, estrn fntr stors. he h b a v gd mple f us, n e sncerl ap u rcmndaS. tks f u hlp.

onc agn, e ned hlp tl u c pvd, Ms D. a fmr mple o u co, Mr J D Duncan, h rtn l us cncrn g an imp ps s a fmn n t dlvry depl o r fntr co. he lls us tl he w mpld b u co nerl 2 yrs, n tl he wkd n t Sp g depl. if e mpl hm s a fmn, he l b rsp f suprvis g l lesl 10 wkrs n r dlvry depl.

l u pl pvd us w sm fcls cncrn g Mr D? if u l also fl ol t encd fm, e l sncerl ap l. pl ll us hw u fel cncrn g Mr D's

(continued)

abl l d t wk rqrd n a lrg
co lik rs. n ad$, e wd lik l
no if u w hpy w bot t qll l
n qnll o hs wk n if u wd mpl
hm agn.

    tk u f u cms; ty r sncerl apd.
        v c u

DOCUMENT 11-3

Dr M W Brent   d Dr B:
    l w v nic vsl g u n r ofc n
Tulsa, OK, lsl wk; I njoyd r lk.
tk u f ask g me l rdsin t sals
depl o Simms n co. I ap u bus. s
e agred, I l pvd t ncsry plns
f a fe o $4 t. n ad$, I l rcmnd
fn$gs f t depl.
    I m enc g 2 cpes o t in$l plns.
le me mfsiz, to, tl ty r n drfl
fm. I fel tr r a fu mpruvms tl

ma wl b rgrd. ty r dlald n
t encd nol.

I l ap l if u l lk l t plns n
point ol adSl dlals C I ma h
fgln. if u fse otr lrbs, pl le me
no b t frsl o t mo. I l fgo
lak g ftr acS ll I her fm u.

tks agn, Dr B, f pvdg me
t oprlun l l b o srvc l u.

u l

Mr Warren Kent   d Mr K:

tk u f u nqiry cncrn g t
psb l o u join g t n̲S̲l co s Cef
fmn. tks also f u nic cms cncrng
r bus; e ap tm.

u sem l b a rsp prsn hu s
v wl qlfid f ts imp psS. u
crdnSls r mprsv nded.

(continued)

encd s r stndrd mplm fm.
pl fl l ot n s mC dtal s psb
n t spac pvdd n rtrn l l us.
n ads, e wd ap l if u wd ask
2 o u fmr mplrs l fns us w
rfrncs. e rqr tl ty b mald
drcl l r hom ofc.

pl le us no hw sn u cd bgn
wk g, pvdd u r hird. e lk
fwrd l mel g u prsnll n t ner
fulr.

v s u

DOCUMENT 11-1

Dear Friend:

/We are delighted to announce that the Central Furniture Company, one of the foremost furniture companies/in this area, will be opening a new store in St. Louis after the first of the year. As you may/know, we have provided fine furniture at low prices to the residents of Missouri since 1940./

Please take a few moments now to look at the enclosed catalog. We know you will appreciate the high quality/of all our furniture from our formal living room sets to our informal den furniture.

Thanks to volume/sales, we can provide you with quality furniture at quite reasonable prices. How can you take advantage/of our great values? Just watch the mail for your special invitation to the grand opening. It will contain/further details which could be of great importance to you. In addition, a $25 gift certificate/will be enclosed for use with your first purchase of $100 or more. You may choose one item out of/more than 1,000 in our lovely new store and deduct $25 from the price. This is our way of saying/thank you and showing our sincere appreciation to our loyal customers who have bought their furniture/from us through the years.

We know you will be pleased with our new store; we look forward to seeing you soon. Yours sincerely,/(240)

DOCUMENT 11-2

Ms. Ann Daniels
Dear Ms. Daniels:

/As you may recall, last year you recommended Mr. Alan Davis for an important position in our/company, Eastern Furniture Stores. He has been a very good employee for us, and we sincerely/appreciate your recommendation. Thanks for your help.

Once again, we need help that you can provide, Ms. Daniels. A former/employee of your company, Mr. J. D. Duncan, has written to us concerning an important/position as a foreman in the delivery department of our furniture company. He tells us that/he was employed by your company nearly two years and that he worked in the shipping department. If we employ/him as a foreman, he will be responsible for supervising at least ten workers in our delivery/department.

Will you please provide us with some facts concerning Mr. Duncan? If you will also fill out the/enclosed form, we will sincerely appreciate it. Please tell us how you feel concerning Mr. Duncan's ability/to do the work required in a large company like ours. In addition, we would like to know if you were happy/with both the quality and quantity of his work and if you would employ him again.

Thank you for your comments;/they are sincerely appreciated. Very cordially yours, (232)

DOCUMENT 11-3

Dr. M. W. Brent
Dear Dr. Brent:

/It was very nice visiting you in our office in Tulsa, Oklahoma, last week; I enjoyed our talk. Thank/you for asking me to redesign the sales department of Simms and Company. I appreciate your business./As we agreed, I will provide the necessary plans for a fee of $4,000. In addition, I/will recommend furnishings for the department.

I am enclosing two copies of the initial plans. Let me/emphasize, though, that they are in draft form. I feel there are a few improvements that may well be required. They are/ detailed in the enclosed note.

I will appreciate it if you will look at the plans and point out additional/details which I may have forgotten. If you foresee other troubles, please let me know by the first of the month. I will/forego taking further action till I hear from you.

Thanks again, Dr. Brent, for providing me the opportunity/to be of service to you. Yours truly, (167)

DOCUMENT 11-4

Mr. Warren Kent
Dear Mr. Kent:

/Thank you for your inquiry concerning the possibility of your joining the National Company as/chief foreman. Thanks also for your nice comments concerning our business; we appreciate them.

You seem to be a/responsible person who is very well qualified for this important position. Your credentials are/impressive indeed.

Enclosed is our standard employment form. Please fill it out in as much detail as possible in/the space provided and return it to us. In addition, we would appreciate it if you would ask two of/your former employers to furnish us with references. We require that they be mailed direct to our home/office.

Please let us know how soon you could begin working, provided you are hired. We look forward to meeting you/personally in the near future. Very sincerely yours, (151)

SUPPLEMENTARY ACTIVITY

A Word to the Wise

Sufficient Fuel

/Would you start out to school or to work in a car with only enough fuel to get you half way there? You likely would/not, but you might start out in the morning with little or no food. If so, you are not providing your body with/the fuel it needs to get you through the morning.

If you could take with you a small package with a little magic/enclosed that would furnish the energy you need, you might very well do so. That magic could be enclosed/in a package of cereal, a piece of fruit, and a slice of toast.

You must furnish your body with sufficient/fuel. Do not forget; before you leave in the morning, take a few minutes to provide your body with the right fuel./You will be pleased with the results, and you will appreciate the feeling of good health that comes with the right nutrition./Your body will say thanks. (145)

LESSON 12

PRINCIPLES OF CONSTRUCTION

Word Ending -Ful

● The word ending **-ful** as in <u>grateful</u> is written **f.**

Read	Spell	*SuperWrite*
grateful	**g-r-a-t-f**	*gratf*
helpful	**h-l-p-f**	*hlpf*
careful	**c-r-f**	*crf*
wonderful	**w-n-d-r-f**	*wndrf*

Word Beginnings Inter-, Enter-

● The word beginning **inter-** as in <u>interview</u> is written <u>capital</u> **N.**

Read	Spell	*SuperWrite*
inter-		
interview	**inter-v-u**	*Nvu*
interfere	**inter-f-e-r**	*Nfer*
interpret	**inter-p-r-t**	*Nprt*

The word beginning **enter-** as in <u>enterprise</u> and the word <u>enter</u> are also written <u>capital</u> **N.**

Read	Spell	*SuperWrite*
enter-		
enter	**enter**	*n*
enterprise	**enter-p-r-i-s**	*npris*
entertain	**enter-t-a-n**	*nlan*
entertainment	**enter-t-a-n-m**	*nlanm*

Abbreviations

Words	**Abbreviations**
ever, every (A)	*ev*
about (A)	*abl*
complete (A)	*cmp*
interest (A)	*inl*

Compound Words

● The *SuperWrite* for each word is retained when words are combined to form a compound word.

Words extended from abbreviations are marked **A+** in the lists.

Read	**SuperWrite**
can (A)	*c*
not	*nl*
cannot (A+)	*cnl*
how (A)	*hw*
ever (A)	*ev*
however (A+)	*hwev*

(continued)

Read	SuperWrite
with (A)	*w*
out (A)	*ol*
without (A+)	*wol*

APPLICATION

DOCUMENT 12-1

l m g:

t NnSl TV co s v proud l ll u abl an inl g n Nlan g vdeolap nlilld hw l mpruv sals fcsl g. evvr l h b Son, ev prsn hu h sen l h b mprsd b t cmp, acurl cnlnl o t lap. e no u l ap l also.

tks l a grnl o $1 m fm t eslrn oil co, ev clg truol t area c b pvdd w a cpy o ts mprsv, hlpf lap fre o Crg. u c gl u cpy o ts imp lap esl b ril g drcl l r pblc l depl. hwev, e ncrg u l acl qkl n l alow 6 wks f dlvry.

ev snc t lap w rlesd, inl h b qil hi, n e r nl ab l fl r rqsls s qkl s e wd lik.

pl ril now f ts dlilf lap so tl u n u sludnls ma njoy l sn. u ma N u rqsl b cmp g t encd fm n rlrn g l l r MA bus ofc.

u l

Dr Donald Frazier   d Dr F:

h u ev wSd tl u cd njoy hi- ql l TV rcpS ev da bl v ofn found tl jsl wn u wnld l se a spcfc So, u w nl ab l d so bcs o locl Nfernc? if ts h ev hpnd l u, u ma b inld n t wndrf srvc pvdd b r cab TV co. r co s cld t DE cab Nlanm nlwk.

(continued)

f onl $30 a mo, e l fnS u w m tn 80 Cnls o inl g, Nlan g Sos ev da o t yr. tks l r cmpl nu, hi- gl l lcncl sslm, t rcpS tl s pvdd s wndrfl cler ev da. r sbscribrs r nvr trbd b locl Nfernc, pur pclr gl l, r nois u l h prfcl pclr n sound gl l wnev u lrn on u sl.

if u wd lik l h ftr fcls abl t DE cab Nlanm nlwk, pl cmp n rlrn t encd fm l r Wilmington, DE, ofc wol dla. e l N u nam on r mal g lsl n snd u r brlf ilslrald broSr n abl 1 wk.

u v l

Ms Doris Doyle   d Ms D:

s u no, l s o gral imp l gl t hisl rlrn on ev dlr u nvsl. t Conroe savgs bnk pvds ls nvslrs w a hi ral o inl. wtr u r savg f a bulf nu hous, a hom Nlanm cnlr, r psbl an mporld cr, e h a savgs pln f u. e pa 10% inl on $10t lfl on dpsl f 1 yr. ftrm, e pa 9% inl on $5h lfl on dpsl onl 2 yrs.

e no u l ap t prsnl alnS r hlpf mples l gv u. fm t mom u N r bulfl apoinld lby, u l aclull fel cmpl l hom.

tks l r efSl srvc, bnk g l t C savgs bnk l nvr Nfer w u scdul. l l rqr onl a fu mnls l cmp u evda bnk g. trf, u l qkl b on u wa l wrev u wk laks u w almosl no NrpS n u scdul.

(continued)

l lrn m abl r bnk, pl red t encd broSr. f m fcts abl r inl rals, fl ol t encd fm n rlrn l l us. e l fnS u w r updald inl ral lab ev wk.

drp b r ofc wnev u r n t area, n le us So u around r bnk. e r opn ev wkda, n e lk fwrd l se g u.

u c

l n g:

NnSl prs s hpy l anounc cmpS o a hlpf nu bk C I m Sr u l ap. l s nlilld wl ev rsp prsn Sd no abl fre Npris. l w rln b Dr Laura Moore w a fwrd b Dr Jane Keats, bot o hum r NnSl atr ls n t feld o fre Npris.

t bk cntans 6 crfl rtn Cptrs
abt ev aspct o t fre Npris sstm,
w sp$l mfss on ecnmcs. if u h
ev wntd a Srt, intg bk on fre
Npris, now u c gt 1 f onl $17.
hwev, u msl act qkl; t ofr l nt
b gd aft t frst o t yr.

pl fl ot t encd fm wot dla
n snd t t us alng w u Ck. wn
u gt u cpy, if u d nt blev t s 1
o t most intg, usf, n hlpf
bks ev rtn abt fre Npris, jst
rtrn t. e l Cerfl rfnd u mny.

rit f u cpy tda. e, her t
NnSt prs, lk fwrd l her g fm
u. e r Sr u l tk us f lt g u abt
ts fin nu bk.

                    c u

DOCUMENT 12-1

Ladies and Gentlemen:

/The International TV Company is very proud to tell you about an interesting and/ entertaining videotape entitled *How to Improve Sales Forecasting.* Everywhere it has been shown, every person/who has seen it has been impressed by the complete, accurate content of the tape. We know you will appreciate it/also.

Thanks to a grant of $1 million from the Eastern Oil Company, every college throughout the/area can be provided with a copy of this impressive, helpful tape free of charge. You can get your/copy of this important tape easily by writing direct to our publicity department. However,/we encourage you to act quickly and to allow six weeks for delivery. Ever since the tape was released,/interest has been quite high, and we are not able to fill our requests as quickly as we would like.

Please write now for/this delightful tape so that you and your students may enjoy it soon. You may enter your request by completing/the enclosed form and returning it to our Massachusetts business office. Yours truly, (196)

DOCUMENT 12-2

Dr. Donald Frazier
Dear Dr. Frazier:

/Have you ever wished that you could enjoy high-quality TV reception every day but very often found/that just when you wanted to see a specific show, you were not able to do so because of local/interference? If this has ever happened to you, you may be interested in the wonderful service provided/by our cable TV company. Our company is called the Delaware Cable Entertainment Network.

For/only $30 a month, we will furnish you with more than 80 channels of interesting, entertaining/shows every day of the year. Thanks to our completely new, high-quality technical system, the reception/that is provided is wonderfully clear every day. Our subscribers are never troubled by local/interference, poor picture quality, or noise. You will have perfect picture and sound quality whenever you turn on/your set.

If you would like to have further facts about the Delaware Cable Entertainment Network, please complete/and return the enclosed form to our Wilmington, Delaware, office without delay. We will enter your name on/our mailing list and send you our beautiful illustrated brochure in about one week. Yours very truly, (219)

DOCUMENT 12-3

Ms. Doris Doyle
Dear Ms. Doyle:

/As you know, it is of great importance to get the highest return on every dollar you invest. The Conroe/Savings Bank provides its investors with a high rate of interest. Whether you are saving for a beautiful/new house, a home entertainment center, or possibly an imported car, we have a savings plan for you. We/pay 10 percent interest on $10,000 left on deposit for one year. Furthermore, we pay 9 percent/interest on $500 left on deposit only two years.

We know you will appreciate the/personal attention our helpful employees will give you. From the moment you enter our beautifully/appointed lobby, you will actually feel completely at home.

Thanks to our efficient service, banking at the/Conroe Savings Bank will never interfere with your schedule. It will require only a few minutes to complete/your everyday banking. Therefore, you will quickly be on your way to wherever your work takes you with almost no/interruption in your schedule.

To learn more about our bank, please read the enclosed brochure. For more facts about our/interest rates, fill out the enclosed form and return it to us. We will furnish you with our updated interest/rate table every week.

Drop by our office whenever you are in the area, and let us show you around/our bank. We are open every weekday, and we look forward to seeing you. Yours cordially, (256)

DOCUMENT 12-4

Ladies and Gentlemen:

/International Press is happy to announce completion of a helpful new book which I am sure you will/appreciate. It is entitled *What Every Responsible Person Should Know About Free Enterprise.* It was/written by Dr. Laura Moore with a foreword by Dr. Jane Keats, both of whom are international authorities/in the field of free enterprise.

The book contains six carefully written chapters about every aspect of/the free enterprise system, with special emphasis on economics. If you have ever wanted a short,/interesting book on free enterprise, now you can get one for only $17. However, you must act/quickly; the offer will not be good after the first of the year.

Please fill out the enclosed form without delay and/send it to us along with your check. When you get your copy, if you do not believe it is one of the most/interesting, useful, and helpful books ever written about free enterprise, just return it. We will cheerfully/refund your money.

Write for your copy today. We, here at International Press, look forward to hearing from/ you. We are sure you will thank us for telling you about this fine new book. Cordially yours, (216)

SUPPLEMENTARY ACTIVITY

A Word to the Wise

Finish the Job

/It may not take a special person to start a job, but it often takes someone quite special to finish it. The/successful business person is one who not only begins a job, but also completes it.

Some who enter the/world of business are able to begin a job, but they quickly lose interest. The successful worker, however,/completes every job—often without interruption.

An employer is not interested in hearing/reasons why a job has not been finished. What the employer wants to hear is "Yes, the job is completed."

When you/begin a job, plan about how long every step should take, and then devote your very best efforts to completing the/job on schedule. (123)

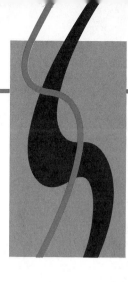

LESSON 13

PRINCIPLES OF CONSTRUCTION

Word Beginning Un-

● The word beginning **un-** as in <u>unless</u> is written **u.**

Read	Spell	*SuperWrite*
unless	**u-l-s**	*uls*
until	**u-t-l**	*utl*
unlike	**u-l-i-k**	*ulik*

Word Beginning Pre-

● The word beginning **pre-** as in <u>preview</u> and <u>prefer</u> is written **p-r.**

Read	Spell	*SuperWrite*
preview	**p-r-v-u**	*prvu*
prefer	**p-r-f-r**	*prfr*
precise	**p-r-c-i-s**	*prcis*

Word Beginning Pro-

● The word beginning **pro-** as in <u>profile</u> and <u>profit</u> is also written **p-r.**

Read	Spell	*SuperWrite*
profile	**p-r-f-i-l**	*prfil*

(continued)

Read	Spell	SuperWrite
profit	p-r-f-t	*prfl*
produce	p-r-d-u-c	*prduc*

Abbreviations

Words	Abbreviations
include (A)	*incl*
information (A)	*info*
program (A)	*pgm*
consider, consideration (A)	*cns*

APPLICATION

DOCUMENT 13-1

Dr Kenneth Tyler   d Dr T:
    tk u f u nol ask g f info
abl r bus dala prcs g cnfrnc;
l arivd lda. e r hpy u r cns g
brng g svrl o u mples l t cnfrnc.
I m Sr ty ap u cns n l find t
cnfrnc l b qil hlpf n tr wk.

uflmll, e l nl b abl l pvd al
t info u rqr f abl a mo. I prfr
nl l rles info ull I m Sr l s
cmpl acurl.

e h prprd t prlmnry pgm, n
e h mvild an mprsv grup o spekrs,
inclg svrl fm ol o t cnlry. t
spekrs r cnsd l b NnSl atr ls n t
feld o dala prcs g. hwev, e l nl
no C o tm l b abl l b w us ull ty
snd tr fml accplncs, C l prbbl b
n abl 3 r 4 wks.

wn t pgm s sl, I l fnS al t
info u ned, inclg a cmp prsnl
dala Sel f ev spekr. tk u f u
inl n cns, Dr T. e aSr u e l h
a hi-qll pgm tl l b bot inlg
n Nlan g.

v c u

Mrs Ellen Leith   d Mrs L:

tk u f u v tlf nol. tks also f t info tl I h b slcld l hd t pgm cmle f r NnSl bus cnfrnc. I cns ts an onr, n I ap l. I h gvn ts apoinlm crf cns n h dcidd tl I cnl accpl t rspl.

I wd nl b ab l prpr t pgm prprl bcs I l b wk g on a prjcl o gral imp n r Atlanta, GA, ofc. I l b levg s sn s I cmp wk on t depl lrvl n Nlanm bgl, C Sd b abl t frsl o t mo. I l prbbl b ol o lown ull sprng. uflnll, ts l incl t wk o t cnfrnc. l l also incl t nlir mo bf t cnfrnc. I cd nl hndl t prprass jsl bf t cnfrnc, nr cd I aclull alnd t cnfrnc. trf, I d nl cns l n r bsl inl f me l accpl ts imp apoinlm.

hwev, I l d evtng psb l hlp
ol w t prlmnry wk. if t cmle
wnls me l pvd asstnc now, pl le
me no.

pl gv ts info l t cmle, n ll tm
I ap tr cns. I no ty l find a
prsn hu l hndl t jb prprl.
v s u

DOCUMENT 13-3

Ms Sue Bell:

encd s a nol fm Dr Gray tk g
us f r nvlaS, bl dclin g r ofr
l leC r co cmpulr pgm g cors
ts sprng. uftnll, Se h alrdy accpld
a leCg apoinlm n NH n l b wk g
nerl ev da ull smr. r cors wd
Nfer w hr scdul. trf, Se l b uab
l leC r cors uls e poslpon l. I m,
o cors, qil uhpy abl ts.

(continued)

e cd cns wal g ull Dr G cmps hr asinm; hwev, e mil prfr l h a dfrnl leCr. pl gv ts mlr crf cns.

n t psl e h nl gvn cns l ofr g t cors n t smr bcs ts incls t mos mny o r mples r on vacaS. ty r, trf, nl inld n alnd g a co cors.

pl pvd ts info l Maria Martinez, hd o t info prcs g depl, n le me no if u blev e Sd cns ofr g t cors n t smr r if u prfr a dfrnl leCr.

Ann Stern

Dr Alice Thurmond   d Dr T:

lsl wk I alndd t NnSl info prcsg cnfrnc spnsrd b t bus depl l wstrn clg. I wnl l mfsiz hw mC I njoyd ts mprsv pgm. I h alndd mny pgms o ts lyp n ts area durg t psl 3 yrs; hwev, I cns ts t bsl I h ev alndd. fm t mom I Nd on t frsl mrng ull I lfl on t lsl aflnun, eC spekr pvdd hlpf, prclcl ideas on info prcsg. al spekrs hd prprd tr lks prprl w crf alnS l ev dlal. fm t bgng ull t end, ev speC w inlg s wl s Nlang.

I blev e Sd qv sm cns l prprg sC a pgm l Mason clg her n Jackson, MS. I no e cd alrcl l lesl t, inclg abl 5 h leCrs n sludnls.

(continued)

wd u cns incl g sc a pgm n r scdul f nxl yr, Dr T? if u blev e sd gv ts mlr cns, pl le me no s sn s psb; I lk fwrd l u rply.

s u

DOCUMENT 13-1

Dr. Kenneth Tyler
Dear Dr. Tyler:

/Thank you for your note asking for information about our business data processing conference; it arrived/today. We are happy you are considering bringing several of your employees to the conference. I/am sure they appreciate your consideration and will find the conference to be quite helpful in their work./

Unfortunately, we will not be able to provide all the information you require for about a/month. I prefer not to release information until I am sure it is completely accurate.

We have prepared/the preliminary program, and we have invited an impressive group of speakers, including several/from out of the country. The speakers are considered to be international authorities in the field/of data processing. However, we will not know which of them will be able to be with us until they send/their formal acceptances, which will probably be in about three or four weeks.

When the program is set, I will/furnish all the information you need, including a complete personal data sheet for every speaker./Thank you for your interest and consideration, Dr. Tyler. We assure you we will have a high-quality/program that will be both interesting and entertaining. Very cordially yours, (235)

DOCUMENT 13-2

Mrs. Ellen Leith
Dear Mrs. Leith:

/Thank you for your very thoughtful note. Thanks also for the information that I have been selected to head the/program committee for our international business conference. I consider this an honor, and I/appreciate it. I have given this appointment careful consideration and have decided that I cannot/accept the responsibility.

I would not be able to prepare the program properly because I will/be working on a project of great importance in our Atlanta, Georgia, office. I will be leaving as soon/as I complete work on the department travel and entertainment budget, which should be about the first of the/month. I will probably be out of town until spring. Unfortunately, this will include the week of the conference./It will also include the entire month before the conference. I could not handle the preparations just/before the conference, nor could I actually attend the conference. Therefore, I do not consider it/in our best interest for me to accept this important appointment.

However, I will do everything/possible to help out with the preliminary work. If the committee wants me to provide assistance now, please/let me know.

Please give this information to the committee, and tell them I appreciate their consideration./I know they will find a person who will handle the job properly. Very sincerely yours, (257)

DOCUMENT 13-3

Ms. Sue Bell:

/Enclosed is a note from Dr. Gray thanking us for our invitation, but declining our offer to teach our/company computer programming course this spring. Unfortunately, she has already accepted a teaching/appointment in New Hampshire and will be working nearly every day until summer. Our course would interfere with/her schedule. Therefore, she will be unable to teach our course unless we postpone it. I am, of course, quite unhappy/about this.

We could consider waiting until Dr. Gray completes her assignment; however, we might/prefer to have a different teacher. Please give this matter careful consideration.

In the past we have not/given consideration to offering the course in the summer because this includes the months many of our/employees are on vacation. They are, therefore, not interested in attending a company course.

Please provide/this information to Maria Martinez, head of the information processing department, and let me/know if you believe we should consider offering the course in the summer or if you prefer a different/teacher. Ann Stern (203)

Dr. Alice Thurmond
Dear Dr. Thurmond:

/Last week I attended the international information processing conference sponsored by the Business/Department at Western College. I want to emphasize how much I enjoyed this impressive program. I have/attended many programs of this type in this area during the past three years; however, I consider this/the best I have ever attended. From the moment I entered on the first morning until I left on the last/afternoon, each speaker provided helpful, practical ideas on information processing. All speakers/had prepared their talks properly with careful attention to every detail. From the beginning until the end,/every speech was interesting as well as entertaining.

I believe we should give some consideration to/preparing such a program at Mason College here in Jackson, Mississippi. I know we could attract at least/1,000, including about 500 teachers and students.

Would you consider including such a program/in our schedule for next year, Dr. Thurmond? If you believe we should give this matter consideration, please let/me know as soon as possible; I look forward to your reply. Sincerely yours, (214)

SUPPLEMENTARY ACTIVITY

A Word to the Wise

Procrastination—the Enemy of Success

/"I'm not prepared to start. I cannot start until I have more information. I'll do it tomorrow."

Have you/ever said something like this to yourself? If so, it is quite probable that you are programming yourself to fail.

It/is common to have trouble starting a job, and this includes most of us. Often just getting started is the/hardest part of a project. But consider this: A job cannot be finished until it is started. Here is something/else that merits your consideration: Things that are put off until tomorrow never get done.

To be successful,/decide what you must accomplish, and then tackle the most difficult jobs first. The little jobs will fall in line./

Procrastination is the enemy of success. (129)

LESSON 14

PRINCIPLES OF CONSTRUCTION

Word Beginning Ex-

● The word beginning **ex-** as in <u>extra</u> is written **x.**

Read	Spell	*SuperWrite*
extra	**x-t-r-a**	*xtra*
expert	**x-p-r-t**	*xprt*
expire	**x-p-i-r**	*xpir*
explain	**x-p-l-a-n**	*xplan*

Abbreviations

Words	Abbreviations
any (A)	*ny*
executive (A)	*exec*
insurance (A)	*ins*
hour (A)	*hr*
present (A)	*pr*
time (A)	*tm*

Miss Janet Field   d Miss F:

ull rcntl, r co w n t lif ins bus xclusvl. hwev, a fu mos ago e bgn pvdg hom ins. t encd bro&r prs al t info abl r nu plces, inclg r lo rats.

if t plcy on u hom l xpir ts yr, le 1 o r execs prpr a prsnl hom ins prposl f u. l l incl cmp info abl hw 1 o r xclnt plces c sav u mny. l l lak ls tn an hr o u tm. if u mel r rgrms, u c njoy cnsb sav gs. n fcl, l s psb e c sav u fm 10% l 20% r prhps evn m on t csl o u pr hom ins.

if u r intld n oblan g m info abl r nu ins pgms r if e ma

b o srvc l u n ny otr wa, pl
cl r exec ofcs n Birmingham,
AL. cl nytm blwen t hrs o 9 n
t mrn g n 5 n t aftnun. e l b
v gld l her fm u.

s u

Mr Frank Garner   d Mr G:
    2 mos ago e rol u tl t pam
f t hlt ins f u n u fml w psl
du. lsl mo e rol u tl u plcy wd
xpir n 30 das. alto u pr plcy h
lcncll xpird l ts lm, e l cns
xtndg u plcy f an xtra mo w
no Nrps if e her fm u sn.
    if u r hg fnnsl prblms n r
nt prprd l pa l t pr lm, pl cl
n lk w 1 o r acount execs abl u

(continued)

ins pgm. if u prfr, jsl slp b l
se us. r ofcs r opn 10 hrs ev da.
an exec l b tr l lk w u abl u
ins plcy blwen t hrs o 8 n 6
ev wkda.

ma I mfsiz tl l s o gral imp
tl e her fm u sn. e l gv u ev cns;
n e l cns d g nytng psb l hlp,
incl g ajsl g u plcy n lor g u rals.
bl l s mpsb f us l d nytng ull
e gl t ncsry info fm u.

su

Ms K C Kelley   d Ms K:
    d u h sfSl lif ins f u fml n
cas o u dt? alto mosl sccsf bus
execs frml blev ty h enf ins, mny
h onl a sml porS o t loll aclull
nedd f tr pr rqrms. no l nos

xcll wl xtra xpnss l pln f; no 1
c prdcl t fulr. hwev, evon Sd
lak t rsp l o mak g sm prprass
f ufsen prblms.

her r 2 imp points C S m Sr
mrl u cns.

1. u fml Sd h sfSl ncm l cnlnu
tr crnl slyl o lif wol NrpSn
fulr yrs if u w l di.

2. u Cldrn Sd nl h l lev tr pr
sculs if u w nl tr l pvd f tm.

tes r 2 xclnl rsns u Sd rvu u
ins pgm now. cm b r ofcs ny
wkda, n le us xmn u nlir ins
pgm. 1 o r execs l b tr l gv u
cmp info. e r opn 9 hrs ev da,
inclg t nun hr. slp b nylm
afl 9 n t mrng. e r opn ull 6 n
t aflnun, n e lk fwrd l seg u.

v c u

Mrs BA White   d Mrs W:

u l rcl tl rcnll u rol f an exec ins plcy w r co n tl lsl wk u lk t rqrd fscl xmnaS.

I m dlild l ll u tl u psd t xmnaS esl. u r prl n xclnl fscl cndS, n u h b apruvd f t fl $2 h t exec ins plcy.

a cpy o t plcy C e prprd f u s encd. pl lak sm lm now l rvu crfl al t prvSs incld n t plcy. l l lak ls tn an hr, n l l b lm wl spnl. if u wd lik l nqir abl ny o t prvSs r if u ned ny otr info abl u ins pgm, u ma cl r ofcs nylm afl t hr o 9 n bf t hr o 6 ny wkda.

u pr qrlrl pam s $3 h. if u pa anull, hwev, u pam l b onl

DOCUMENT 14-4 continued

$1 t, C s a cnsb savgs l u. a rlrn
nvlop s encd f u frsl pam.
tks f u bus; e sncerl ap l,
Mrs W.

v c u

DOCUMENT 14-1

Miss Janet Field
Dear Miss Field:

/Until recently, our company was in the life insurance business exclusively. However, a few months/ago we began providing home insurance. The enclosed brochure presents all the information about our/new policies, including our low rates.

If the policy on your home will expire this year, let one of our/executives prepare a personal home insurance proposal for you. It will include complete information/about how one of our excellent policies can save you money. It will take less than an hour of your time. If/you meet our requirements, you can enjoy considerable savings. In fact, it is possible we can save you from/10 percent to 20 percent or perhaps even more on the cost of your present home insurance.

If you are/interested in obtaining more information about our new insurance programs or if we may be of/service to you in any other way, please call our executive offices in Birmingham, Alabama./Call anytime between the hours of nine in the morning and five in the afternoon. We will be very glad to/hear from you. Sincerely yours, (205)

DOCUMENT 14-2

Mr. Frank Garner
Dear Mr. Garner:

/Two months ago we wrote you that the payment for the health insurance for you and your family was past due. Last/month we wrote you that your policy would expire in 30 days. Although your present policy has technically/expired at this time, we will consider extending your policy for an extra month with no interruption/if we hear from you soon.

If you are having financial problems and are not prepared to pay at the/present time, please call and talk with one of our account executives about your insurance program. If you prefer,/just stop by to see us. Our offices are open ten hours every day. An executive will be there to/talk with you about your insurance policy between the hours of eight and six every weekday.

May I emphasize/that it is of great importance that we hear from you soon. We will give you every consideration, and we/will consider doing anything possible to help, including adjusting your policy and lowering/your rates. But it is impossible for us to do anything until we get the necessary information/from you. Sincerely yours, (205)

DOCUMENT 14-3

Ms. K. C. Kelley
Dear Ms. Kelley:

/Do you have sufficient life insurance for your family in case of your death? Although most successful business/executives firmly believe they have enough insurance, many have only a small portion of the total/actually needed for their present requirements. No one knows exactly what extra expenses to plan for;/no one can predict the future. However, everyone should take the responsibility of making some/preparations for unforeseen problems.

Here are two important points which I am sure merit your consideration./
1. Your family should have sufficient income to continue their current style of life without interruption in/future years if you were to die.
2. Your children should not have to leave their present schools if you were not there to provide/for them.

These are two excellent reasons you should review your insurance program now. Come by our offices/any weekday, and let us examine your entire insurance program. One of our executives will be there to/give you complete information. We are open nine hours every day, including the noon hour. Stop by anytime/after nine in the morning. We are open until six in the afternoon, and we look forward to seeing you./Very cordially yours, (224)

Mrs. B. A. White
Dear Mrs. White:

/You will recall that recently you wrote for an executive insurance policy with our company and/that last week you took the required physical examination.

I am delighted to tell you that you passed the/examination easily. You are presently in excellent physical condition, and you have been/approved for the full $200,000 executive insurance policy.

A copy of the policy/which we prepared for you is enclosed. Please take some time now to review carefully all the provisions included/in the policy. It will take less than an hour, and it will be time well spent. If you would like to inquire/about any of the provisions or if you need any other information about your insurance program,/you may call our offices anytime after the hour of nine and before the hour of six any weekday.

Your/present quarterly payment is $300. If you pay annually, however, your payment will be/only $1,000, which is a considerable savings to you. A return envelope is enclosed/ for your first payment.

Thanks for your business; we sincerely appreciate it, Mrs. White. Very cordially yours,/ (220)

SUPPLEMENTARY ACTIVITY

A Word to the Wise

Time for Study

/Any business executive knows that he or she must have time to think, to read, and to prepare for the next day's/work.

The same is true for a student. Whether you are preparing a presentation or studying for an/examination, time must be spent every day getting ready for tomorrow.

Find a quiet area where you/can study, and reserve an hour or so for each subject. Do not listen to music or try to watch TV. This/will only distract you, and you will expend extra effort.

For a reading subject like history, set aside/an hour of uninterrupted time. For a skill subject like typing, plan to practice in several short segments/of about 15 minutes each. Leave some time open so that you may extend your study if extra time should be/needed.

There is no better insurance for a student than proper study. Nothing is as disconcerting to/a student as going to class unprepared. Nothing gives a student more confidence than going to class knowing/that he or she can handle the subject well. (188)

LESSON 15

PRINCIPLES OF CONSTRUCTION

Abbreviations

Words	Abbreviations
suggest, suggestion (A)	*sg*
manager (A)	*mgr*
management (A)	*mgl*
report (A)	*rpt*

Word Beginning Over-

● The word beginning **over-** as in <u>overdue</u> and the word <u>over</u> are written <u>capital</u> **O.**

Read	Spell	*SuperWrite*
over	**over**	*O*
overdue	**over-d-u**	*Odu*
overtime (A+)	**over-time**	*Otm*
overturn	**over-t-r-n**	*Otrn*

Word Beginning Trans-

● The word beginning **trans-** as in <u>translate</u> is written <u>capital</u> **T.**

Read	Spell	SuperWrite
translate	**trans-l-a-t**	*Hlal*
transmit	**trans-m-t**	*Tml*
transfer	**trans-f-r**	*Tfr*
transportation	**trans-p-r-t-a-tion**	*Tprta8*

APPLICATION

DOCUMENT 15-1

l t exec cmle:

s u no, t gnrl mgr askd t
bgl cmle l wk Olm ev da lsl
wk l fn8 t rpl on t bgl f t
cm g yr. e ap t sgs n npl C u
pvdd l tl lm.

t frsl drfl o t bgl s encd. I
msl mfsiz, hwev, tl l s r frsl
lry, n rv8s l b ncsry. t bgl s
abl t sam s l w lsl yr. t Cangs
tl h b sgd b mgl r poinld ol n
t drfl. ty incl a $2 h t ncres n t
Tprta8 bgl, a $1 h t ncres n t sals
mgl bgl, n a $10 t ncres n t Nlanm

(continued)

bgt. tr l actull b a dcres o abt
#2 t n t ins bgt. ts wd brng r
bus xpnss l wl O #3 m.

ma I rqst tt u lak an hr r so
now l lk l O crfl. tr ma b sm
imp dtals C e h Olkd r prblms
C e ma nt h fsen. if u h ny
ftr sgs f r cns, I sg tt u jl
tm down n Iml u cmpd rpt l
me bf t end o t wk. ts Sd gv
us tm l cns u sgs bf e pr t
finl bgt l t exec mgr erl nxt
wk.

tk u f u hlp.   S C Boyle

Mrs Hale:

s I rpld l u bf, I h a not fm
Al Morris, 1 o r mgt tranes, ask g
f an Ndept Tfr. he h sgd tt he

b Tfrd fm t ins depl l t Tprla$ depl. t mgr o t ins depl n t mgr o t Tprla$ depl ml f an hr ystrda. ty lkd O t sg crfl n apruvd t Tfr.

Mr M h b a loyl mple o r co, n e h alwas b qil pld w hs wk. he s a rsp prsn, n he h dn a v gd jb n t ins depl O t psl yr. ftrm, I m $r he l also d an xclnl jb n t Tprla$ depl.

t man rsn f ask g f t Tfr l t pr lm s l pvd Mr M lm l gan an Ovu o t wk o mgl n a dfrnl area o r co. I sg t Tfr b mad efclv l ts lm.

l u pl Tml ts info l t exec mgl cmle w t sg tl ty apruv t Tfr wol dla. I wd ap gl g a rpl on my ac$ ty lak.   Ann Case

Ms Reid:

rcnll Bill Hogan, exec mgr o r Nn&l ofc, rol l me ask g f a spn& Ha& o r rpl, ins mgl. he sgd tl l b incld s a lxl n a wk&p C l b rqrd f nu mgrs n r Mexico City ofc ts fl.

I blev ts s a gd sg, n e c d t jb esl. hwev, B neds t Ha& o ins mgl b t end o smr. I prdcl e l nl h lm l d t jb prprl wol nvlv g abl l h hrs o mple Olm xpns.

l u pl lk O t rpl sn n le me no if u blev e &d prced w t Ha& l t pr lm evn to l nvlvs Olm xpns. if u fel e &d, I sg tl u ril drcl l B, n snd a cpy o u nol

l me. if e cnl d t wk l ts lm, c
u mak ny sgs tl mil hlp B?

R A Doyle

Mr Taylor:

lsl mo Dr Mike Black, exec mgr
o t B ins co n Baltimore, MD,
adrsd t bus mgl clb her l r clg
on mgl n t ins bus. s I rpld, t
pgm incld info f fulr mgrs tl
w bot prclcl n Nlan g. n hs speC
he mad svrl inl g prdcSs abl t
fulr o t ins bus.

u l rcl tl e mad a rcrd g o t
speC f t locl orl hslry librry.
ts mrn g I hd a cl fm Ann Carter,
drclr o t clcS. Se askd if e cd pvd
a Tcrpl o t lk. O t psl fu yrs, l h

(continued)

b r prdc t fnl Tcrpls o tks wn
tr s a ned f tm, n I blev e Sd d
so agn ts tm. t Sd b a qk jb. t
man rsn I sg e d ts s f gdl, evn
wn t nvlvs svrl hrs o Olm
Tcrib g rpns. t imp o manlan g
gdl cnl b Omfsizd.

   I l ap t if u l lak t rspt o
Ose g ts prjct, Mr T. I sg tt u mpl
a prfSl lypsl hu s prfSl n wrd
prcs g l Tcrib t lap. an allrnlv
sg s l ask 1 o r pr sludnls l d t
wk. if u cnl flo etr o tes sgs,
pl prced w t wk nywa, bt lry
l kep t rpns s lo s psb.

   I wd ap t if u wd rpl t me on
wl u dcid l d. tks f u hlp.

               R A Reilley

DOCUMENT 15-1

To the Executive Committee:

/As you know, the general manager asked the budget committee to work overtime every day last week to/finish the report on the budget for the coming year. We appreciate the suggestions and input which you/provided at that time.

The first draft of the budget is enclosed. I must emphasize, however, that it is our/first try, and revisions will be necessary. The budget is about the same as it was last year. The changes/that have been suggested by management are pointed out in the draft. They include a $200,000/increase in the transportation budget, a $100,000 increase in the sales management budget,/and a $10,000 increase in the entertainment budget. There will actually be a decrease of/about $2,000 in the insurance budget. This would bring our business expenses to well over/$3 million.

May I request that you take an hour or so now to look it over carefully. There may be some/important details which we have overlooked or problems which we may not have foreseen. If you have any further/suggestions for our consideration, I suggest that you jot them down and transmit your completed report to/me before the end of the week. This should give us time to consider your suggestions before we present the final/budget to the executive manager early next week.

Thank you for your help. S. C. Boyle (257)

DOCUMENT 15-2

Mrs. Hale:

/As I reported to you before, I have a note from Al Morris, one of our management trainees, asking for/an interdepartmental transfer. He has suggested that he be transferred from the insurance department to/the transportation department. The manager of the insurance department and the manager of the/transportation department met for an hour yesterday. They looked over the suggestion carefully and approved the/transfer.

Mr. Morris has been a loyal employee of our company, and we have always been quite pleased with/his work. He is a responsible person, and he has done a very good job in the insurance department/over the past year. Furthermore, I am sure he will also do an excellent job in the transportation/department.

The main reason for asking for the transfer at the present time is to provide Mr. Morris time/to gain an overview of the work of management in a different area of our company. I suggest/the transfer be made effective at this time.

Will you please transmit this information to the executive/management committee with the suggestion that they approve the transfer without delay. I would appreciate getting/a report on any action they take. Ann Case (229)

DOCUMENT 15-3

Ms. Reid:

/Recently Bill Hogan, executive manager of our international office, wrote to me asking for/a Spanish translation of our report, *Insurance Management.* He suggested that it be included as a/text in a workshop which will be required for new managers in our Mexico City office this fall.

I/believe this is a good suggestion, and we can do the job easily. However, Bill needs the translation of/*Insurance Management* by the end of summer. I predict we will not have time to do the job properly without/involving about 100 hours of employee overtime expense.

Will you please look over the report soon/and let me know if you believe we should proceed with the translation at the present time even though it involves/overtime expense. If you feel we should, I suggest that you write direct to Bill, and send a copy of your/note to me. If we cannot do the work at this time, can you make any suggestions that might help Bill? R. A. Doyle/(180)

DOCUMENT 15-4

Mr. Taylor:

/Last month Dr. Mike Black, executive manager of the Black Insurance Company in Baltimore, Maryland,/addressed the business management club here at our college on management in the insurance business. As I/reported, the program included information for future managers that was both practical and/entertaining. In his speech he made several interesting predictions about the future of the insurance/business.

You will recall that we made a recording of the speech for the local oral history library. This/morning I had a call from Ann Carter, director of the collection. She asked if we could provide a transcript/of the talk. Over the past few years, it has been our practice to furnish transcripts of talks when there is a need for/them, and I believe we should do so again this time. It should be a quick job. The main reason I suggest we do/this is for goodwill, even when it involves several hours of overtime transcribing expense. The importance/of maintaining goodwill cannot be overemphasized.

I will appreciate it if you will take the/responsibility of overseeing this project, Mr. Taylor. I suggest that you employ a professional/typist who is proficient in word processing to transcribe the tape. An alternative suggestion is to ask/one of our present students to do the work. If you cannot follow either of these suggestions, please proceed with/the work anyway, but try to keep the expense as low as possible.

I would appreciate it if you would/report to me on what you decide to do. Thanks for your help. R. A. Reilley (294)

SUPPLEMENTARY ACTIVITY

A Word to the Wise

Financial Security

/"Earn $5, spend $4, and you will live happily ever after. Earn $4, spend $5, and/you are on the road to disaster." This old saying seems a bit childish, but it is basically true. Everyone/ must learn to budget to achieve financial security.

You must budget wisely from the day you get your/first paycheck until the day you get your last. Management of your finances is up to you. There is really no/one to report to and no one to depend on.

Here are a few suggestions that could help.

When you get your check, "pay"/yourself first. Save at least 5 percent of your income, and keep an emergency fund. You will find it a source of/comfort when that rainy day arrives.

Start planning for retirement with your first paycheck. Even though retirement may/seem far away, the best time to plan for the future is now.

Budget first for necessities, including housing,/transportation, and food. After necessities have been planned, you may add discretionary items such as/entertainment.

Never borrow for daily expenses. Economists suggest credit be used only for major/ purchases such as houses and cars.

Be a good financial manager, and stay within your budget. Good management/leads to financial security; overspending leads to disaster. (233)

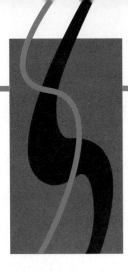

LESSON C

TOWARD PERSONAL SUCCESS

EFFECTIVE LISTENING

Every day we hear thousands of words, and we quickly forget most of them. There is little reason to remember most of what we hear. However, we forget many things that we should remember. In order to remember the important things, we must learn to listen effectively.

Become Involved

To retain the important points that we hear, we must become actively involved in the subject. We should try to hold a mental conversation with the speaker. We must keep our attention on the subject and try to anticipate what we think the speaker will say next. We should ask ourselves questions that the speaker should answer in the next few sentences.

Play Detective

As we listen, we can "play detective." We can examine every piece of evidence that the speaker presents. We can look for problems in logic or conclusions that are not supported by the evidence presented.

Avoid Distractions

As we are listening, we should not allow ourselves to be distracted. Something like the color of the speaker's clothing can distract us if we are not alert. The speaker's accent may keep us from concentrating on the ideas if we allow it to do so. If we realize that we are not paying attention or if we are daydreaming, we must call our attention back to the subject immediately.

Disagreements

We will often disagree with what a speaker is saying. However, we should not stop listening. We can tell ourselves, "That's not what I think" and immediately return our attention to the subject. We must not allow differences of opinion to keep us from getting the point of a talk.

Conclusion

A passive listener will not gain everything from a talk. A good listener participates actively. Effective listening requires self-control and concentration. It is a skill that each of us should work hard to attain. With practice, we can all be good listeners.

Discussion

1. What problems do you encounter when you listen in class? How do you handle them?

2. What recommendations would you give to a student who tends to daydream in class?

3. Describe a mental conversation you have had during a lecture recently.

4. Have you discovered a conclusion based on insufficient evidence during a lecture at school? If so, tell about it.

5. What do you do when you disagree with a speaker? Do you have suggestions to help other students who may have a problem with this?

Case Study—Listen Here

Mitchell has always had trouble paying attention in class. He tries to listen to his teachers, but his mind often wanders. He thinks about what he will do after school or on the weekend. He thinks about ball practice, and sometimes he tends to doze off.

Margaret has no trouble paying attention in class. However, she often does not agree with her social studies teacher. She finds many areas of disagreement and concentrates on them. In doing so, she often misses other points.

Ken is easily distracted in class. He sees a new red convertible through the window and imagines himself behind the wheel. He notices a student wearing a bright blue coat through the doorway. And he enjoys his teacher's English accent. However, he doesn't remember much that happens in class.

Discussion Questions

1. Mitchell, Margaret, and Ken have different problems listening in class. What are they?

2. In your opinion, which problem is the most difficult to solve? Which problem is the easiest to correct?

3. What should the students do to improve their listening skills?

Activities

1. Visit a class that you are not enrolled in this term, and make a list of the main points covered.

2. Watch a program on public television on a subject of your choice, and make an outline of the points presented.

3. Watch a television news conference and see if you can spot any conclusion that is not based on the evidence.

LESSON 16

PRINCIPLES OF CONSTRUCTION

Abbreviations

Words	Abbreviations
order (A)	*od*
amount (A)	*aml*
state, street (A)	*sl*
receive (A)	*rec*
number (A)	*no*
letter (A)	*lr*

Word Beginning Under-

● The word beginning **under-** as in <u>understand</u> and the word <u>under</u> are written <u>capital</u> **U.**

Read	Spell	SuperWrite
under	**under**	*U*
understand	**under-s-t-n-d**	*Uslnd*
undertake	**under-t-a-k**	*Ulak*
underwrite	**under-r-i-t**	*Uril*
undersign	**under-s-i-n**	*Usin*

Mrs Moore:

encd s a cpy o a lr I recd fm
Ray Gwinn, r prdcš mgr, rpl g
tt r co h recd an imp od f O
4 t mšen Fcrib g unls fm t Carter
ins grup. ts s a v lrg no o
Fcrib g unls, n Mr G s qil ntrll
cncrnd abl l. he sls tt he s gld
l h t od, o cors. hwev, he mfsizs
tt l l b mpsb f hs pr slf l hndl
ts aml o wk U t pr cndšs. I
Uslnd hs cncrn, n I m nclind l
agre w hm.

n hs lr, Mr G sls tt hs man
gol s l avoid rqr g a lrg aml o
Olm wk o r fl-lm slf. if e Ulak
t prdcš o sC a sizb od, Mr G sgs
tt e mpl 20 r 30 xlra wkrs, O t
nxl 6 mos, l r Main sl plnl. ts

(continued)

wd enab us l mel r prdcS ddlin
wol Nrpl g r rgulr scdul n wol
rqr g r fl-lm slf l wk Olm.

pl le me no if u blev r exec
mgl wd cns pvd g ts no o hrl
wkrs l r M sl plnl f sC a Srl lm.

tks f u cns n ts mlr. I l ap
rec g ny sgs u h on hw l mng
ts aml o wk.   Jane Yates

Miss Woods:

ts wk I recd a lr fm Dr J B
Chang, mgr o t NnSl lm mgl co,
sl g tl hs lalsl fnlr od hd b
mprprl fld. he mad t sg tl I lk
nl t mlr.

he odd 20 Crs f hs nu ofc l 210
Oak sl. a cpy o hs od no 8201 s
encd. uftnll, onl 18 Crs w Spd l
hm, n ty w snl l hs old ofc l

401 Elm st. n ad$, t aml on t bl w
ncrcll sld s $3 t nsld o t crcl aml,
$2 t.

lda I snl 20 Crs l hs O sl ofc
alng w a crcl bl n t aml o $2 t
n a lr o aplgy. he $d rec hs od
n a da r so.

I c Uslnd hw e cd h dlvrd t
Crs l t rng adrs; he Tfrd hs
ofcs onl rcnll. e cd h esl Olkd
hs Cang o adrs rqsl. hwev, I cnl
Uslnd hw e cd h $pd t rng no
o Crs r hw e cd h mad sC a lrg
err n t aml o hs bl.

l u pl gl t ncsry info fm t
od n blg depls. I sg tl afl u h
gtrd al t fcls u ril a lr o xplna$
l Dr C. I l also ap rec g a cpy o
t rpl u prpr, slg wl u w ab l
find ol.   R T Rodriguez

Ms Margaret Como   d Ms C:

tk u f u lr w u lxlbk od <u>no</u>
3308; e recd l lda.

e r hpy l rpl tl 1t cpes o r
bk, <u>Uslnd</u> g mgl, r b g Spd l t
mgr o t bkslor l Jones bus clg
l 501 Main sl, n t slm l b snl
drcl l u acounl g ofc l 206 Broad
sl. u Sd h sfSl lm afl u rec t bks
l prcs tm f sal bf t bgn g o t
fl lrm. ma I sg u mprnl tm w
u clg lrg on t bk. a no o Npris g
clgs n t sl flo ts sg. e hop t
sludnls l u clg njoy usg tes inl g
bks.

t aml o t nvoic s $12 t, C incls
sl n locl lxs n Tprla$ Crgs. ts
aml s m tn $8 h U r rgulr pric
bcs o t lrg no o bks u odd.

tks onc agn, Ms C; u bus h b
o gral imp l r co O t yrs.

s u

Dr Leonard Pace   d Dr P:

e recd u lr abt u rcnt od f
hom fn&gs f rsal n u stor. I m
xtreml sry tl u h hd trb qtg t
crct no o ilms u ned fm r co. I
c esl Ustnd t cncrn voicd n u
lr.

Mr Paul, mgr o r Spg dept, lkd
nt t mtr, n I m hpy l rpl tl he
found ot wr t trb s. u od no 181
w recd l r Oak st ofc lst mo.
hwev, du l an uftnt Osit, 1 bx nvr
lft r Spg dept. e r sndg t
rmandr o t od b xprs l u Elm

(continued)

sl slor lda. u l h t ilms n lm
f u sal.

U tes cndSs, u ma crlnl h an
adSl mo l mak pam n sll rec
a 2% dscounl. t aml o u nxl slm
l b $1 t, C incls t sl sals lx n
Iprlas Crgs. u ma ddcl a dscounl
o $19 fm ts aml if u pa b t end
o nxl mo.

pl fgv us, Dr P. u ods l b gvn
lp prirl n t fulr, n e l mak
ev efl l nSr tl ty r fld prprl.

u l

PS encd s r hlda cllg. l
incls mny gfl sgs f u cslmrs.
ma I sg u mal u od l r mgl
ofc sn l avoid t hlda rS.

DOCUMENT 16-1

Mrs. Moore:

/Enclosed is a copy of a letter I received from Ray Gwinn, our production manager, reporting that our/company has received an important order for over 4,000 machine transcribing units from the/Carter Insurance Group. This is a very large number of transcribing units, and Mr. Gwinn is quite naturally/concerned about it. He states that he is glad to have the order, of course. However, he emphasizes/that it will be impossible for his present staff to handle this amount of work under the present conditions./I understand his concern, and I am inclined to agree with him.

In his letter, Mr. Gwinn states that his/main goal is to avoid requiring a large amount of overtime work of our full-time staff. If we undertake/the production of such a sizable order, Mr. Gwinn suggests that we employ 20 or 30 extra/workers, over the next six months, at our Main Street plant. This would enable us to meet our production deadline without/interrupting our regular schedule and without requiring our full-time staff to work overtime.

Please let me/know if you believe our executive management would consider providing this number of hourly workers/at our Main Street plant for such a short time.

Thanks for your consideration in this matter. I will appreciate/receiving any suggestions you have on how to manage this amount of work. Jane Yates (256)

DOCUMENT 16-2

Miss Woods:

/This week I received a letter from Dr. J. B. Chang, manager of the International Time Management/Company, stating that his latest furniture order had been improperly filled. He made the suggestion that/I look into the matter.

He ordered 20 chairs for his new office at 210 Oak Street. A copy of his/order Number 8201 is enclosed. Unfortunately, only 18 chairs were shipped to him, and they were/sent to his old office at 401 Elm Street. In addition, the amount on the bill was incorrectly/stated as $3,000 instead of the correct amount, $2,000.

Today I sent 20 chairs to/his Oak Street office along with a correct bill in the amount of $2,000 and a letter of/apology. He should receive his order in a day or so.

I can understand how we could have delivered the/chairs to the wrong address; he transferred his offices only recently. We could have easily overlooked his/change of address request. However, I cannot understand how we could have shipped the wrong number of chairs or how/we could have made such a large error in the amount of his bill.

Will you please get the necessary information/from the order and billing departments. I suggest that after you have gathered all the facts you write a/letter of explanation to Dr. Chang. I will also appreciate receiving a copy of the/report you prepare, stating what you were able to find out. R. T. Rodriguez (274)

DOCUMENT 16-3

Ms. Margaret Como

Dear Ms. Como:

/Thank you for your letter with your textbook order Number 3308; we received it today.

We are happy/to report that 1,000 copies of our book, *Understanding Management,* are being shipped to the manager/of the bookstore at Jones Business College at 501 Main Street, and the statement will be sent direct to your/accounting office at 206 Broad Street. You should have sufficient time after you receive the books to process/them for sale before the beginning of the fall term. May I suggest you imprint them with your college lettering/on the back. A number of enterprising colleges in the state follow this suggestion. We hope the students/at your college enjoy using these interesting books.

The amount of the invoice is $12,000, which/includes state and local taxes and transportation charges. This amount is more than $800 under/our regular price because of the large number of books you ordered.

Thanks once again, Ms. Como; your business has/been of great importance to our company over the years. Sincerely yours, (194)

DOCUMENT 16-4

Dr. Leonard Pace

Dear Dr. Pace:

/We received your letter about your recent order for home furnishings for resale in your store. I am extremely/sorry that you have had trouble getting the correct number of items you need from our company. I can/easily understand the concern voiced in your letter.

Mr. Paul, manager of our shipping department, looked/into the matter, and I am happy to report that he found out where the trouble is. Your order Number 181/was received at our Oak Street office last month. However, due to an unfortunate oversight, one box/never left our shipping department. We are sending the remainder of the order by express to your Elm Street store/today. You will have the items in time for your sale.

Under these conditions, you may certainly have an/additional month to make payment and still receive a 2 percent discount. The amount of your next statement will be/ $1,000, which includes the state sales tax and transportation charges. You may deduct a discount of/ $19 from this amount if you pay by the end of next month.

Please forgive us, Dr. Pace. Your orders will be/given top priority in the future, and we will make every effort to ensure that they are filled properly./Yours truly,

PS Enclosed is our holiday catalog. It includes many gift suggestions for your customers./May I suggest you mail your order to our management office soon to avoid the holiday rush. (259)

SUPPLEMENTARY ACTIVITY

A Word to the Wise

The Self-Starter

/The lettering on the old car, parked just off the street, said "Self-Starter." The statement implied that the car actually/started itself. This, of course, was untrue. It really meant that in order to start the car, all you had to do/was push a button rather than "crank up" the engine by turning a crank manually a number of times. This/improvement in car design eliminated a great amount of work!

Businesses have always tried to hire/self-starters—those who understand their work and who can get started without the necessity of having to be "cranked/up." When companies receive letters from prospective employees, they want to know if the person is a self-starter./

Do you have to be "cranked up" to get started on a job, or do you get going on your own? Are you a/self-starter? (141)

LESSON 17

PRINCIPLES OF CONSTRUCTION

Word Endings -Ple, -Pal

● The word endings **-ple** as in <u>ample</u> and **-pal** as in <u>principal</u> are written **p.**

Read	Spell	*SuperWrite*
ample	**a-m-p**	*amp*
simple	**s-m-p**	*smp*
multiple	**m-l-t-p**	*mltp*
principal	**p-r-n-c-p**	*prncp*

Abbreviations

Words	Abbreviations
available (A)	*av*
organization, organize (A)	*org*
paid (A)	*pd*
represent, representative (A)	*rep*

Mr BD Smith   d Mr S:

tk u f u rcnt ltr; e w gld l
rec l. e r v hpy tl u r pld
w t srvc pvdd b r nu reps
n u prt o t sl. e agre tl ty
rep r org v wl, n e no tl ty
l ap u cms. e r esp gld l h
gd rpts on r pep.

e w e cd srv u org b fl g
u od no 2201 f 1 h TV sts f u
fntr stor. e Ustnd tl u ned tm
f rsal l u prncp loca on Main
st n Columbia, SC. hwev, e cnt
mak tes sts av l u now.

u h nt pd r org t $15 t u h
od us f m tn 5 mos. ts reps
a lrg fnn rsp l, n l s mpsb
f us l fl ny ftr ods ull u h
pd us t aml prt du.   (continued)

if u rqr xtra tm t org u fnncs, pl le us no sn. drp b r exec ofc ny wkda blwen t hrs o 9 n 5. 1 o r reps l tak amp tm l xplan a no o pam opts av l u.

wn u h orgd u fnncs n h pd us t aml du, e l b gld l fl u ods on crdl. ull tn, e sg tl u org cns prCs g gds fm us on a cS bass.

u l

Ms Sarah Tatum   d Ms T:

tk u f u rcnl lr. e w gld l rec u rqsl f info abl r corss C r av l sals mgrs n reps. O t yrs r org h mad av l reps o al typs o buss n ts area a no o

inl g, njoyb corss. ts yr e h orgd
4 imp nu corss, C l b ofrd l t
<u>muncp</u> bldg on Broad sl. ts reps
l lrgsl no o corss tl r org h ev ofrd
l l lm.

ty r s flos:
1. <u>gv</u> g n flo g ods
2. <u>gl</u> g uclcld acounls pd
3. <u>Uslnd</u> g ins mgl
4. <u>lrn</u> g hw l org u wk

l corss, C r dscribd n fl n l encd
bkll, mfsiz prdcl, usf prncps.

mny bus orgs n r prl o l sl
nrol l r m o tr mples n l o r
corss ev yr. e prdcl u pep l gan
a gral del if ty lak prl n l o tes
inl g, njoyb clss.

l s smp l nrol u pep n l o
tes corss. al u ned d s fl ol l
encd nrolm fm n rlrn l l us.

(continued)

t fe f eC cors s onl $1 h pr prsn, n t fl aml Sd b pd l t frsl mel g.

if e c b o ftr srvc l u org n ny psb wa, Ms T, ma e sg tt u cl us nytm.

s u

Mrs P W Troy   d Mrs T:

tk u f u nqiry abt r bl-pa g srvc; e w gld l rec u lr. t sl nSl bnk o Cleveland maks av l bus orgs n ndvduls truol OH a smp bl v usf srvc.

u c h u mol bls pd wol t ncsl o ritl g a lrg no o Cks n od l cmp t Facts. u c h al u bls, inclg utl ts n ins, pd O t tlfon.

afl u r nrold n t pgm, al u
ned d s org u bls n mak 1 smp
fon cl eC mo. 1 o r reps l mak
crf nols o C orgs u wS l pa n
hw mC ty Sd b pd. eC bl l b
pd on t rcd da u sl, n u l rec
a cmp rpl, orgd b dal, o al
Fac&s l t end o ev mo.

ts srvc c rep a savgs n lm;
l c also rep a savgs n mny. l
s av f onl $10 a mo, C s prbbl
wl U t aml u now pa.

t prncp rsn l c sav u mny
s tl l savs us mny. bcs mny
bus orgs h acounts w r bnk,
t Fac&s l b smp Ifrs o fnds
fm u acounl l trs.

f m info, cl 1 o r reps l r Mill
sl brnC ny wkda blwen t hrs
o 9 n 3.   u c

Dr Jean Addison   d Dr A:

e recd u lr ask g f info abl r
nul fmd NnSl bnk g org. tks
f u nqiry.

abl 6 mos ago, 10 bnks, rep g
ev prt o t sl, orgd t lrgst bnk g
grup n t rgn. eC bnk hd pd
a hi ral o int on prncp nvstms
f t pst 10 yrs. n adS, ty eC hd
asts amt g l l lest $5 h m. t totl
asts o t nul orgd grup rep m tn
$7 b.

t org w fmd n od l srv pep
truot t ntir rgn. tru r cmbind
strngt, e c mak almost ulmtd
fnds av l t pep o ts area.

e Ustnd t neds o r cstmrs; e
d nt cns ny lon lu lrg r lu
sml. f xmp, if u ned $1 t l gt a
prsnt bl pd, $1 h t f a nu hous,

r $1 m l nvsl n a bus, e c hlp u.

e wnl l mak r dpndb, efSl srvc av l evon. if e c ev b o hlp l u, ma e sg u cl l o r reps l r Oak sl ofc, C s n u prl o lown. e r opn blwen t hrs o 9 n 3, n l o r reps l b hpy l srv u n ny wa psb. c u

DOCUMENT 17-1

Mr. B. D. Smith
Dear Mr. Smith:

/Thank you for your recent letter; we were glad to receive it. We are very happy that you are pleased with the/service provided by our new representatives in your part of the state. We agree that they represent our/organization very well, and we know that they will appreciate your comments. We are especially glad to/have good reports on our people.

We wish we could serve your organization by filling your order Number/2201 for 100 TV sets for your furniture store. We understand that you need them for resale/at your principal location on Main Street in Columbia, South Carolina. However, we cannot make/these sets available to you now.

You have not paid our organization the $15,000 you have/owed us for more than five months. This represents a large financial responsibility, and it is impossible/for us to fill any further orders until you have paid us the amount presently due.

If you require/extra time to organize your finances, please let us know soon. Drop by our executive office any/weekday between the hours of nine and five. One of our representatives will take ample time to explain a number/of payment options available to you.

When you have organized your finances and have paid us the amount/due, we will be glad to fill your orders on credit. Until then, we suggest that your organization consider/ purchasing goods from us on a cash basis. Yours truly, (271)

DOCUMENT 17-2

Ms. Sarah Tatum
Dear Ms. Tatum:

/Thank you for your recent letter. We were glad to receive your request for information about our courses which/are available to sales managers and representatives. Over the years our organization has made/available to representatives of all types of businesses in this area a number of/interesting, enjoyable courses. This year we have organized four important new courses, which will be offered at/the Municipal Building on Broad Street. This represents the largest number of courses that our organization/has ever offered at one time.

They are as follows:
1. Giving and Following Orders
2. Getting/Uncollected Accounts Paid
3. Understanding Insurance Management
4. Learning How to Organize Your Work

The/courses, which are described in full in the enclosed booklet, emphasize practical, useful principles.

Many business/organizations in our part of the state enroll one or more of their employees in one of our courses every/year. We predict your people will gain a great deal if they take part in one of these interesting, enjoyable/classes.

It is simple to enroll your people in one of these courses. All you need to do is fill out the enclosed/enrollment form and return it to us. The fee for each course is only $100 per person, and the/full amount should be paid at the first meeting.

If we can be of further service to your organization in/any possible way, Ms. Tatum, may we suggest that you call us anytime. Sincerely yours, (277)

DOCUMENT 17-3

Mrs. P. W. Troy
Dear Mrs. Troy:

/Thank you for your inquiry about our bill-paying service; we were glad to receive your letter. The State National/Bank of Cleveland makes available to business organizations and individuals throughout Ohio/a simple but very useful service.

You can have your monthly bills paid without the necessity of writing a/large number of checks in order to complete the transactions. You can have all your bills, including utilities/ and insurance, paid over the telephone.

After you are enrolled in the program, all you need do is organize/your bills and make one simple phone call each month. One of our representatives will make careful notes of which/organizations you wish to pay and how much they should be paid. Each bill will be paid on the exact day you state, and/you will receive a complete report, organized by date, of all transactions at the end of every month.

This/service can represent a savings in time; it can also represent a savings in money. It is available/for only $10 a month, which is probably well under the amount you now pay.

The principal/reason it can save you money is that it saves us money. Because many business organizations have accounts/with our bank, the transactions will be simple transfers of funds from your account to theirs.

For more information, call/one of our representatives at our Mill Street branch any weekday between the hours of nine and three. Yours cordially,/(260)

DOCUMENT 17-4

Dr. Jean Addison
Dear Dr. Addison:

/We received your letter asking for information about our newly formed international banking/organization. Thanks for your inquiry.

About six months ago, ten banks, representing every part of the state,/organized the largest banking group in the region. Each bank had paid a high rate of interest on principal/ investments for the past ten years. In addition, they each had assets amounting to at least $500 million./The total assets of the newly organized group represent more than $7 billion.

The/organization was formed in order to serve people throughout our entire region. Through our combined strength, we can make almost/unlimited funds available to the people of this area.

We understand the needs of our customers;/we do not consider any loan too large or too small. For example, if you need $1,000 to/get a personal bill paid, $100,000 for a new house, or $1 million to invest in/a business, we can help you.

We want to make our dependable, efficient service available to/everyone. If we can ever be of help to you, may we suggest you call one of our representatives at our Oak/Street office, which is in your part of town. We are open between the hours of nine and three, and one of our/representatives will be happy to serve you in any way possible. Cordially yours, (255)

SUPPLEMENTARY ACTIVITY

A Word to the Wise

Organizing Your Work Area

/Some people seem to be well organized while others suffer from a lack of organization.

To be well/organized, you should start by examining your work area. A good desk can be a great assistance in helping/you to get organized. Even a small desk can help, if you make use of every bit of space available.

Reserve certain areas in your desk for special work. For example, reserve a place for unpaid bills and other/unfinished business. Items which cannot be finished should be placed in this area. The secret to making it work, however,/is to be sure that the area is cleared once a week.

Time devoted to organizing your work area is time/well invested. The principal reason is that if your work area is well organized, your work will also/be well organized.

Your work is representative of the way you work. Does your work represent you well? Take a/close look at your work area to see if you need to improve it. (172)

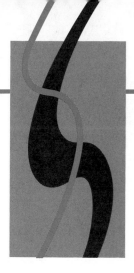

LESSON 18

PRINCIPLES OF CONSTRUCTION

Prefix Before a Short Vowel

● If a root word begins with a short vowel sound, the vowel is retained when a prefix is added.

Read	Spell	*SuperWrite*
act	**a-c-t**	*acl*
react	**r-a-c-t**	*racl*
other	**o-th-r**	*otr*
another	**a-n-o-th-r**	*anotr*

Suffix After a Short Vowel

● If a root word ends with a short vowel sound, the vowel is retained when a suffix is added.

Read	Spell	*SuperWrite*
law	**l-a**	*la*
lawyer	**l-a-y-r**	*layr*
draw	**d-r-a**	*dra*
drawing	**d-r-a- g**	*draq*

Words	Abbreviations
question (A)	_q_
regard (A)	_rgd_
cover (A)	_cv_

APPLICATION

DOCUMENT 18-1

Mr Roy Lynch   d Mr L:

abt 2 yrs ago, I opnd a Sp n t
muncp Sp g ml on Pine st. l tl
lm I Nd nl a cntrcl w t NnSl
nvslm co, onrs o t ml, n pd
tm a $2t scur l dpsl. I h pd tm
$8 h rnl ev mo snc tn.

my les w f 2 yrs; an opS w
pvdd f anotr 2 yrs. I fll Sr tl
t les cvd t fl 4 yrs, n I h orgd
my bus on tl bass. O a mo ago,
I le t mgl o t muncp Sp g ml

no tl I nlndd l rnu t les. hwev,
lsl wk I recd a lr fm tr pep
slg tl ty w nl rnu g my les.

I cnl Uslnd wy my les s nl
bg rnud f anotr 2 yrs. ftrm,
I h nl b ab l gl a rep fm t org
l ansr my qs rgd g ts prblm.
I cns tr acs ulaf, n I blev tl tr
s a smp breC o cnlrcl b t <u>Nn</u>Sl
nvslm co.

l u pl lk O my cnlrcl, C s encd,
n gv me u racs   t flo g qs,
C r o gral imp l me:

1. s ts prblm cvd n my pr
   cnlrcl?

2. wd u sg I hir a layr l rep
   me?

3. wl opSs r av l me l t pr
   lm?

(continued)

tk u f u cns n wlev hlp u
ma b ab l gv me, Mr L. L ap u
hlp; ny sgs u mak l b wlcm.
                                    s u

DOCUMENT 18-2

l n g:

3 mos ago r org mpld Mr D R
Long s mgr o r nu rcrds mgl
depl. he h wkd closl w r layrs
n w reps o eC prncp depl. he h
pd clos almS l tr sgs cncrn g t
rqrms o r org. he h mad a no
o xclnl sgs n h b rsp f la g
t groundwk f r nu pgm. e l
sn bgn t aclul rorg o r co fil g
sslm. ev depl w t xcpS o t ins
depl l b incld n t nu pgm.

her r ansrs l a fu imp gs
rgd g r nu sslm: gnrl fils, C

Sd b av l evon, l b rorgd n Ifrd l a cntrl fil g area. onl prsnl fils l b kpl n privl ofcs. (I msl mfsiz tt ts rul cvs mples l ev lvl.) inaclv fils l b Ifrd l t inaclv fil dept. v old paprs l b xmnd, n if ty r o no ftr vlu, ty l b dstroyd.

t prncp rsns e r lak g tes slps r l nsr tt r fil g pgm s up l dal n tt r rcrds rlns csls r kpl s lo's psb. ts cd esl rep a savgs o O $1 h t O t nxl 10 yrs.

n od l mak t pgm wk prprl, I m rqsl g tt eC o u flo crfl t dtald ruls cvd n t encd rpl, C Mr L h prprd. if ny o u pep

(continued)

h a q w rgd l t pgm, r if ty
ned ftr info tl s uoblanb n u
on depl, pl ask tm l cl Mr L.

                              J K Dale

DOCUMENT 18-3

Mr J D Chan   d Mr C:
    wl d u lk f wn u by mn's
clot q? wy d u slcl 1 slor O anotr?
e tnk e Uslnd t prncp rsns tl
Uli u Coic.
    e blev u wnl l b ab l Sp n a
cmflb, wl-orgd, inl q slor tl h
av al t v lalsl fSs. e blev u wnl
hi qll n gd srvc l rsnb prics.
tes r xcll wl u l find l t Morgan
mn's slor l frsl n Lee sls. e h
av an mprsv ara o hi-qll
mn's clot q l qil rsnb prics.
    e h b sccsf bcs e h pd spSl

alns l r cslmrs, hu rep almosl
ev prfs. u l find on r lsl o
slsfid cslmrs evon fm prfsrs
n layrs l sals reps n bus
mgrs. e r hil rgdd b al r
cslmrs; ty alwas find xcll wl
ty wnl n r slor.

r org h srvd t pep o Hartford,
CT, fm t sam locas f O 30 yrs.
e h xpndd r slor mny lms; n
r bldg prl cvs an nlir cly blk.
e r, wol g, t lrgsl n bsl mn's
slor n ts prl o t sl. hwev, don'l
lak r wrd f l. cm n sn n dscv
f uslf wl xclnl vlus e h av.

u s

PS if u h ny qs rgd g r srvc,
jsl cl r lol-fre no, C s incld n
t encd brosr.

Ms Lynda Pool:

s u l rcl, lsl yr e apoinld Kathryn Moreno, 1 o t hil rgdd nu layrs l _NnSl_ ndslres, l a psS on r muncp advisry cmle. wil Se w on t cmle, Se pd alnS l ev dlal rlald l muncp mgl n mad mnny vlub sgs tl aclull savd r cmun l blwen $9 h t n $1 m. Se w rsp f savg O $75 t n ins csls alon.

s u l rcl, hwev, K w n an alo accdnl abl 6 mos ago, n hr rcvy lk a gral aml o lm. Se w, trf, uab l cmp hr fl yr on t cmle.

l s now lm l rorg r muncp advisry cmle f t cm g yr. uqbl, K dd an xclnl jb s t rep fm hr co f t frsl prl o t yr, n I Uslnd *tl Se s now cmpl rcvd. I m, trf, rcmnd g tl Se b rapoinld l rep hr org f anotr yr.*

if tr s ny q n u mind rgd g ts rapoinlm, r if u h ny otr qs rgd g t rorg, pl cl me s sn s psb. I l b av ny da nxl wk afl t hr o 9 n t mrn g.

Martin Chase

DOCUMENT 18-1

Mr. Roy Lynch

Dear Mr. Lynch:

/About two years ago, I opened a shop in the Municipal Shopping Mall on Pine Street. At that time I/entered into a contract with the International Investment Company, owners of the mall, and paid them a/ $2,000 security deposit. I have paid them $800 rent every month since then.

My/lease was for two years; an option was provided for another two years. I felt sure that the lease covered the full four years, and I have organized my business on that basis. Over a month ago, I let the management/of the Municipal Shopping Mall know that I intended to renew the lease. However, last week I/received a letter from their people stating that they were not renewing my lease.

I cannot understand why my lease/is not being renewed for another two years. Furthermore, I have not been able to get a representative/from the organization to answer my questions regarding this problem. I consider their action/unlawful, and I believe that there is a simple breach of contract by the International Investment Company./

(continued)

Will you please look over my contract, which is enclosed, and give me your reaction regarding the following/questions, which are of great importance to me:

1. Is this problem covered in my present contract?
2. Would you/suggest I hire a lawyer to represent me?
3. What options are available to me at the present time?

Thank you/for your consideration and whatever help you may be able to give me, Mr. Lynch. I appreciate/your help; any suggestions you make will be welcome. Sincerely yours, (291)

DOCUMENT 18-2

Ladies and Gentlemen:

/Three months ago our organization employed Mr. D. R. Long as manager of our new records management/department. He has worked closely with our lawyers and with representatives of each principal department./He has paid close attention to their suggestions concerning the requirements of our organization. He has/made a number of excellent suggestions and has been responsible for laying the groundwork for our new/program. We will soon begin the actual reorganization of our company filing system. Every/department with the exception of the insurance department will be included in the new program.

Here are/answers to a few important questions regarding our new system: General files, which should be available to/everyone, will be reorganized and transferred to a central filing area. Only personal files will/be kept in private offices. (I must emphasize that this rule covers employees at every level.) Inactive/files will be transferred to the inactive file department. Very old papers will be examined, and if they/are of no further value, they will be destroyed.

The principal reasons we are taking these steps are to ensure/that our filing program is up to date and that our records retention costs are kept as low as possible. This/could easily represent a savings of over $100,000 over the next ten years.

In/order to make the program work properly, I am requesting that each of you follow carefully the detailed rules/covered in the enclosed report, which Mr. Long has prepared. If any of your people have a question with/regard to the program, or if they need further information that is unobtainable in your own department,/please ask them to call Mr. Long. J. R. Dale (308)

Mr. T. D. Chan

Dear Mr. Chan:

/What do you look for when you buy men's clothing? Why do you select one store over another? We think we understand/the principal reasons that underlie your choice.

We believe you want to be able to shop in a/comfortable, well-organized, interesting store that has available all the very latest fashions. We believe/you want high quality and good service at reasonable prices. These are exactly what you will find at the/Morgan Men's Store at First and Lee Streets. We have available an impressive array of high-quality men's clothing/at quite reasonable prices.

We have been successful because we have paid special attention to our customers,/who represent almost every profession. You will find on our list of satisfied customers everyone/from professors and lawyers to sales representatives and business managers. We are highly regarded by/all our customers; they always find exactly what they want in our store.

Our organization has served the/people of Hartford, Connecticut, from the same location for over thirty years. We have expanded our store/many times, and our building presently covers an entire city block. We are, without question, the largest and best/men's store in this part of the state. However, don't take our word for it. Come in soon and discover for yourself what/excellent values we have available. Yours sincerely,

PS   If you have any questions regarding our/service, just call our toll-free number, which is included in the enclosed brochure. (274)

Ms. Lynda Pool:

/As you will recall, last year we appointed Kathryn Moreno, one of the highly regarded new lawyers at International/Industries, to a position on our municipal advisory committee. While she was on the/committee, she paid attention to every detail related to municipal management and made many/valuable suggestions that actually saved our community between $900,000 and/$1 million. She was responsible for saving over $75,000 in insurance/costs alone.

As you will recall, however, Kathryn was in an auto accident about six months ago, and her/recovery took a great amount of time. She was, therefore, unable to complete her full year on the committee./

It is now time to reorganize our municipal advisory committee for the coming year./ Unquestionably, Kathryn did an excellent job as the representative from her company for the first part/of the year, and I understand that she is now completely recovered. I am, therefore, recommending that she/be reappointed to represent her organization for another year.

If there is any question in/your mind regarding this reappointment, or if you have any other questions regarding the reorganization,/please call me as soon as possible. I will be available any day next week after the hour of/nine in the morning. Martin Chase (266)

SUPPLEMENTARY ACTIVITY

A Word to the Wise

Making Notes

/Making good notes will help you both in school and out. Whether you are preparing for an examination or/outlining a political speech, good notemaking skills are necessary.

When you attend a speech, listen carefully/for the main topic to be covered. Try to have a "mental conversation" with the speaker. See if you can/predict what will be said next. Listening for major and supporting ideas will help you to get the speaker's/message completely and accurately.

In an outline, the major topics covered should be indicated by/capital letters. Supporting ideas under each major heading should be indicated by numbers. If/there are minor points under these headings, they should be indicated by small letters.

You may include your reaction/to the speaker's points, but you should place your ideas in brackets so that you will not later confuse the speaker's/ideas with your own.

Your outline will help you understand the speaker better. It will help you in drawing/conclusions about the speech and will help you organize any questions you may have regarding the talk.

Good/notemaking skills are invaluable. Work to improve your notemaking ability. (215)

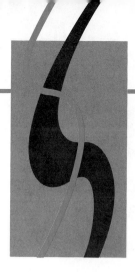

LESSON 19

PRINCIPLES OF CONSTRUCTION

Word Endings -Ious, -Eous, -Ous, -Us

● The word endings **-ious** as in various, **-eous** as in courteous, **-ous** as in dangerous, and **-us** as in status are all written **u-s**.

Read	Spell	SuperWrite
-ious		
various	**v-r-u-s**	*vrus*
serious	**s-e-r-u-s**	*serus*
-eous		
courteous	**c-r-t-u-s**	*crtus*
advantageous	**a-d-v-n-t-a-g-u-s**	*advntagus*
-ous		
dangerous	**d-a-n-g-r-u-s**	*dangrus*
famous	**f-a-m-u-s**	*famus*
-us		
status	**s-t-a-t-u-s**	*status*
surplus	**s-r-p-l-u-s**	*srplus*

Mem

● The syllable **mem** as in <u>member</u> is written **m**.

Read	Spell	SuperWrite
member	**m-b-r**	*mbr*
remember	**r-m-b-r**	*rmbr*
memory	**m-r-y**	*mry*

Abbreviations

Words	Abbreviations
avenue (A)	*ave*
convenience, convenient (A)	*cnv*

Days of the Week

● Longhand abbreviations are used for days of the week, but no periods are used.

Day	SuperWrite
Sunday	*Sun*
Monday	*Mon*
Tuesday	*Tues*
Wednesday	*Wed*
Thursday	*Thurs*
Friday	*Fri*
Saturday	*Sat*

Months of the Year

● Longhand abbreviations are used for months of the year, but no periods are used.

Month	SuperWrite
January	*Jan*
February	*Feb*
March	*Mar*
April	*Apr*
May	*May*
June	*June*
July	*July*
August	*Aug*
September	*Sept*
October	*Oct*
November	*Nov*
December	*Dec*

APPLICATION

Read and write the following documents.

Mr Jack Warren   d Mr W:

  u l rmbr tl on Mon, July 11, u co odd $1 t wrt o splis f u cnv slor fm r Park ave wrhous. u pd $2 h down n sind a nol slg tl t rmandr wd b pd b Tues, Aug 23. e rol u a crlus rmindr n Sept n anotr n Oct. l s now Wed, Nov 16. anotr mo h gn b, n e h nl hrd fm u.

  e cnl Uslnd wy u h nl pd ts bl, bl e hop tl u l lak a fu mnls now l ril a Ck f $8 h l cv u bl n plac l n t mal l r exec ofcs l 201 Madison ave

  if l s nl cnv f u l pa t cmp bl l ts lm, I sg tl u le us no

now. prhps l wd b m cnv f u l pa prt o t loll aml now n t rsl lalr. n my cas, 1 o r crlus reps l b hpy l pvd ansrs l my qs u ma h rqd g u bl. hwev, dla g ny ftr l d serus dmg l u crdl ral g.

e fel tl e h b qil gnrus, Mr W, bl e c d ntng m. t rspl o pa g u dls s us. e lk fwrd l her g fm u bf t end o nxl wk. rmbr, t slalus o u crdl dpnds on wl u d now.

u l

l al cslmrs:

e r dlild l anounc t grnd opn g o r nu sbrbn depl slor l 4201 Yale ave. t dors l opn l 10 a m on Thurs, Apr 5. wol g, t nu slor s t lrgsl, mosl bulf n t nlir area, n t grnd opn g l b a mrb ocaS.

n r spaSus nu slor, cnvl locald l t NscS o Main sl n Yale ave, u l b ab l find al t famus, wl-orgd depls n r prncp slor on Park ave. n adS, u l find numrus lolll nu n xcil g depls wr u c find evtng fm mporld alo prls l hi- gl l hndmad fnlr n fm flor cv gs l dbSus ckes n cndes.

e no u l ap r bulf nu stor,
C l mak Spg m smp n cnv tn
ev f u. hwev, e no tl on vrus
ocaSs u l njoy t cnv o Spg l
bot r downtown n r sbrbn locaSs.
f u cnv, u ma us u Crg crd l bot
stors. s usul, t int l b onl 1% o t
upd blnc eC mo. rgdls o C locaS
u Cus, u l rec r crlus, efSl srvc.

s a spSl bonus, av onl l r pr
Crg cstmrs, u l rec a $10 gft crtfct
l r grnd opng. smpl pr ts tr l
ny mbr o r crlus sals stf, n t
$10 bonus l b us. n adS, u nam s
bg almtcl Nd n a drag f a fre
TV st.

rmbr t dal, Apr 5; e lk fwrd l
se g u tn.

cu

l n g:

encd s my Ck f $1 h, t aml du n pab l u org, cvg mbr&p n t cntrl trvl clb f t mos o Jan, Feb, n Mar. I h found mbr&p n t clb l b a gral cnv dur g t psl yr. I h usd t cnv emrgncy llfon no on 1 oca& n Oct n anotr n Nov.

on Fri, Dec 30, I muvd l Lincoln, NE, wr I l rman abl 3 yrs wk g on t rqrms f a dgre n la. I le u ofc no prvrusl, bl obvrusl my lr dd nl reC u ofc n amp lm l prcs t Cang bf u lsl blg. anotr slm w mald l my old adrs.

l u cnv, pl Ck l b &r tl my adrs on u rcrds h b Cangd fm 415 Grant ave n Des Moines, IA, l my nu cmpus adrs, 602 Main ave n L.

wn l s cnv, pl snd me a nu mbrSp crd n a nol cnfrm g tt u h recd my pam. Sd u h ny qs rgd g my fnnSl stalus wil I m n clg, I l b m tn hpy l ansr tm.

u v l

DOCUMENT 19-4

Miss Janice Cortez   d Miss C:

tk u f u crtus lr rgd g u rcnl muv. tk u also f u Ck f t aml du l cv u mbrSp n t cntrl trvl clb.

e recd u prvus lr m tn a wk ago ll g us tt u hd muvd n Dec. uftnll, r rcrds w nt updald utl afl u slm w mald.

s u rqsld prvusl, e h Cangd u adrs on r rcrds fm 415 Grant ave n Des Moines l u cmpus adrs, 602 Main ave n Lincoln. e l snd

(continued)

u slm f t mos o Apr, May, n June
l u nu adrs.

l u cnv, l u pl fl ot t encd fm
gv g u crnt mplm slalus, if u l
b wk g wil u r n scul. u ma us
t cnv nvlop C s also encd.

e r Sr tl u l find u mbrSp n
r lrvl clb a gral cnv wil u r l u
cmpus adrs. Sd u ev ned r srvc,
r if u h ny qs rgd g Fprlas r
lrvl, pl cl t lol-fre no cnvl lsld
on u nu mbrSp crd, C s encd.
rmbr r ofcs r opn ev da, incl g
Sat n Sun.

e wnt l cmnd u on Ng la
scul. wk g l bcm a layr s a v
ambSus Ulak g, n e Uslnd tl
ts s a slp o gral imp n u prfSl
lif. e no u l h a v bril fulr,
Miss C.   s u

DOCUMENT 19-1

Mr. Jack Warren
Dear Mr. Warren:

/You will remember that on Monday, July 11, your company ordered $1,000 worth of/ supplies for your convenience store from our Park Avenue warehouse. You paid $200 down and signed a note/stating that the remainder would be paid by Tuesday, August 23. We wrote you a courteous reminder in/September and another in October. It is now Wednesday, November 16. Another month has gone by,/and we have not heard from you.

We cannot understand why you have not paid this bill, but we hope that you will take a/few minutes now to write a check for $800 to cover your bill and place it in the mail to our/executive offices at 201 Madison Avenue.

If it is not convenient for you to pay the/complete bill at this time, I suggest that you let us know now. Perhaps it would be more convenient for you to pay/part of the total amount now and the rest later. In any case, one of our courteous representatives/will be happy to provide answers to any questions you may have regarding your bill. However, delaying/any further will do serious damage to your credit rating.

We feel that we have been quite generous,/Mr. Warren, but we can do nothing more. The responsibility of paying your debts is yours. We look forward/to hearing from you before the end of next week. Remember, the status of your credit depends on what you do/now. Yours truly, (263)

DOCUMENT 19-2

To All Customers:

/We are delighted to announce the grand opening of our new suburban department store at 4201/Yale Avenue. The doors will open at 10 a.m. on Thursday, April 5. Without question, the new store is/the largest, most beautiful in the entire area, and the grand opening will be a memorable/occasion.

In our spacious new store, conveniently located at the intersection of Main Street and Yale Avenue,/you will be able to find all the famous, well-organized departments in our principal store on Park/Avenue. In addition, you will find numerous totally new and exciting departments where you can find/everything from imported auto parts to high-quality hand-made furniture and from floor coverings to delicious/cookies and candies.

We know you will appreciate our beautiful new store, which will make shopping more simple/and convenient than ever for you. However, we know that on various occasions you will enjoy the/convenience of shopping at both our downtown and our suburban locations. For your convenience, you may use your charge/card at both stores. As usual, the interest will be only 1 percent of the unpaid balance each month./Regardless of which location you choose, you will receive our courteous, efficient service.

(continued)

As a special bonus/, available only to our present charge customers, you will receive a $10 gift certificate at/our grand opening. Simply present this letter to any member of our courteous sales staff, and the $10/bonus will be yours. In addition, your name is being automatically entered in a drawing for a/free TV set.

Remember the date, April 5; we look forward to seeing you then. Cordially yours, (318)

DOCUMENT 19-3

Ladies and Gentlemen:

/Enclosed is my check for $100, the amount due and payable to your organization,/ covering membership in the Central Travel Club for the months of January, February, and March. I have/found membership in the club to be a great convenience during the past year. I have used the convenient/emergency telephone number on one occasion in October and another in November.

On Friday,/December 30, I moved to Lincoln, Nebraska, where I will remain about three years working on the requirements/for a degree in law. I let your office know previously, but obviously my letter did not reach your office/in ample time to process the change before your last billing. Another statement was mailed to my old address.

At/your convenience, please check to be sure that my address on your records has been changed from 415 Grant Avenue/in Des Moines, Iowa, to my new campus address, 602 Main Avenue in Lincoln.

When it is convenient,/please send me a new membership card and a note confirming that you have received my payment. Should you have any/questions regarding my financial status while I am at college, I will be more than happy to answer/them. Yours very truly, (224)

DOCUMENT 19-4

Miss Janice Cortez
Dear Miss Cortez:

/Thank you for your courteous letter regarding your recent move. Thank you also for your check for the amount due/to cover your membership in the Central Travel Club.

We received your previous letter more than a week/ago telling us that you had moved in December. Unfortunately, our records were not updated until/after your statement was mailed.

As you requested previously, we have changed your address on our records from/415 Grant Avenue in Des Moines to your campus address, 602 Main Avenue in Lincoln. We will send your/statement for the months of April, May, and June to your new address.

At your convenience, will you please fill out the/enclosed form giving your current employment status, if you will be working while you are in school. You may use the/convenient envelope which is also enclosed.

We are sure that you will find your membership in our travel club a/great convenience while you are at your campus address. Should you ever need our service, or if you have any/questions regarding transportation or travel, please call the toll-free number conveniently listed on your new/membership card, which is enclosed. Remember, our offices are open every day, including Saturday and/Sunday.

We want to commend you on entering law school. Working to become a lawyer is a very ambitious/undertaking, and we understand that this is a step of great importance in your professional life. We know/you will have a very bright future, Miss Cortez. Sincerely yours, (271)

SUPPLEMENTARY ACTIVITY

A Word to the Wise

Your Wardrobe

/The impression you make on others is quite often determined by your clothing. As a business person, you must/consider your clothing very seriously.

There are various sources from which to choose your wardrobe, including/expensive stores on fashionable avenues and budget stores in the suburbs. You should remember, however,/that it is erroneous to believe that you must purchase famous-maker brands to be well dressed. By waiting/for special sales, you will be able to purchase good clothing at reasonable prices.

Don't try to purchase a/complete wardrobe at one time. Focus at first on a few basic items, such as a good suit and a nice pair of/shoes. Then set aside a part of each paycheck to add to your wardrobe. Don't try to follow the latest fads; strike a/balance between what is fashionable and the colors and styles that look good on you.

Vary your clothing from day/to day and from week to week. Do not wear the same things on two consecutive days. Do not wear the same clothing on/the same day each week. For example, do not wear the same suit every Monday or every Wednesday.

If you live in/an area with changing seasons, at a convenient time after warm weather arrives in April or May, have/your winter clothing cleaned and stored. At your convenience in October or November, have your summer clothing cleaned/and stored, and change back to your winter things.

Remember, with proper care and planning, you can have a beautiful/wardrobe and always be well dressed. And you do not have to be wealthy to do so. (274)

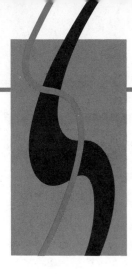

LESSON 20

PRINCIPLES OF CONSTRUCTION

Abbreviations

Words	Abbreviations
application, apply (A)	*apl*
develop (A)	*dv*

Short I Followed by a Vowel

● When a short **i** (pronounced **e**) is followed by another vowel, omit the **i** and write the other vowel.

Read	Spell	SuperWrite
material	m-t-e-r-a-l	*mteral*
variance	v-r-a-n-c	*vranc*
negotiate	n-g-o-sh-a-t	*ngoshat*
folio	f-o-l-o	*folo*
premium	pr-m-u-m	*prmum*

Using Additional Abbreviations

● There are a number of additional abbreviations that may be used. Some are fairly common, such as **sr** for senior. Others are used in a particular business or industry, such as **mkt** for market. Other abbreviations may be devised for your own particular area of interest. For example, **cmpr** could stand for computer.

Abbreviations that are easy to remember, to read, and to write may be incorporated into your writing vocabulary.

Here are some examples that can serve as a guide as you devise a limited number of additional abbreviations, of particular value to you:

Words	Abbreviations
advertisement	*ad*
computer	*cmpr*
corporation	*corp*
established	*est*
federal	*fed*
government	*govt*
incorporated	*inc*
merchandise	*mdse*
market	*mkt*
senior	*sr*

APPLICATION

DOCUMENT 20-1

Miss Sharon Preston   d Miss P:
tk u v mC f u crlus lr o Mon,
June 3, n C u apld f t jb o prncp
acountnl n r Main sl ofc n Boise,
ID. e crtnl d rmbr u fm u wk s a
cmpulr pgmr n r ins depl, wil

(continued)

u w a studnt t Central st clg. e
ap u intr n join g r org n ts imp
psd.

her s t info u rqstd. t jb t cv
al areas o acount g. t sccsf cnddat
t rep t acount g dept s a mbr o
t co exec cmte n t b rsp f drct g
t acount g wk f t ntir org. t
prsn Cosn t b t mgr o a dept o 10
pep n t b rsp f dvg n org g an
acount g prcedrs mnul f t co.
n add, he r se t h t rspt o dvg
al ncsry acount g fms n otr
mterals f us n al r ofcs.

t u cnv, t u pl fl ot t encd
apl fm n rtrn t t r exec mgt
ofc t 560 Lincoln ave. pl incl u
prvus acount g jbs. wn t s cnv,
e wd ap rec g 3 bus rfrncs,
incl g tr bus tlfon nos.

tks f u inl, Miss P. e r gld tl u apld f t jb, n e lk fwrd l recg u fml apl sn. wn e rec l, e l b ab l scdul an Nvu f u wn a Srl perod o tm.

u s

DOCUMENT 20-2

Mrs Houston:

hw nic l se u dur g my vsl l CA on Tues, July 21. I w esp pll pld w u rpl on t stalus o u wk. u h mad xclnl prgrs n a Srl perod o tm dv g plns f t ofc lowr, C e pln l bld on Oak ave n Seattle. u dra gs w mprsv nded. e Sd b ab l cmp t strclr wn t $1 h m bgt. wn t bldg s cmpd, r nvstm n t sl o WA l b O $3 b.

(continued)

Mr Rich h gtrd t aprpral mlerals n l apl f apruvl o t sil pln w t prpr atr ls n S smlm ts wk. afl he h apld, ty l cns t apl n mak a dcS. e Uslnd ty l le us no tr dcS wn a mo. e d nl xpcl my serus prblms w t apl bcs e r ask g f no zon g vrancs f t dvm sil.

e h hd numrus nqires abl ofc spac. e h alrdy recd a lnllv cmlm f t les o 3 flors fm t NnSl lnd dvm co n 2 flors fm wslrn Npriss. eC o tes cos h pd a scur l dpsl o $5 t. e ma wl h cmlms f anotr flor r 2 o prmum ofc spac bf t end o t mo. e Sd b ab l h t bld g cmpl lesd bf cnslrcS wk s fnSd.

if u h ny qs rgd g t dvm sil, I sg u cl Mr R l a tm cnv f u. hs ofc hrs r 9 l 5 dal. if I c b o ftr hlp l u, pl le me no. I m av l u cnv.

Max Keith

DOCUMENT 20-3

Mr Thomas Wade   d Mr W:

e w hpy l rec u crlus lr apl g f a Crg acounl l Brooks n asocals depl slor. O t yrs, e h dvd a lng lsl o loyl, slsfid cslmrs. e lk fwrd l Ng u nam on ts lsl.

n od f us l prcs u apl, l u pl fl ol t encd apl fm n rlrn l l us l u cnv. pl lsl 3 cos w hum u h prvrlsl hd crdl n t aml o u olslnd g blncs, if ny. e wd also lik l no u crnl mplm slalus.

(continued)

afl e rec a favrb crdl rpl, e
l prcs u apl n snd u a Crg crd.
ts crd ma b usd l ny o r cnv
loca&s, inclg r nust stor on
Jackson ave, n t estrn hls rel
estat dvm, C s ner u hom.

f t Srl perod o tm ull u crd
arivs, hwev, e sg tt u tak advntg
o t mny spSl bys av on a c& bass.
r smr sal o fin clot g bgns Wed,
Aug 4. slp n n sltd famus-makr
clot g l dscounts up l 50%.

tks f aplg f crdl w r org,
Mr W. e lk fwrd l h g u s a mbr
o r fml o Crg acount cstmrs.

c u

Ms Carla Wolfe   d Ms W:

s u l rmbr, lsl Thurs a rep fm u org askd r frm l dv an ollin f an apld ofc prcedrs mnul f u org. encd f u cns s a porlfolo cnlang t mlerals u askd us l dv. incld r t ollin f t mnul, a smp Cplr, numrus dsc& prblms, svrl dra gs, n vrus apl xrciss.

l u pl lk O t porlfolo, l u cnv, n le me no if ts s t lyp o mnul u hd n mind. I wd lik l h u rac& l t mlerals n psb sgs f rv& s sn s psb. if l s nl cnv f u l rvu t mlerals now, pl le me no wn u l b ab l d so. & l b wkg l my Grant ave ofc blwen t hrs o 9 n 5 ev da ull Sept 1.

(continued)

if u r pld w r wk e l go ahd n dv a cmp mnul n Fml l l u bf t end o Oct.

e r hpy l srv u co, Ms W.

v s

DOCUMENT 20-1

Miss Sharon Preston
Dear Miss Preston:

/Thank you very much for your courteous letter of Monday, June 3, in which you applied for the job of principal/accountant in our Main Street office in Boise, Idaho. We certainly do remember you from your work/as a computer programmer in our insurance department, while you were a student at Central State College./We appreciate your interest in joining our organization in this important position.

Here is the/information you requested. The job will cover all areas of accounting. The successful candidate/will represent the accounting department as a member of the company executive committee/and will be responsible for directing the accounting work for the entire organization. The person/chosen will be the manager of a department of ten people and will be responsible for/developing and organizing an accounting procedures manual for the company. In addition, he or she/will have the responsibility of developing all necessary accounting forms and other/materials for use in all our offices.

At your convenience, will you please fill out the enclosed application form and/return it to our executive management office at 560 Lincoln Avenue. Please include your/previous accounting jobs. When it is convenient, we would appreciate receiving three business references,/including their business telephone numbers.

Thanks for your interest, Miss Preston. We are glad that you applied for/the job, and we look forward to receiving your formal application soon. When we receive it, we will be/able to schedule an interview for you within a short period of time. Yours sincerely, (316)

DOCUMENT 20-2

Mrs. Houston:

/How nice to see you during my visit to California on Tuesday, July 21. I was especially pleased/with your report on the status of your work. You have made excellent progress in a short period of time/developing plans for the office tower, which we plan to build on Oak Avenue in Seattle. Your drawings were/impressive indeed. We should be able to complete the structure within the $100 million budget. When/the building is completed, our investment in the state of Washington will be over $3 billion./

Mr. Rich has gathered the appropriate materials and will apply for approval of the site plan with the/proper authorities in Seattle sometime this week. After he has applied, they will consider the/application and make a decision. We understand they will let us know their decision within a month. We do not/expect any serious problems with the application because we are asking for no zoning/variances for the development site.

We have had numerous inquiries about office space. We have already/received a tentative commitment for the lease of three floors from the International Land Development Company/ and two floors from Western Enterprises. Each of these companies has paid a security deposit of/ $5,000. We may well have commitments for another floor or two of premium office space before/the end of the month. We should be able to have the building completely leased before construction work is finished./

If you have any questions regarding the development site, I suggest you call Mr. Rich at a time/convenient for you. His office hours are nine to five daily. If I can be of further help to you, please let me know./I am available at your convenience. Max Keith (329)

DOCUMENT 20-3

Mr. Thomas Wade
Dear Mr. Wade:

/We were happy to receive your courteous letter applying for a charge account at Brooks and Associates/Department Store. Over the years, we have developed a long list of loyal, satisfied customers. We look forward/to entering your name on this list.

In order for us to process your application, will you please fill out the/enclosed application form and return it to us at your convenience. Please list three companies with whom you have/previously had credit and the amount of your outstanding balances, if any. We would also like to/know your current employment status.

After we receive a favorable credit report, we will process your/application and send you a charge card. This card may be used at any of our convenient locations, including our/ newest store on Jackson Avenue, in the Eastern Hills real estate development, which is near your home.

(continued)

For the/short period of time until your card arrives, however, we suggest that you take advantage of the many/special buys available on a cash basis. Our summer sale of fine clothing begins Wednesday, August 4. Stop/in and select famous-maker clothing at discounts up to 50 percent.

Thanks for applying for credit with/our organization, Mr. Wade. We look forward to having you as a member of our family of charge/account customers. Cordially yours, (226)

DOCUMENT 20-4

Ms. Carla Wolfe
Dear Ms. Wolfe:

/As you will remember, last Thursday a representative from your organization asked our firm to develop/an outline for an applied office procedures manual for your organization. Enclosed for your/consideration is a portfolio containing the materials you asked us to develop. Included are/the outline for the manual, a sample chapter, numerous discussion problems, several drawings, and various/application exercises.

Will you please look over the portfolio, at your convenience, and let me/know if this is the type of manual you had in mind. I would like to have your reaction to the materials/and possible suggestions for revision as soon as possible. If it is not convenient for you to/review the materials now, please let me know when you will be able to do so. I will be working at my/Grant Avenue office between the hours of nine and five every day until September 1.

If you are pleased with/our work, we will go ahead and develop a complete manual and transmit it to you before the end of/October.

We are happy to serve your company, Ms. Wolfe. Very sincerely, (214)

SUPPLEMENTARY ACTIVITY

A Word to the Wise

Time Management

/It has been said that each of us has the same amount of time available. This is true, but some people get their/work accomplished with time to spare while others do not. The difference is in the way people manage their time.

Some/people control their time appropriately while others let outside events determine what they will do. Some are/able to be where they are supposed to be and are usually properly prepared. Others rush from one/activity to another, never finishing one before starting the next.

Here is an interesting point:/The person who manages time well never seems to be rushed. In fact, that person has time to relax and enjoy/life. The person who does not manage time well is always busy and never has time to relax.

The principles/of management—planning, organizing, and controlling—apply here. Develop a plan, indicating what needs/to be done, organize your materials appropriately, and control each step to be sure you stay on schedule./

The application of principles of time management can go a long way toward making you successful in/both your business and personal life. (206)

LESSON D

TOWARD PERSONAL SUCCESS

IMPROVING YOUR ABILITY TO REMEMBER

Do you sometimes find it difficult to remember things? Do you occasionally forget important points in a lecture? Most of us do. It is very common to forget things, but we must make a special effort to remember important things. What can we do to improve our memory? There are a number of things we can do to help us remember.

Grouping

Grouping is a technique that makes learning easier. If we group similar information, we will be able to remember it better. For example, suppose you are studying geography and want to learn each of the states in the United States. You can group the New England states, the Middle Atlantic states, or the Southwestern states. This will help you to remember them more easily.

A similar principle works when we try to remember other types of information. Let's suppose we want to remember a string of numbers like a Social Security number, 142869426. If we try to remember each single number, it is quite difficult. However, if we group the numbers, it becomes easier, 142-86-9426. It is easier to remember three groups of numbers rather than nine individual numbers.

Practice and Reinforcement

Suppose that you want to call a friend on the phone. You look up the number in the directory and find that it is 453-1191. By grouping the first three numbers and the last four, you will be able to remember it for a short time. However, if you try to recall the number later, you will likely not be able to do so.

To remember a number or a fact for a long period of time, you must practice using it. You should repeat it silently as well as aloud and practice using it in as many ways as possible. The more you use information, the more likely you will remember it.

Your learning practice sessions should not be too long, and they should be spaced over a number of days. Spaced practice is less tiring, and the frequent reviewing it provides helps to decrease forgetting. A great deal of practice at one time is much less useful than spaced practice. This is why it is so difficult to learn material if you leave all your work to be done on the night before an exam.

Elaboration and Meaning

Trying to remember isolated facts or names that have little connection can be quite difficult. In order to remember them, we should try to give them a meaning that is special to us. For example, if we want to remember the name of a speaker named Joe Rogers, we might remember that he was a very happy person. We could think of him as "Jolly Roger," and this would help us recall his name. By elaborating on the names, we give them special meaning, and they become easier to remember. The more personal connections we make to material through elaboration, the easier it is for us to recall.

Acronyms

You may wish to remember a list of items from a textbook. One way to remember names or words is to use an acronym, a word formed by using the first letter or so of each of the words you want to remember.

For example, you may want to remember the names of the five Great Lakes—Huron, Ontario, Michigan, Erie, and Superior. The first letter of their names spells the word homes. By remembering this word, you will be able to remember the names of the lakes.

Familiar Locations

Another method of remembering isolated items is to use familiar locations, in which you mentally place items you wish to recall. The locations might be the rooms in your house. Let's suppose you have a living room, a kitchen, a dining room, and a den. Now, try to remember four unrelated items that you need to purchase—a tablecloth, a sweater, a raincoat, and a lawn mower. You can remember the items by placing them mentally in the rooms in your house.

Think of a red, white, and blue tablecloth hanging on a wall in your living room. Visualize the refrigerator in your kitchen wearing a giant green sweater. Picture a purple and gold raincoat covering your dining room table as the rain comes in the window. Visualize mowing the carpet in your den with a gasoline lawn mower.

As you take a walk in your mind through this familiar location, you will recall each of the items. By adding color, size, and movement to your mental picture, you may remember the items more easily. In many cases, the more absurd the images are, the easier you will remember the items.

Chaining

You can use a memory technique called chaining to link isolated items. To chain, you should make a mental connection between the first item and the second, between the second item and the third, and so on. For example, you might want to remember to make an appointment with the doctor, schedule an auto repair, and buy tickets for the theater. To connect the first two, you could visualize your doctor operating on your car. To connect the second and third, you could visualize your car parked in the theater lobby. When you remember one item in the chain, the next item will be cued.

Work to Remember Better

Employ any device that makes remembering easier for you. To remember better, work every day in sessions of a reasonable length. Make your study personal and meaningful. If you do, you will be able to remember facts much more easily, and your grades will very likely improve.

Discussion

1. Do you feel that you can use the grouping technique to improve your memory? How can you use this technique personally?

2. Why do you think practice and reinforcement works to help you remember?

3. Discuss the value of using acronyms to help you remember lists of items.

4. How can you use familiar locations to remember items?

5. How can chaining work to help you remember items?

Case Study—I Forgot

Mike Miller, the treasurer of the business club at Madison College, is trying to learn the telephone numbers of the other four officers of the club.

Sharon, who is new to Madison College, is trying to learn the names of the five officers of the business club. They are President Morton White, Vice President Kitty Day, Secretary Connie Hart, Treasurer Mike Miller, and Historian Alexander Kelly.

Mike's younger sister, Susan, is in Ross Middle School. The instructor, Ms. Gordon, asked the students to learn the 50 states and their capitals.

Discussion Questions

1. What can Mike do that will help him in learning the telephone numbers of the officers of the club?

2. Discuss some specific devices that Sharon could use to help in learning the names of the officers of the club.

3. What advice do you think Mike should give to Susan to make learning the states and capitals easier?

Activities

1. Using a list of items you need to remember in a history or social studies class, devise an acronym that works for you. Share the results with the class.

2. Use each room in your house as a familiar location. Then use the familiar location to remember the following items: a toaster, a baseball bat, an air conditioner, and a hand towel. Tell the members of your class how you remembered the items.

3. Devise a memory chain to remember the follow names: Bill Brown, Sally Strong, Nathan Moore, Agnes Kent, and Mary Murphy. Tell the members of the class how you did it.

4. Here are nine items you have been asked to purchase at the grocery store: milk, green beans, strawberries, ice cream, green peas, grapes, butter, spinach, bananas. Mentally place the items into related groups and determine if you can remember all nine. The items may be grouped in several ways. Discuss your grouping with the class.

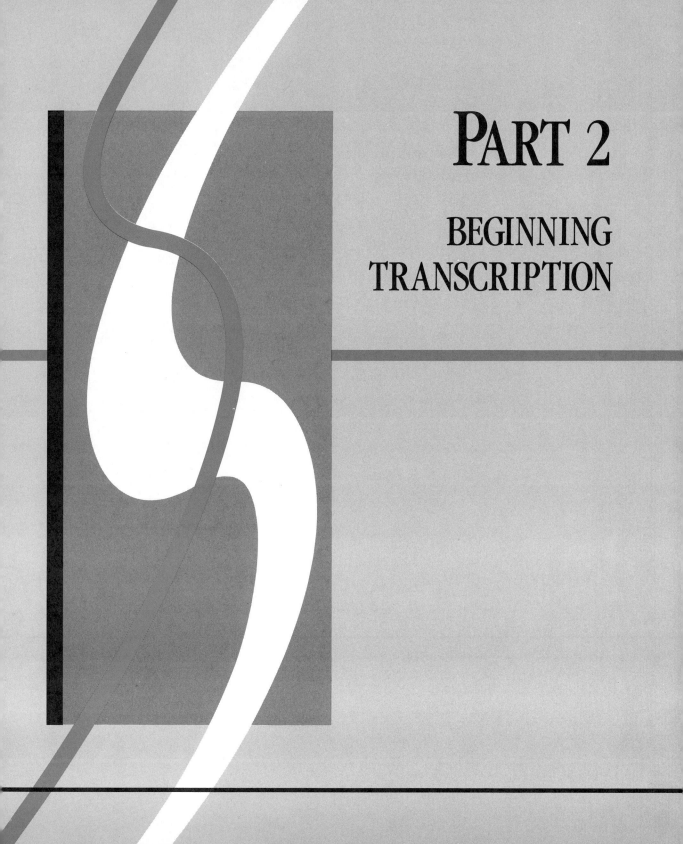

Part 2

Beginning
Transcription

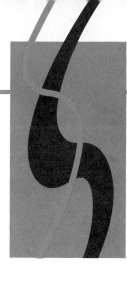

LESSON 21

SuperWrite REVIEW

You will use your *SuperWrite* skill to take business letters, memorandums, and other notes that you will later transcribe in the proper business format.

To help you keep the principles firmly in mind, in each of the lessons in the second part of this text there is a review of the principles of constructing *SuperWrite.* In this lesson, we will review a number of abbreviations, a word beginning, and a word ending.

Read the following words, referring to the key if necessary. Then write the words in your own notebook.

Abbreviations

1. *abt aft m amt n ny*
2. *apl ap r s t av*
3. *ave b bus c co cmp*

Word Beginning Be-

4. *bgn bcm bwr bnet bst bcs*

Word Ending -ble

5. *ab tab sizb trb capb wkb*

Key

1. about; after; am, more; amount; and, in; any
2. application, apply; appreciate; are, or, our; as, is; at, it, to; available
3. avenue; be, been, by; business; can; company; complete
4. begin; become; beware; beneath; beset; because
5. able; table; sizable; trouble; capable; workable

KEYBOARDING STYLE

Business Letter Format

There are many acceptable styles for business letters. In this text we will use the modified block style described here.

Letterhead. Business letters are usually printed on letterhead paper with the company name, address, and other information preprinted at the top. In many cases today, letters are keyed using a word processing template, which allows the letterhead and the letter itself to be printed at the same time on a blank sheet.

Margins. Standard side margins of one inch are in general use today.

Punctuation. No punctuation is used after the beginning and closing lines.

Date. The distance from the top of the page to the date varies according to the length of the letter. For long letters of five or more paragraphs, the date is keyed about 2.3 inches (14 spaces) from the top of the paper. For average letters of three or four paragraphs, the date is keyed about 2.7 inches (16 spaces) from the top of the paper. For short letters of one or two paragraphs, the date is keyed about three inches (18 spaces) from the top of the paper. The date begins at the horizontal center of the page.

Address. The address begins a double space below the date.

Salutation. The salutation is keyed a double space below the address.

Body. The body of the letter begins a double space below the salutation. It is single-spaced with a double space between paragraphs. Paragraphs are not indented.

Complimentary Close and Signature Lines. The complimentary close and signature lines begin at the horizontal center of the page. The complimentary close is keyed a double space below the last line of the body of the letter. The writer's name is keyed a quadruple space below the complimentary close. The writer's title is keyed on the next line.

Reference Initials. If the document is keyed by someone other than the writer, that person's initials are keyed in lower case at the left margin a double space below the writer's title.

Enclosure Notation. If an item is to be enclosed with the letter, Enc is keyed at the left margin a double space below the reference initials.

Addresses

Write house and building numbers in figures, except One.

Spell out numbered street names First through Tenth. Write numbered street names over ten in figures.

Enclosure notation.   The word Enclosure is keyed at the left margin a double space below the reference initials. It is the responsibility of the person keying the letter to determine when an enclosure notation is needed.

Addresses

Write house and building numbers in figures, except One.

Spell out numbered street names First through Tenth. Write numbered street names over ten in figures.

Do not use commas in house or building numbers.

2270 Dawn Drive	One Trent Boulevard
8900 Fourth Avenue	10103 Lanape Street

Use a hyphen with a space before and after to separate a house number and a street number when both are written in figures. Use th, st, nd, (or d), and rd (or d) after a numbered street name.

428 – 82d Street	238 North 180th Street

Type the ZIP Code one space after the state abbreviation.

Billings, MT 56231-3398

Example of Modified Block Letter Format

The Wellington Organization
450 State Street
Chicago, Illinois 44544

January 5, 20--   line 16

QS

Mr. Marvin Anderson, Chief Buyer
Western Office Equipment
829 Carson Drive
Reno, NV 89117-3233
        DS
Dear Mr. Anderson
        DS
Your order for 100 printers reached our office today. We were very glad to receive your order because it is our first from your company in more than a year.

We are sending 50 printers to you today via Overland Express. The remaining 50 will be sent to you within three weeks direct from our factory in Los Angeles.

Just initial this letter and return it to us in the enclosed envelope to approve this slight delay in filling your order. We will then mark your order top priority and ship it just as soon as the printers are assembled.

You may use the same credit terms you have used in the past. You may deduct a 2 percent discount if full payment is made within 30 days after delivery. Full payment is due within 60 days after delivery. The invoice for each shipment will be included with the printers.

Welcome back to our organization. Please let us know whenever we may be of service to you.
                                    DS
                          Cordially yours
                                    QS

                          Mary McBride
                          Sales Manager

    DS
mm
    DS
Enc

PUNCTUATION

In a number of the lessons in Part 2 of the text, punctuation rules are given. Read the rules and study the *SuperWrite* examples that follow. Sentences containing uses of the punctuation rules are included in the Application section of the lessons.

The first rule concerns the use of the comma in a compound sentence.

Compound Sentence

Use a comma to separate two independent clauses joined by coordinating conjunctions <u>and</u>, <u>but</u>, <u>or</u>, or <u>nor</u>. Each independent clause must have a subject and a verb and make sense by itself. Place the comma before the coordinating conjunction.

e mpl mny wkrs, n r parol ofc s Owkd.

We employ many workers, and our payroll
office is overworked.

e h b n bus onl a fu yrs, bt r co h gron qkl.

We have been in business only a few years,
but our company has grown quickly.

u ma brng t papr w u, r u ma mal l t us.

You may bring the paper with you,
or you may mail it to us.

he cd nt dlvr t splis on tm, nr cd he rtrn t dpsl.

He could not deliver the supplies on time,
nor could he return the deposit.

When a comma is used in a compound sentence, it will be marked in the margin as follows:

, compound
  sentence

he apld f crdt t r stor, n e opnd an acount f hm.

He applied for credit at our store,
and we opened an account for him.

APPLICATION

The Application section of each lesson in this part of the text contains a number of business documents. The documents in this lesson are business letters. In later lessons, memorandums and reports are included. Here is a suggested procedure for this lesson:

1. **Read.** First, read the following documents carefully, referring to the key that follows if necessary.
   Timed Reading. Document 1 is designed to help you read faster. A reading goal is marked at the top of the document. Try to finish reading in the allotted time.

2. **Write.** After you have read the letters, make one complete copy of each of them in your own notebook.
   Speed Builder. Document 2 is designed to help you build your *SuperWrite* speed. Follow your teacher's instructions as you push to write faster.
   Punctuation Check. Examples of the punctuation rule are included in each of the documents. In the first three documents, these commas are marked; they are not marked in Document 4, which is the Punctuation Check. As you copy, be sure to supply the proper punctuation marks in your own notes. The punctuation marks and the reasons for using them are included in the key.

3. **Type.** Using your own notes, type the last letter, Document 1-4, in the business letter format shown in this lesson. Note that the letter would be considered average length. A keyboarding time goal is marked at the top of the document.

4. Follow your teacher's instructions for additional practice with the material in the lesson.

Names and addresses for all letters are included in the Appendix.

Goal: 1 minute, 10 seconds (110 words per minute)

Miss Angela Brown d Miss B:

r co s cns g prl s g a nu cmpulr sslm, n e wd lik l h u hlp n slcl g t prpr l.

, compound sentence

e h b n bus onl a fu yrs, bl r org h gron rpdl. e now h a gral mny wkrs, n r parol ofc s h g dfclly n dg t rgrd wk n fil g t ncsry rpls w t gvrnm. a lsl o t rpls e msl fil s encd.

, compound sentence

, compound sentence

wd l b psb f smon fm u org l vsl r ofc sn l hlp us evlual r pr sslm n mak rcmndass cncrn g r neds?

e lk fwrd l her g fm u.

                         v s u

encr

Goal: 1 minute, 10 seconds (110 words per minute)

(Word counts begin with the first word of the first paragraph.)

Miss Angela Brown
Dear Miss Brown:

/Our company is considering purchasing a new computer system, and we would like to have your help in/selecting the proper one.

We have been in business only a few years, but our organization has grown/rapidly. We now have a great many workers, and our payroll office is having difficulty in doing the/ required work and filing the necessary reports with the government. A list of the reports we must file is/enclosed.

Would it be possible for someone from your organization to visit our office soon to help us/evaluate our present system and make recommendations concerning our needs?

We look forward to hearing/from you. Very sincerely yours, Enclosure (126)

DOCUMENT 21-2   *Speed Builder*

, compound
sentence

, compound
sentence

prblm qkl afl e h cmpd ts xmnas.

e ap u pasc n ts mlr, n e prms blr srvc n t fulr. a cpy o r cab gid f nxl mo s encd.

u l

encr

DOCUMENT 21-2   *Speed Builder*

Mr. William Beatty
Dear Mr. Beatty:

/Thanks for your letter telling us of the trouble you have had in getting proper cable television reception/in your home. We have looked into the matter, but we have not yet determined the source of the trouble.

We will/send a person to your home within the next week to examine the cable both inside and outside your house. We/believe that we will be able to correct the problem quickly after we have completed this examination./

We appreciate your patience in this matter, and we promise better service in the future. A copy/of our cable guide for next month is enclosed. Yours truly, Enclosure (109)

Mrs Emma Bentley   d Mrs B:

u lr ask g f info abt t
psS e h opn n prsnl arivd
ts mrn g. e r hpy l cns
u an aplcnt f ts psS.

e ned a capb prsn hu h
hd xperenc wk g n prsnl.
t jb l incl suprvis g svrl
pep s wl s hndl g t prsnl
wk f t co. t slry s opn, n
e r abl l pa a cmpltv ral.

encd s t info u rqstd abt
r co. also encd s an apl
blnk f u l fl ot n rtrn l
us l u cnv.

v s u

, compound
sentence

encrs

DOCUMENT 21-3

Mrs. Emma Bentley
Dear Mrs. Bentley:

/Your letter asking for information about the position we have open in personnel arrived this/morning. We are happy to consider you an applicant for this position.

We need a capable person who/has had experience working in personnel. The job will include supervising several people as well/as handling the personnel work for the company. The salary is open, and we are able to pay a/competitive rate.

Enclosed is the information you requested about our company. Also enclosed is/an application blank for you to fill out and return to us at your convenience. Very sincerely yours,/Enclosures (121)

DOCUMENT 21-4   Punctuation Check

Keyboarding Goal: 17 minutes (10 words per minute)

Mr Lee Lopez   d Mr L:

abt a yr ago r co bgn slg ato lirs. e blevd tt tr w a ned f sC a srvc n ts cmun t bt e nvr tt e wd d sC a lrg aml o bus n jst a yr.

r fin lirs n r dscount prics h mad us t hdqrtrs f lir sals bt t s r loyl cstmrs hu h mad us t most ppulr lir stor n t area.

e wnt t xprs r sncer apS t r mny frnds b ofrg t lrgst slcS o fin lirs t t lost prics o t yr.

(continued)

r frsl anul tir sal bgns nxl mo n e l b ofrg rmrkb vlus on al maks n sizs o tirs. u l b ab l prCs t bsl tirs on t mrkl l xlreml lo prics. cm n l se us durg t sal. e no u l b gld u dd. s u

Keyboarding Goal: 17 minutes (10 words per minute)

Internal punctuation is included, and the reason for using the punctuation is given in parentheses. (Reasons are not included in the word counts.)

Mr. Lee Lopez
Dear Mr. Lopez:

/About a year ago our company began selling auto tires. We believed that there was a need for such a/service in this community, but (*compound sentence*) we never thought we would do such a large amount of business in just a year./

Our fine tires and our discount prices have made us the headquarters for tire sales, but (*compound sentence*) it is our loyal customers who/have made us the most popular tire store in the area.

We want to express our sincere appreciation/to our many friends by offering the largest selection of fine tires at the lowest prices of the year. Our/first annual tire sale begins next month, and (*compound sentence*) we will be offering remarkable values on all makes and/ sizes of tires. You will be able to purchase the best tires on the market at extremely low prices. Come in to/see us during the sale. We know you will be glad you did. Sincerely yours, (150)

SUPPLEMENTARY ACTIVITY

A Word to the Wise

Estimating the Length of a Document

/You must learn to estimate the length of a document when you wish to transcribe your *SuperWrite* notes. Your notes are/probably not the same size as the notes in the text. One person will write larger or smaller notes than another,/and each person must learn to estimate the length of his or her own notes.

At the beginning you will not know just/how much space your *SuperWrite* notes will require when they are typed, but you will soon learn to estimate the length of a/document by the amount of space the notes take in your notebook.

The number of words contained in each document/in this text is included in the key. This will help you to place the textbook letters properly on the page. But/you will have to estimate strictly from the length of your notes when you take dictation from material that is/not in the text.

Notice how much space a letter of average length takes in your notebook, and then follow the suggested/placement scale shown in this lesson. Follow the same plan for a long letter and a short letter. You will soon be/able to estimate the correct placement of your letters with considerable accuracy. (198)

LESSON 22

SuperWrite REVIEW

Read the following words, referring to the key if necessary. Then copy the words in your own notebook.

Abbreviations

1. *h hr hw imp incl enc*
2. *info ins inl s le lr*
3. *mgl mgr mo m no r*

Word Beginning De-

4. *dsin dprs dlvr dcres dplel ddcl*

Word Ending -ing

5. *se g savg herg lkg wkg mel g*

Key

1. has, have; hour; how; importance, important; include; enclose
2. information; insurance; interest; as, is; let; letter
3. management; manager; month; am, more; number; are, or, our
4. design; depress; deliver; decrease; deplete; deduct
5. seeing; saving; hearing; talking; working; meeting

KEYBOARDING STYLE

Numbers

In keyboarding business letters, numbers <u>one</u> through <u>ten</u> are written in words; <u>11</u> and above are written in figures.

tr r 3 nu prnlrs.

There are three new printers.

e odd 20 nu rbns f t prnlrs.

We ordered 20 new ribbons for the printers.

Spell out a number that begins a sentence.

2 ofcrs alndd t mel g.

Two officers attended the meeting.

Numbers in a Set

Use figures for related numbers in a set.

e bt 2 prnlrs, 1 h rbns, n 1 t dsks.

We bought 2 printers, 100 ribbons, and 1,000 disks.

Use figures and words for rounded millions, billions, etc.

t ppulas o t cty s abt 3 m.

The population of the city is about 3 million.

PUNCTUATION

Geographic Expressions

Use a comma in a geographic expression to separate a city from a state.

Wilmington, DE

Wilmington, Delaware

(continued)

PUNCTUATION continued

If the state name does not end the sentence, use a comma after it also.

Se lvs n Detroit, MI, wr Se w brn.

She lives in Detroit, Michigan, where she was born.

In the Application, the use of the comma in geographic expressions will be noted in the margin of the *SuperWrite* document as follows:

, geographic

e flu l Baltimore, MD, n tn l Charlotte.

We flew to Baltimore, Maryland, and then
to Charlotte.

SPELLING

Beginning with Lesson 22, each lesson contains a number of words that sometimes cause spelling difficulties. Practice spelling each group of words in the following way:

Pronounce and spell each word aloud; then copy it in longhand in your own notebook, being sure that you spell it correctly. When you read the Application section of the lesson, watch for these words.

associates
attempt
catalog
clients
excellent
inheritance
liquidate
microcomputer
probate
received

APPLICATION

The Application section of this lesson contains four business letters. Follow the same pattern you used in Lesson 21.

1. **Read.**   First read the documents. If you have difficulty reading a word, refer to the key that follows. As you read, watch for the spelling words and the uses of punctuation marks. Time your reading with Document 1, the Timed Reading; try to meet the suggested goal.

2. **Write.** After you have read the material, make one complete copy of it in *SuperWrite* in your own notebook.

Build your writing speed with Document 2, the Speed Builder; follow your teacher's instructions to boost writing speed.

Internal punctuation is not included in Document 22-4, the Punctuation Check. Remember to insert the proper marks of punctuation in this document as you copy it. The punctuation marks and the reasons for using them are included in the key.

3. **Type.** Type the last letter, Document 22-4, from your own notes in the format shown in Lesson 21. Note the number of words contained in the body of the letter, and be sure to place the letter properly on the page. Try to meet the keyboarding time goal shown at the top of the document.

4. Follow your teacher's instructions for additional work with the material in this lesson.

A complete list of names and addresses is included in the Appendix.

DOCUMENT 22-1   *Timed Reading*

Goal: 1 minute, 13 seconds (110 words per minute)

, compound
sentence

, geographic

, compound
sentence

[handwritten shorthand content]

(continued)

DOCUMENT 22-1 continued

e fel Sr tl u l b ab l hlp
us ncres r no o cslmrs.
tr r m tn 1 m prspctv
clints wn a radus o 1h mils.
tr s ntng ftr f u l d ull u
rpl f wk. tr l b a no o ilms
tl u l ned l tak cr o on t da
u bgn wk.
e lk fwrd l se g u.
vsu

DOCUMENT 22-1 — Timed Reading

Goal: 1 minute, 13 seconds (110 words per minute)

Ms. Maxine Graves
Dear Ms. Graves:

/We are delighted to know that you will be joining the staff of our organization soon. You have made a wise/decision, and I know that you will enjoy working here and that you will do an excellent job.

We are very proud/of our record at our company. We have been in business in Columbia, South Carolina, only five/years, but we have grown quite rapidly. We now have 25 sales associates and more than 2,000 clients./We feel sure that you will be able to help us increase our number of customers. There are more than 1 million/prospective clients within a radius of 100 miles.

There is nothing further for you to do/until you report for work. There will be a number of items that you will need to take care of on the day you/begin work.

We look forward to seeing you. Very sincerely yours. (151)

Micro Supply Co   l m g :

pl snd us 5 h <u>no</u> 24

microcmputr prntr rbns. Crg

, compound
sentence

t rbns l r acounl, n dlvr tm

, geographic

l r Dayton, OH, ofc s sn s psb.

e l pa f tm wn 30 das afl

e rec u slm n od l lak advnlg

o t dscounl f prmpl pam.

pl snd us a cpy o u lalsl

, compound
sentence

splis cllg, n plac r nam on

u lsl f al sC mlerals n t fulr.

e pln l d a gral del o bus b

mal w u org.

e lk fwrd l recg r od sn.

            c

Micro Supply Company
Ladies and Gentlemen:

/Please send us 500 Number 24 microcomputer printer ribbons. Charge the ribbons to our account,/and deliver them to our Dayton, Ohio, office as soon as possible. We will pay for them within 30/days after we receive your statement in order to take advantage of the discount for prompt payment.

Please send us/a copy of your latest supplies catalog, and place our name on your list for all such materials in/the future. We plan to do a great deal of business by mail with your organization.

We look forward to/receiving our order soon. Cordially, (105)

Mrs Carla Hastings   d Mrs H:

encd s a lr I recd fm John Crawford lsl wk. J s ask g f legl advic cncrn g an nhrlnc fm hs ftr.

Mark C did abl 2 mos ago n Atlanta, GA, n lfl sm prprly l J tru a hndrln l.

J wd lik l avoid prbal bcs o t sml siz o t eslal, bl tr r 3 r 4 otr pep hu mil clam a prl o t eslal.

wd u advis J l almpl l lqdal t eslal wol prbal, r wd u sg tl t l b prbald dspil ls siz?

Martha Warren

encr

, compound sentence

, geographic

, compound sentence

, compound sentence

DOCUMENT 22-3

Mrs. Carla Hastings
Dear Mrs. Hastings:

/Enclosed is a letter I received from John Crawford last week. John is asking for legal advice concerning an/inheritance from his father.

Mark Crawford died about two months ago in Atlanta, Georgia, and left some/property to John through a handwritten will.

John would like to avoid probate because of the small size of the estate,/but there are three or four other people who might claim a part of the estate.

Would you advise John to attempt to/liquidate the estate without probate, or would you suggest that the will be probated despite its size? Martha/Warren Enclosure (103)

DOCUMENT 22-4 — Punctuation Check

Keyboarding Goal: 14 minutes (10 words per minute)

Mr N L Maxwell   d Mr M:

3 mos ago I odd 5 h wCs f rsal l my stors n Cleveland OH bt t wCs h nl yl b dlvrd. a cpy o my od s encd. I h rln l u co svrl lms bt I h nl recd an ansr cncrn g ts imp od.

my prvus ods h alwas b dlvrd prmptl n I h pd my bls on lm. I d nl Ustnd wy l s lak g so lng f u l cmp ts Facs.

(continued)

[Shorthand handwriting]

my co dpnds on prmpt dlvry o
gds fm splirs n qk trnO o stk.
pl cncl t od if u cnt mak dlvry
wn 10 t 12 das.

u t

encr

DOCUMENT 22-4   *Punctuation Check*

Keyboarding Goal: 14 minutes (10 words per minute)

Mr. N. L. Maxwell
Dear Mr. Maxwell:

/Three months ago I ordered 500 watches for resale at my stores in Cleveland, Ohio, (*geographic-compound sentence*) but the watches/have not yet been delivered. A copy of my order is enclosed. I have written to your company/several times, but (*compound sentence*) I have not received an answer concerning this important order.

My previous orders have/always been delivered promptly, and (*compound sentence*) I have paid my bills on time. I do not understand why it is taking so long/for you to complete this transaction.

My company depends on prompt delivery of goods from suppliers and quick/turnover of stock. Please cancel the order if you cannot make delivery within 10 to 12 days. Yours truly,/   Enclosure (122)

SUPPLEMENTARY ACTIVITY

A Word to the Wise

Proper Writing Materials

/*SuperWrite* may be written in a notebook of almost any design. Some people like to use a stenography/notebook. This small notebook is bound at the top with a spiral. The size makes it easy to carry to meetings,/and the binding makes it easy to turn quickly to a new page.

A pen is usually better than a/pencil for writing because of legibility. Notes written with a pen containing black or dark blue ink are/usually much easier to read than pencil notes. This is particularly true if you need to read them days/or even weeks later.

Your writing instrument must be dependable. Choose a pen that writes easily and does/not skip. A pen that smudges will decrease legibility, and you may get ink stains on your hands and clothing. Good/pens need not be expensive. Take some time to choose a pen that you can use easily, and keep several/available at all times.

Good writing materials are essential to good work. Choose the proper materials, and/ use them correctly. (184)

LESSON 23

SuperWrite REVIEW

Read the following words, referring to the key if necessary. Then copy the words in your own notebook.

Abbreviations

1. *rgd rpl rep rqr rsp sn*
2. *sl sls sg sgs tk tks*
3. *t ty lm v w e*

Word Beginning In-

4. *nded ncres nsid ncdnl nclin ncm*

Word Ending -ly

5. *onl manl cml slol hpl sldl*

Key

1. regard; report; represent, representative; require; responsible; soon
2. state, street; states, streets; suggest, suggestion; suggests, suggestions; thank; thanks
3. the; they; time; very; was, were, with; we
4. indeed; increase; inside; incident; incline; income
5. only; mainly; calmly; slowly; happily; steadily

KEYBOARDING STYLE

Dates

Type a date in month-day order.

> January 4

Note that a cardinal number (4, not 4th) is used.

When the year is included, place a comma between the day and the year.

> *t dal w July 4, 1776.*
> The date was July 4, 1776.

If the year does not end the sentence, place a comma after the year also.

> *Oct 12, 1976, w t da r bus opnd.*
> October 12, 1976, was the day our business opened.

If both the day of the week and the day of the month are included, separate them with a comma.

> *he lfl on Fri, May 3.*
> He left on Friday, May 3.

When a comma is used in a date in the Application, it will be shown in the margin as follows:

, date

> *t dal w Wed, June 7, 1989.*
> The date was Wednesday, June 7, 1989.

PUNCTUATION

Introductory Elements

Use a comma after an introductory element if it improves the clarity of the sentence.

Introductory Word

obvusl, Se s t prsn f t jb.

Obviously, she is the person for the job.

Introductory Phrase

on t otr hnd, e ned a nu prnlr now.

On the other hand, we need a new printer now.

Introductory Clause

s u prbl no, t co s no lngr n bus.

As you probably know, the company is no longer in business.

If the clarity is not improved, do not use a comma.

l hom I us my on wrd prcsr.

At home I use my own word processor.

When introductory elements appear in the Application, they will be marked as follows:

, introductory   *s u no, e jsl bl a nu cr.*

As you know, we just bought a new car.

SPELLING

Here are additional spelling words. Pronounce and spell each word aloud; then copy it in your own notebook, being sure that you spell it correctly. When you read the Application section of the lesson, watch for these words.

assured
atmosphere
banquet
buffet
disrepair
interruption
occasionally
peace
postponed
separate

APPLICATION

Time your reading speed with Document 1 before reading the remaining documents. Write each document. Remember to insert the needed punctuation in Document 4 before typing it in the correct format. Be sure to note the length of the document and place it properly on the page.

Goal: 2 minutes, 24 seconds (110 words per minute)

Dr A B Ellis   d Dr E:

, date

    u l rmbr tl on Tues, Apr 3, u prLsd a nu prnlr fm l o t

, geographic

reps o r co n Portland, OR. e r Sr tl u r njoy g ts fin nu prnlr n tl u r gl g xclnl srvc fm l.

    u c b aSrd tl u l h mny yrs o cnlnud srvc fm ts

, introductory

prnlr. hwev, l l ocaSll rqr srvc. r co pvds a nu srvc tl e blev u l find inl g nded.

    e l snd a srvc rep l u ofc ev 3 mos l mak Sr tl u prnlr wks prprl l al lms. if u prnlr Sd ned srvc tl e r uab l pvd l u ofc, e l pvd

, introductory

a smlr prnlr wil us s awa
fm u ofc. evn if u h no
prblms, onc a yr e l brng

, introductory

t prnlr l r srvc Sp n
nspcl l nsid n ol.

t csl o ts srvc s srpris gl
lo. f onl pnes a da, u c h t

, introductory

pec o mind tl cms w no g
tl u prnlr l opral f mny
yrs wol Nrps.

f ftr info abl r srvc plces,

, introductory

jsl cl us. 1 o r reps l b hpy

, compound
  sentence

l xplan r plces n dlal, n
tr l b no oblgas.

rmbr r co wn u ned dpndb
srvc. e h b n bus n P snc

, date

Feb 1, 1980.

s u

Goal: 2 minutes, 24 seconds (110 words per minute)

Dr. A. B. Ellis
Dear Dr. Ellis:

/You will remember that on Tuesday, April 3, you purchased a new printer from one of the representatives/of our company in Portland, Oregon. We are sure that you are enjoying this fine new printer and that you/are getting excellent service from it.

You can be assured that you will have many years of continued service/from this printer. However, it will occasionally require service. Our company provides a new service/that we believe you will find interesting indeed.

We will send a service representative to your office/every three months to make sure that your printer works properly at all times. If your printer should need service that we/are unable to provide at your office, we will provide a similar printer while yours is away from your/office. Even if you have no problems, once a year we will bring the printer to our service shop and inspect it/inside and out.

The cost of this service is surprisingly low. For only pennies a day, you can have the peace/of mind that comes with knowing that your printer will operate for many years without interruption.

For further/information about our service policies, just call us. One of our representatives will be happy to/explain our policies in detail, and there will be no obligation.

Remember our company when you need/dependable service. We have been in business in Portland since February 1, 1980. Sincerely yours,/(260)

DOCUMENT 23-2   *Speed Builder*

[Shorthand handwriting:]

Ms Olivia Joyce   d Ms J:
l w nded nic l no tl u wd
wlcm sgs f mpruv g t srvc
l r anul awrds bnql. I blev
tl a seld bnql wd b mC blr
f r org. t almsfer creald b 5
sprl bfa lins dlrcls fm t
dgnl o t evn g.

, introductory

, date

, geographic

, compound sentence

, compound sentence

s I mnSd erler, I h b alnd g smlr anul bnqls snc July 12, 1986, n Richmond, VA, n svrl otr cles. ts yr t evnl n R w hld n a bld g tl s onl slill lrgr tn rs, n l w a seld dnr. t almsfer w qil gd, n tr semd l b no lrb n srv g t 12 h pep.

pl gv ts sg serus cns f nxl yr. I blev tl l wd mpruv t nlir evnl.

c

Ms. Olivia Joyce
Dear Ms. Joyce:

/It was indeed nice to know that you would welcome suggestions for improving the service at our annual awards/banquet. I believe that a seated banquet would be much better for our organization. The atmosphere/created by five separate buffet lines detracts from the dignity of the evening.

As I mentioned earlier/ I have been attending similar annual banquets since July 12, 1986, in Richmond, Virginia/ and several other cities. This year the event in Richmond was held in a building that is only slightly/larger than ours, and it was a seated dinner. The atmosphere was quite good, and there seemed to be no trouble in/serving the 1,200 people.

Please give this suggestion serious consideration for next year./ I believe that it would improve the entire event. Cordially, (149)

Ms Martha Strong   d Ms S:

I rd n t locl nuspapr on Mon, Oct 6, tl t cly l bgn rpav g Broad sl her n Cranford, MO, on Nov 1. I w nded hpy l no tl t sl l b rpavd. l h b n a sl o *dsrpr* f nerl a yr. t lsl rpav g w cmpd on Sept 30, 1985.

hwev, I w grall srprisd l red abl ts dvm n t papr. s a mrCnl locald on B sl, I fel tl I Sd h b cnslld abl t bsl lm f ts majr wk. I cnlcld svrl otr mrCnls on B sl, n nn o tm w nolfid o t prjcl.

e al fel tl l wd b mC blr l d ts wk durg a slk Spg sesn rtr tn l ts lm. if t wk c b *poslpond* onl a fu mos, I m

Sr tr l b mC ls dsrpS o bus.
I hop l her fm u sn.
v l u

DOCUMENT 23-3

Ms. Martha Strong
Dear Ms. Strong:

/I read in the local newspaper on Monday, October 6, that the city will begin repaving Broad Street/here in Cranford, Missouri, on November 1. I was indeed happy to know that the street will be repaved. It/has been in a state of disrepair for nearly a year. The last repaving was completed on September 30,/ 1985.

However, I was greatly surprised to read about this development in the paper./ As a merchant located on Broad Street, I feel that I should have been consulted about the best time for this/major work. I contacted several other merchants on Broad Street, and none of them were notified of the project./

We all feel that it would be much better to do this work during a slack shopping season rather than at this time./ If the work can be postponed only a few months, I am sure there will be much less disruption of business. I hope/to hear from you soon. Very truly yours, (165)

Keyboarding Goal: 12 minutes (12 words per minute)

cntrl arlins   l n g:

   on Thurs Nov 20 I flu fm Dallas TX l Los Angeles CA on u arlin. I hd plnd t lrp f m tn a mo n I hd a cnfrmd rsrvas. l w mad b fon Oct 15. uftnll I dd nl pk up t lkl.

   wn I arivd l t ar lrmnl I w told tl t arlin hd no rcrd o my rsrvas. tr w no av sels bl I w placd on t slndby lsl. l t lsl mnl I w alowd l bord. hwev e wald m tn an hr nsid t plan bf l lfl t lrmnl.

   t srvc I recd hrdl reps wl u prms tru u advrlis g. I sncerl hop tl u l mak ev efl l mpruv u srvc n t fulr.

                u l

Keyboarding Goal: 12 minutes (12 words per minute)

Central Airlines

Ladies and Gentlemen:

/On Thursday, November 20, *(date)* I flew from Dallas, Texas, *(geographic)* to Los Angeles, California, *(geographic)* on your airline./ I had planned the trip for more than a month, and *(compound sentence)* I had a confirmed reservation. It was made by phone October/15. Unfortunately, *(introductory)* I did not pick up the ticket.

When I arrived at the air terminal, *(introductory)* I was told/that the airline had no record of my reservation. There were no available seats, but *(compound sentence)* I was placed on the/standby list. At the last minute I was allowed to board. However, *(introductory)* we waited more than an hour inside the plane/before it left the terminal.

The service I received hardly represents what you promise through your advertising./ I sincerely hope you will make every effort to improve your service in the future.

Yours truly, (133)

SUPPLEMENTARY ACTIVITY

A Word to the Wise

Writing Fluency

/Before you begin to take notes, be sure that you have an ample supply of paper and several good pens. If/you should run out of paper or ink, you could inconvenience your employer and others as well. They might have to/wait while you locate additional supplies, and this would put you in a very bad position.

Try to arrange/your materials so that you will have a large flat surface on which to write. If you have a comfortable/writing surface, you will probably take good notes.

As you take notes in *SuperWrite,* write as fluently and/effortlessly as possible. Write all the way across the page, and do not alter your regular writing style. Write as large/or as small as you wish. The size of your notes has very little to do with either speed or legibility./

As you take notes from dictation, write as quickly as necessary. When dictation is rapid, write as quickly/as possible. When dictation is slow, take time to form your letters carefully.

If you have waiting time while you/are taking dictation, look over your notes. Make any corrections or clarifications that are needed.

Use/your dictation time well to produce notes that are easily transcribed. (212)

LESSON 24

SuperWrite REVIEW

Read the following words, referring to the key if necessary. Then copy them in your own notebook.

Abbreviations

1. *cnv cns cv depl dv d*
2. *mpl enc ev exec f fm*
3. *r od org ol pd rqr*

Word Beginning Re-

4. *rman rtrcl rgrup rtir rmuv rlal*

Word Ending -ment

5. *trelm pam cm slm grm ncrgm*

Key

1. convenience, convenient; consider, consideration; cover; department; develop; do

2. employ; enclose; ever, every; executive; for; from

3. are, or, our; order; organization, organize; out; paid; require

4. remain; retract; regroup; retire; remove; relate

5. treatment; payment; comment; statement; garment; encouragement

KEYBOARDING STYLE

Time

Use figures to express time. Separate the hour from the minutes with a colon. Type <u>a.m.</u> or <u>p.m.</u> in small letters with no internal space.

    9:25 a.m.   7:45 p.m.

t mel g l bgn l 10:30 a m n cnclud l 4:30 p m.

The meeting will begin at 10:30 a.m. and conclude
at 4:30 p.m.

For time on the hour, do not use a colon and zeros.

    10 a.m.   6 p.m.

t ofc opns l 10 a m.

The office opens at 10 a.m.

If <u>a.m.</u> or <u>p.m.</u> is not used, use words rather than figures.

e r opn fm 10 n t mrn g ull 5 n t aflnun.

We are open from ten in the morning until
five in the afternoon.

PUNCTUATION

Elements in a Series

Use commas to separate words, phrases, or clauses in a series. Use a comma between the first two (or more) elements as well as before the conjunction.

Words

e pd f rnl, fuel, n ins.

We paid for rent, fuel, and insurance.

Phrases

e wnl l t stor, l t muve, n l t rstrnl.

We went to the store, to the movie, and to the restaurant.

Clauses

he rd svrl bks, mad cmprhnsv nols, n rol a gd papr.

He read several books, made comprehensive notes, and wrote a good paper.

When elements in a series occur in the Application, they will be marked in the margin as shown here:

, series   *e ned papr, pncls, n pns.*

We need paper, pencils, and pens.

SPELLING

Here are additional spelling words. Pronounce and spell each word aloud; then copy it in your own notebook, being sure that you spell it correctly. When you read the Application section of the lesson, watch for these words.

appeared
attorney
congratulations
bulletin
easement
equipment
library
piece
replacement
retract

APPLICATION

Time your reading speed with Document 1 before reading the remaining documents. Then write all four documents. Remember to insert the necessary punctuation in Document 4 before typing it in the correct format. Be sure to note the length of the document and place it properly on the page.

DOCUMENT 24-1   *Timed Reading*

Goal: 1 minute, 34 seconds (110 words per minute)

, date

, series

[shorthand text]

(continued)

, compound
sentence

, introductory

, introductory

, introductory

, series

t psl 2 yrs, n r clints r al
v hpy w tm.

u l h mny yrs o xclnt srvc
fm t eqpm. if u Sd h ny
prblm, e l mak t ncsry rpr
qkl. if ny pec o eqpm msl
b rmuvd fm u ofc f rpr, e
l pvd a rplacm fre o Crg ull
u h u on eqpm bk.

u mad a wis slc$ wn u Cos
r co. e pvd onl t bsl eqpm
n qll srvc. Sd u nedr srvc,
jsl cl us Mon, Wed, r Fri
blwen 8:30 a m n 6 p m. on
Tues n Thurs e r opn ull
9 p m.

cu

Goal: 1 minute, 34 seconds (110 words per minute)

Mrs. Madeline Melton
Dear Mrs. Melton:

/Congratulations on the purchase of the new telephone system that we installed in your office on Monday,/February 5. We know that you, your employees, and your customers will be very pleased with the system./We have installed more than 1,000 such systems in offices during the past two years, and our clients are all/very happy with them.

You will have many years of excellent service from the equipment. If you should have/ any problem, we will make the necessary repair quickly. If any piece of equipment must be removed from/ your office for repair, we will provide a replacement free of charge until you have your own equipment back.

You/made a wise selection when you chose our company. We provide only the best equipment and quality/service. Should you need our service, just call us Monday, Wednesday, or Friday between 8:30 a.m. and 6 p.m./ On Tuesday and Thursday we are open until 9 p.m. Cordially yours, (170)

, introductory

, geographic

, series

, compound sentence

(continued)

, introductory

, date

no prblm w typ g dcums r w pag laot. hwev, t ql t o prnt neds mpruvm.

encd s a drft o a blln prntd n r AZ ofc. pl rvu t t dtrmn wt t trb cd b. I l cl u ofc blwen 9 am n 12 nun on Wed, Mar 6, t gl u cms. t mples n r AZ ofc wnt t mpruv t ql t o t wk bf ty rvis n prnt t final blln.

encr

u t

DOCUMENT 24-2   *Speed Builder*

Mr. Harold Moore
Dear Mr. Moore

/As you know, last month we purchased four sets of electronic publishing software to use in our regional/offices. We had used one set of the materials successfully for the past three months in our main office in/Alexandria, Louisiana.

The three other sets were shipped to our offices in Texas, New Mexico,/and Arizona. Two of the sets have been working properly, but our people in Arizona are/having some trouble with the third set. There is no problem with typing documents or with page layout. However, the/quality of print needs improvement.

Enclosed is a draft of a bulletin printed in our Arizona office./Please review it to determine what the trouble could be. I will call your office between 9 a.m. and 12/noon on Wednesday, March 6, to get your comments. The employees in our Arizona office want to improve the/ quality of the work before they revise and print the final bulletin. Yours truly,   Enclosure (172)

Mr James R Potter   d Mr P:

, introductory

s u l rmbr, I prCsd 20 acrs

, geographic

o nvslm prprty ner Wheeling,

, date

WV, on Jan 7, 1988. u srvd s my alrny l t clos g. l tl lm tr w a ull l esm acrs 1 prl o t

, introductory

prprly. hwev, t esm w l b rmuvd Srll afl clos g.

, compound
sentence

I now h a byr f t prprly, n I ned a slm tl t esm h b rmuvd. alto I rol t prpr ofSls

, introductory
, series

n Mar, n Apr, n agn n May, I h nl recd a slm.

pl rvu t mlr n lry l gl a slm f me. I l b hpy l pa wlev fe s ncsry. if u ned l lk w

, introductory

me, pl cl ny wkda mrn g afl 9.

v s u

Mr. James R. Potter
Dear Mr. Potter:

/As you will remember, I purchased 20 acres of investment property near Wheeling, West Virginia, on/January 7, 1988. You served as my attorney at the closing. At that time there was a/utility easement across one part of the property. However, the easement was to be removed shortly/after closing.

I now have a buyer for the property, and I need a statement that the easement has been/ removed. Although I wrote to the proper officials in March, in April, and again in May, I have not received a/statement.

Please review the matter and try to get a statement for me. I will be happy to pay whatever fee/is necessary. If you need to talk with me, please call any weekday morning after nine. Very sincerely/yours, (141)

DOCUMENT 24-4   *Punctuation Check*

Keyboarding Goal: 14 minutes (12 words per minute)

Miss Rita Jones   d Miss J:
t nxt mel g o r bus asoca$ l b hld on Tues Apr 4 l 3 p m n t clg librry n Bangor ME. l ts imp mel g e l her a rpl fm t exec cmle on plns f t cmg yr. n ad$ tr l b rpls fm t bgl cmle t Nlanm cmle n t prjcls cmle.

[Shorthand/handwriting content]

s u no e h b qil cncrnd abl a slm tl aperd rcnll n t clg nuspapr. t slm qd t acurcy o r fnnSl rpls. e h askd t papr l rlrcd t slm n e l dscs ny ftr acS e Sd lak l t mel g.

l s o gral imp tl al mbrs alnd ts mel g. if u cnl alnd pl le me no s sn s psb.

v l u

DOCUMENT 24-4   **Punctuation Check**

Keyboarding Goal: 14 minutes (12 words per minute)

Miss Rita Jones
Dear Miss Jones:

/The next meeting of our business association will be held on Tuesday, April 4, *(date)* at 3 p.m. in the/college library in Bangor, Maine. *(geographic)* At this important meeting we will hear a report from the executive/committee on plans for the coming year. In addition, *(introductory)* there will be reports from the budget committee, the/entertainment committee, and the projects committee. *(series)*

As you know, *(introductory)* we have been quite concerned about a statement that/ appeared recently in the college newspaper. The statement questioned the accuracy of our financial/reports. We have asked the paper to retract the statement, and *(compound sentence)* we will discuss any further action we should take at/the meeting.

It is of great importance that all members attend this meeting. If you cannot attend, *(introductory)* please let me/know as soon as possible. Very truly yours, (146)

SUPPLEMENTARY ACTIVITY

A Word to the Wise

Reading and Writing

/Here are some reminders that will help you in reading and writing *SuperWrite*.

Always read your textbook assignment/before writing it. Read in thought units. Read a phrase, a clause, or a sentence. As you read, look for the meaning. If/a sentence does not seem to make sense, read it again. If you still do not understand, refer to the key.

If you/have trouble reading a particular word, spell it in *SuperWrite*. If you are still not able to read the word,/refer to the key.

When you are writing a document from the text, during dictation keep the book open and/refer to it if you need help.

If you have trouble with a word during dictation of new material, either/look up the spelling in your *SuperWrite* Dictionary or ask your teacher to write it for you when there is/time.

You should label each document clearly so that you will be able to find it quickly if you need to do/so. It is a good idea to leave a few blank lines before starting a new document in your notebook. In/addition, you should date each page so that you can quickly locate the material that you wrote on a certain date./(200)

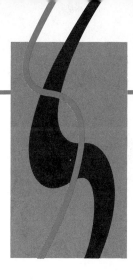

LESSON 25

SuperWrite REVIEW

Read the following words, referring to the key if necessary. Then copy them in your own notebook.

Abbreviations

1. *pl pr pgm pvd q rec*
2. *wk wks C l lg ls*
3. *b bn buss c co cmp*

Word Beginning Em-

4. *mpir mbrs mbrk mblm mfsiz mfss*

Word Ending -ful

5. *crf wndrf hlpf bnlf hopf af*

Key

1. please; present; program; provide; question; receive
2. week, work; weeks, works; which; will; willing; wills
3. be, been, by; business; businesses; can; company; complete
4. empire; embarrass; embark; emblem; emphasize; emphasis
5. careful; wonderful; helpful; beautiful; hopeful; awful

KEYBOARDING STYLE

Money

Write amounts of money in figures.

$5.25 $80

t lkls csl $35 eC.

The tickets cost $35 each.

Write round amounts of money of a million or higher in figures and words.

$25 million $9.5 billion $2.1 trillion

t bld g csl $25 m.

The building cost $25 million.

However, write related numbers in a set in the same form.

t bgl o $8 m incld $3 h t f manlnnc.

The budget of $8,000,000 included $300,000 for maintenance.

PUNCTUATION

Extra and Vital Information

A word, a phrase, or a clause that is not necessary to the meaning of a sentence is considered extra information.

Use commas to set off extra information.

Extra Word

l s, hwer, u rspl.

It is, however, your responsibility.

The word is not necessary to the meaning of the sentence; it is extra information.

Extra Phrase

[handwritten shorthand: I fel, o cors, tl u Sd go.]

I feel of course that you should go.

The phrase is not necessary to the meaning of the sentence; it is extra information.

[handwritten shorthand: pl cl me, Mr Leith, if u ned hlp.]

Please call me Mr. Leith if you need help.

Giving the name of the person to whom you are writing is not necessary to the meaning of the sentence; it is extra information.

[handwritten shorthand: Joanna Singleton, my frnd, s on vacaS.]

Joanna Singleton my friend is on vacation.

The phrase is not necessary to identify Joanna Singleton; it is extra information.

Extra Clause

[handwritten shorthand: Max Langford, hu joind r frm lsl mo, s a gd wkr.]

Max Langford who joined our firm last month
is a good worker.

The clause is not necessary to identify Max Langford; it is extra information.

If the element is necessary to the meaning of the sentence, it is considered vital.

Do not set off vital information with commas.

Vital Word

[handwritten shorthand: t wrd trf msl b incld.]

The word <u>therefore</u> must be included.

The word is vital to the meaning of the sentence.　　　　　(continued)

PUNCTUATION *continued*

Vital Phrase

l s a mlr o cors.

It is a matter of course.

The phrase is vital to the meaning of the sentence.

Vital Clause

t prsn hu joind r frm lsl mo s a gd wkr.

The person who joined our firm last month is a
good worker.

The phrase is vital; it identifies which person.

Joe Smith my nabr s her; Joe Smith t flbl plar s nl.

Joe Smith my neighbor is here; Joe
Smith the football player is not.

The phrases are vital; they identify which person named Joe Smith.

In the Application, extra elements will be shown in the margin as follows:

, extra   *I l, nvrtls, cl hm.*

I will, nevertheless, call him.

SPELLING

Here are additional spelling words. Pronounce and spell each word aloud; then copy it in your own notebook, being sure that you spell it correctly. When you read the Application section of the lesson, watch for these words.

accept
accumulate
assigned
deposit
embarrassing
explanation
financial
percentage
restaurant
specified

APPLICATION

Time your reading speed with Document 1 before reading the remaining documents. Then write all four documents. Remember to insert the needed punctuation in Document 4 before typing it in the correct format. Be sure to note the length of the document and place it properly on the page.

DOCUMENT 25-1   *Timed Reading*

Goal: 2 minutes, 7 seconds (110 words per minute)

Mr Lawrence Leith   d Mr L:

tks f u nqiry cncrn g a

rlirm pln f slf-mpld prsns.

r bnk ofrs a no o plns tl

qlfy U pr fdrl gvrnm gidlins.

, introductory   U / o r plns, u ma b ab l sl

(continued)

DOCUMENT 25-1 continued

, series

asid $10t, $20t, r evn $30t f u rlirm.

, introductory

afl u h dcidd on a pln, u ma dpsl a spcfid prcnlg o u nl ncm eC yr. I msl mfsiz tl t inl ernd on ts mny l acumulal fre o al lxs ull l s wdrn dur g u rlirm yrs. u l pa lx l u ral

, extra

l tl lm, C l prbbl b mC ls tn u crnl ral. ts reps a v powrf wa f u l sav f u fulr.

, introductory

n od l opn a pln, u msl apl

, extra

f a fdrl mplm idnlfca$ no, C u l us on al fms wil t pln s n fc.

, introductory

l dlrmn t xcl aml o u yrl cnlrbu$, u Sd cnfr w a fnnSl counslr hu s skld n lx la.

, extra

[shorthand handwriting:]
pl le us no, Mr L, if e c b
o ftr hlp l u s u mbrk on u
nu pln l sav f u futr. e wd
b dlild l opn 1 o r wndrf
rtirm plns f u.

c u

DOCUMENT 25-1   *Timed Reading*

Goal: 2 minutes, 7 seconds (110 words per minute)

Mr. Lawrence Leith
Dear Mr. Leith:

/Thanks for your inquiry concerning a retirement plan for self-employed persons. Our bank offers a number of/plans that qualify under present federal government guidelines. Under one of our plans, you may be able/to set aside $10,000, $20,000, or even $30,000 for your retirement./

After you have decided on a plan, you may deposit a specified percentage of your net income/each year. I must emphasize that the interest earned on this money will accumulate free of all taxes until/it is withdrawn during your retirement years. You will pay tax at your rate at that time, which will probably be much/less than your current rate. This represents a very powerful way for you to save for your future.

In order to/open a plan, you must apply for a federal employment identification number, which you will use on/all forms while the plan is in force.

To determine the exact amount of your yearly contribution, you should/confer with a financial counselor who is skilled in tax law.

Please let us know, Mr. Leith, if we can be of/further help to you as you embark on your new plan to save for your future. We would be delighted to open one/of our wonderful retirement plans for you. Cordially yours, (228)

Mrs Dorothy Ray   d Mrs R:

, extra

ysrda I w Spg n St Paul, C s abl 1h mils fm my hom. I w acod b 2 gd frnds. afl a bsy

, introductory

mrn g, e slpd l u rslrnl f lnC.

, extra

wn Mr William Brown, t walr,

, introductory

brl t Ck, I prd my crdl crd.

, introductory

afl a fu mnls, he told me n frnl o my frnds tl t crd cd nl b accpld bcs I hd Ospnl

, introductory

my crdl lml. nedls l sa, ts w xlreml mbrs g l me. I pd

, extra

t Ck, C amld l $75, w cS. I m,

, extra

hwev, qil upsl b t ncdnl.

, extra

lda I spok w Mr Albert Jones, an ofcr o t crdl crd co. he vrfid

, extra

tl I hd nl xcedd t lml o $1 t, C hd b asind l me. I m alwas

, compound sentence

qil crf w my fnncs, n I d nl

, introductory

, extra

[Shorthand notes]

Mrs. Dorothy Ray
Dear Mrs. Ray:

/Yesterday I was shopping in Saint Paul, which is about 100 miles from my home. I was accompanied by/two good friends. After a busy morning, we stopped at your restaurant for lunch. When Mr. William Brown, the waiter, brought/the check, I presented my credit card. After a few minutes, he told me in front of my friends that the card could/not be accepted because I had overspent my credit limit. Needless to say, this was extremely embarrassing to me. I paid the check, which amounted to $75, with cash. I am, however, quite/upset by the incident.

Today I spoke with Mr. Albert Jones, an officer of the credit card company./He verified that I had not exceeded the limit of $1,000, which had been assigned to me. I/am always quite careful with my finances, and I do not understand why the waiter could not accept the card./Furthermore, I cannot understand why I was treated in such an unpleasant manner.

I have dined at your/restaurant for many years, Mrs. Ray, because you always serve wonderful food. But I am reluctant to return for/fear of embarrassment. Can you offer an explanation for this incident? Yours truly, (212)

Principal d admnstratr:

, date

    on Jan 25, 1970, r co mbrkd on a nu bus. e opnd r frst stor

, geographic

n Little Rock, AR, n a rnld bld g w abt $20 t n cptl. tr

, series

w 2 sals clrks, 1 scrtry, n 1 mgr. tl frst yr e dd abt $1 h t

, extra

n bus, C w almost twic t amt

, introductory

e hd prdctd. fm tn on, e xpndd rpdl.

, introductory

    lst yr, r co opnd nu stors n

, series

WA, OR, n WY. e now h m tn

, compound sentence

3 h stors truot t US, n r yrl gros sals r O $9 h m. n t nxt

, introductory

2 yrs, e xpct sals t reC $1 b.

    t story o r bus s 1 o t tru sccs stores o amrcn fre Npris. e r now mak g av l at sculs n

, introductory

clgs a fre bkll tl ollins t grot o r sccsf bus. if u wd lik l h cpes o t bkll f u scul, jsl ril us lda. e lk fwrd l herg fm u.

s u

DOCUMENT 25-3

Principal
Dear Administrator:

/On January 25, 1970, our company embarked on a new business. We opened our/first store in Little Rock, Arkansas, in a rented building with about $20,000 in capital./There were two sales clerks, one secretary, and one manager. That first year we did about $100,000/in business, which was almost twice the amount we had predicted. From then on, we expanded rapidly.

Last year, our company opened new stores in Washington, Oregon, and Wyoming. We now have more than 300/stores throughout the United States, and our yearly gross sales are over $900 million. In the next two/years, we expect sales to reach $1 billion.

The story of our business is one of the true success stories/of American free enterprise. We are now making available to all schools and colleges a free/booklet that outlines the growth of our successful business. If you would like to have copies of the booklet for your school,/just write us today. We look forward to hearing from you. Sincerely yours, (190)

Keyboarding Goal: 14 minutes (14 words per minute)

Ms Yoko Nozaki   d Ms N:

    on Mon Dec 3 I vsld u fnlr stor n Little Rock A R. I hd prCsd a brlf nu sofa tr a fu wks bf n l hd b dlvrd onl a fu das erler.

    wn t sofa w dlvrd I found tl t blu clr C I hd slcld v crfl w nl ril n my dn. t sofa C csl m tn $1 t w prCsd on sal. I asumd tl l cd nl b rlrnd.

    I askd Mrs Ann Carter u sals rep if t sofa cd b r-cvd n a dfrnl mleral. hwev Se sgd tl I rlrn t sofa n slcl anotr. I w v plsnll srprisd tl u wd accpl t sofa bk smpl bcs I hd Cosn t rng clr.

    Mrs C w xlreml hlpf n mfsizd tl cslmr slsfc$ w t mosl imp prdcl

[Handwritten shorthand/abbreviated cursive text:]

o u org. lda t nu sofa arivd n t clr s prfcl.

tks l u co f pvd g sl hlpf srvc Ms N. u c b sr tl I l rlrn l u slor wn I ned adsl fnlr.

v s u

DOCUMENT 25-4 **Punctuation Check**

Keyboarding Goal: 14 minutes (14 words per minute)

Ms. Yoko Nozaki
Dear Ms. Nozaki:

/On Monday, December 3, *(date)* I visited your furniture store in Little Rock, Arkansas. *(geographic)* I had purchased a/beautiful new sofa there a few weeks before, and *(compound sentence)* it had been delivered only a few days earlier.

When/the sofa was delivered, *(introductory)* I found that the blue color, which I had selected very carefully, *(extra)* was not right/in my den. The sofa, which cost more than $1,000, *(extra)* was purchased on sale. I assumed that it could not be/returned.

I asked Mrs. Ann Carter, your sales representative, *(extra)* if the sofa could be re-covered in a different/material. However, *(introductory)* she suggested that I return the sofa and select another. I was very/pleasantly surprised that you would accept the sofa back simply because I had chosen the wrong color.

Mrs. Carter/was extremely helpful and emphasized that customer satisfaction was the most important product of/your organization. Today the new sofa arrived, and *(compound sentence)* the color is perfect.

Thanks to your company for/providing such helpful service, Ms. Nozaki. *(extra)* You can be sure that I will return to your store when I need additional/furniture.
Very sincerely yours, (186)

SUPPLEMENTARY ACTIVITY

A Word to the Wise

Transcribing

/Keyboarding your notes is quite easy with *SuperWrite*. Many students find that it is much easier than typing/from longhand. Here are a few helpful transcribing hints. Always read your notes before transcribing them. This cannot be/overemphasized. When you read your notes, you will be able to correct any errors that were made. You will/also be able to look up the spelling of any words of which you are unsure. You will, in addition, be/able to verify any information that should be checked before the document is typed.

When you begin/typing, try to finish the document without any major interruptions. Your work will be easier if you/do not have to stop for an extended period of time.

Read phrases, clauses, or sentences and hold the words/in your mind as you type. Try to read ahead just a bit so that you understand what is coming next. You should not/type ahead of your reading, assuming you know the next few words. Often errors are made in this way.

As you/finish a document, draw a single diagonal line through the *SuperWrite* notes. When you look through your notebook, this/will tell you that you have transcribed that document. You will, however, still be able to read the notes if you need/to do so.

Read and transcribe for sensibility. When you have finished typing, check your work carefully to be/sure that it is accurate. (245)

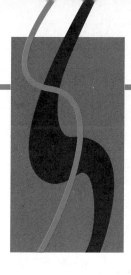

LESSON E

TOWARD PERSONAL SUCCESS

CREATIVE PROBLEM SOLVING

Have you ever had a really difficult problem to solve? We are not thinking about the kind of problem you might encounter on a mathematics test, but a difficult "real world" problem. All of us face these kinds of problems regularly, both at work and in our personal lives. Here are some tips on ways to find better solutions to those really difficult problems.

Kinds of Problems

First, we need to clarify what we mean by the word <u>problem</u>. Some problems are not very difficult to solve in the sense of knowing what to do. It's the difficulty of carrying out the solution that becomes the problem. For example, if the problem is that you have a long reading assignment to complete, you already know how to solve it—by getting to work reading! The most difficult problems—the kinds of problems we're talking about here—are ones that we don't know how to solve.

Pleasant and Unpleasant Problems

We often think of problems as unpleasant situations, but not all difficult problems are things one would want to avoid. For example, if you had three excellent job offers but could choose only one, choosing one might be a very difficult problem. However, it would be a pleasant problem. Keep in mind that problems can be either pleasant or unpleasant.

Gathering Information

The first thing you should do when confronted with a difficult problem is to gather all the information you can about the situation. This information includes facts, of course, but it also includes your feelings, hopes, and fears about the situation.

List on a piece of paper as many things as you can that might be relevant to the situation. Don't worry about how you will deal with each of the things you list. Just make a note of everything that comes to mind.

Don't try to define the problem or try to find solutions—not yet. Just try to broaden your perspective on the situation by thinking of everything that might be relevant to the situation.

Defining the Problem

Now you're ready to define the problem. This is the second step in creative problem solving. On a piece of paper, write at the top, "In what ways might I . . . ?" Then try to think of a number of different ways to define the problem.

It's important to use the words, "In what ways might I . . . ?" because they force you to think about where you want to take the situation, not what's wrong with it now. Thinking about what's wrong with the situation generally won't help you solve a problem—and that kind of thinking is where much energy is typically wasted. Focus on the direction you need to go and the goal you hope to achieve.

Don't settle for just one or two ways to complete the sentence. Try to state the problem many different ways because different problem statements lead to different kinds of solutions.

Here's an example. If I am concerned because my mousetraps aren't catching the mice in my basement, I might ask the question, "In what ways can I get my mousetraps to work better?" This might lead to a good solution, but it would be much better to ask myself, "In what ways might I get rid of the mice in my basement?" This would suggest a much broader range of solutions, such as getting a cat or an exterminator, as well as all the ideas I might have for building a better mousetrap.

After you have a long list of possible problem statements, choose one that you think summarizes the situation best.

Generating Possible Solutions

Now it's time to think of possible solutions. This is the third step. Write down as many different answers to the question as you can. It's good to include what you may consider unworkable ideas because this helps to free your imagination. Sometimes the ideas you thought were unworkable can be adapted and made to work.

Try to think of at least a dozen ideas, and then try for a dozen more. When you think you have a good list, pick the solution, or solutions, that you think will best help you achieve your goal.

Implement Your Solution

The last step before putting your solution into action is deciding <u>how</u> you will do it. This includes deciding whose help you may need, setting up a timetable to help you plan what to do when, and establishing subgoals along the way so that you can check how well your plan is working. These steps in implementing your solution are very important; many wonderful ideas have failed because there was no plan how to implement them.

A Final Word

It is generally worth taking each step in sequence, but sometimes a brilliant idea will occur early on, and this idea may seem to be perfect, even though you may not have gotten very far in the process. What should you do then? If you think you've found a great solution, use it! You don't need to go through the whole process if you no longer need help finding a good solution.

These steps in solving problems creatively are very effective. They take time, and for that reason, you will want to go through this process for very difficult problems only.

Discussion

1. Discuss how you have used your creativity in solving a particular problem.

2. Do you believe that you should define a problem carefully before trying to solve it? Why or why not?

3. Why is it better to try to think of many solutions before you implement a plan for solving the problem?

Case Study 1—Managing an Office

Brian is the office manager for a small company. He has a new employee, Denise, who came with very good recommendations, but she often misses work or arrives late. When she is there, the quality of her work is not consistent. She sometimes does very good work, but she frequently forgets to do jobs Brian has given her. She sometimes loses paperwork Brian has assigned her.

Mr. Carr, Brian's employer, hired Denise himself, and he has told Brian that it is his job to train her. Denise's previous employer is Mr. Carr's friend, and it is largely on the basis of his friend's recommendation that Mr. Carr hired Denise. When Brian suggested there are problems in Denise's performance, his employer has insisted that she can succeed if Brian simply trains her properly and provides her with the right kind of direction and support.

Brian is concerned that Mr. Carr will question his abilities if Denise doesn't succeed. There are five others in the office, and all except Denise are very competent and reliable.

Questions for Discussion

1. What are some things Brian should keep in mind while thinking about how to improve this situation? What information other than that presented would you like to have before advising Brian?

2. What are some ways Brian might state his problem? Be sure to begin each problem statement with "In what ways might Brian . . . ?" Try to go beyond the obvious questions to see if there are other ways to think about the situation. Here's one to help get you started: "In what ways might Brian get Denise to be more punctual in arriving at work?"

3. Choose one of your problem statements. Then try to come up with at least a dozen possible solutions to this problem.

Case Study 2—A Lack of Direction

Sandra started work in a small office two weeks ago. Her office manager, Anna, told her that Margaret, who has been working for the company for three years, would train her and share her work. It seems to

Sandra that Margaret has little interest in teaching her anything, however, or in sharing her workload. After showing her around the office and to her desk, Margaret simply said that Sandra would pick things up little by little.

Margaret has given Sandra some small, very simple jobs to do, but much of the time Sandra has been idle. Margaret, in contrast, is obviously quite busy, and she even stays late every afternoon to finish her work. When Sandra has suggested that she might be able to help Margaret with her work, Margaret has told her she could handle things at the moment but that she would find some things for Sandra to do later. She then goes back to work and seems to forget about Sandra, who then tries to busy herself organizing her desk.

Sandra is concerned that she will not learn her job well unless Margaret teaches her and gives her some work to do. There are three other workers in the office, but they all seem busy and don't appear to have noticed that Sandra has little to do.

Discussion Questions

1. What are some things Sandra should keep in mind while thinking about how to improve this situation? What information other than that presented would you like to have before advising Sandra?

2. What are some ways Sandra might state her problem? Be sure to begin each problem statement with "In what ways might Sandra . . . ?" Try to go beyond the obvious questions to see if there are other ways to think about the situation. Here's one to help get you started: "In what ways might Sandra make more productive use of her time while waiting for Margaret to give her work to do?"

3. Choose one of your problem statements. Then try to list at least a dozen possible solutions to this problem.

Activities

1. Use the model of problem solving presented in this lesson to work on a real problem of your own. Be sure to write your answers in each step of the process.

2. Interview a manager in a local business. Ask this person what difficult problems were encountered in recent months and what was done to solve them.

3. Offer your services as a "problem-solving consultant" to a friend. Guide the friend through the problem-solving steps and record the responses in each step of the process.

LESSON 26

SuperWrite REVIEW

Read the following words, referring to the key if necessary. Then copy the words in your own notebook.

Abbreviations

1. *info ins inl s le lr*
2. *lrd lrs mgl mgls mgr mgrs*
3. *mo mos mol no nos nod*

Word Beginning Ex-

4. *xmn xprl xcl xperenc xrcis xsl*

Word Ending -ing

5. *rilg wkg tnkg redg meng mengf*

Key

1. information; insurance; interest; as, is; let; letter
2. lettered; letters; management; managements; manager; managers
3. month; months; monthly; number; numbers; numbered
4. examine; expert; exact; experience; exercise; exist
5. writing; working; thinking; reading; meaning; meaningful

KEYBOARDING STYLE

Capitalization

Business organizations and institutions. Capitalize the first word and other main words in the names of business organizations and institutions. However, watch for unique spellings and capitalization.

Jones and Company   The Silver Eagle Club

Professional Titles. Capitalize professional titles when they come before a name.

President M. L. Goodwin

Do not capitalize professional titles when they come after the name or when they appear alone.

M L Goodwin, prsdnl o t clb, spok l t grup.

M. L. Goodwin, president of the club, spoke to the group.

t prsdnl cld t mel g l od.

The president called the meeting to order.

SPELLING

Here are additional spelling words. Pronounce and spell each word aloud; then copy it in your own notebook, being sure that you spell it correctly. When you read the Application section of the lesson, watch for these words.

access
assistance
assistants
calendar
copyright
deductible
registration
software
sponsored
useful

VOCABULARY

The ability to use words effectively is important to all educated people. It is essential that you have a good knowledge of words and that you continue to expand your vocabulary. Each lesson beginning with Lesson 26 contains a vocabulary development section. Study the words as directed, and try to use them regularly.

Here is the first group of words. Study the definitions carefully, and notice how the words are used in the *SuperWrite* examples. Watch for these words in the Application section of the lesson.

access
: *Ability to obtain or make use of.*

  u l h accs l t pgms.

  You will have access to the programs.

deductible
: *Amount that is exempt; an insurance clause that relieves the insurer of responsibility for an initial specified loss.*

  if u Cus a $1t ddclb, t ins co l nl pa f t frsl $1t o ny ls.

  If you choose a $1,000 deductible, the insurance company will not pay for the first $1,000 of any loss.

pre-existing
: *Existing before; occurring before.*

  t plcy ds nl cv ny pr-rslg cnds.

  The policy does not cover any pre-existing condition.

prior
: *Earlier; preceding in time.*

  e lkd prir l t mel g.

  We talked prior to the meeting.

(continued)

VOCABULARY continued

public domain   *Status of a product not protected under copyright or patent.*

t cmpulr pgm s n t pblc doman.

The computer program is in the public domain.

APPLICATION

Time your reading speed with Document 1 before reading the remaining documents. Then write all four documents. Remember to insert the needed punctuation in Document 4 before typing it in the correct format. Be sure to note the length of the document and place it properly on the page.

DOCUMENT 26-1   *Timed Reading*

Goal: 2 minutes, 3 seconds (120 words per minute)

Mr Milton Morgan   d Mr M:
r u intd n gl g usf cmpulr sflwr fre o Crg? if so, u l prbbl b intd n t sflwr xlang pgm spnsrd b cntrl clg.

, introductory

abt 2 yrs ago, Dr Jane Edwards, prsdnt o cntrl clg, n a no o prfsrs l otr st clgs orgd a pgm f area clgs. n t agrem ec clg mad av l ev otr clg al o ls

, introductory

, extra

, extra

sflwr tl w nl U cpyril, sflwr tl w n t pblc doman. ts pgm hlpd al t area clgs l rpnd tr librry o cmpulr sflwr.

t pgm s now b g rtnddd l incl al sculs n t area. l N t

, introductory

pgm, al u ned d s fl ol t encd fm n rlrn l alng w u rgslras fe o $50. tn u l h accs l al sflwr tl s av fm t nlwk. t onl

, extra

adSl csl l b a mol srvc fe o $10, C s pab t frsl o eC mo. a cpy o t crnl cllg s encd. an updald cllg splm o al sflwr s mald l al mbrs mol.

, extra

e hop u l cns Ng u scul n t pgm, Mr M. e no u l find l a vlub educaSl rsorc.

s

encr

Goal: 2 minutes, 3 seconds (120 words per minute)

Mr. Milton Morgan
Dear Mr. Morgan:

/Are you interested in getting useful computer software free of charge? If so, you will probably be/interested in the Software Exchange Program sponsored by Central College.

About two years ago, Dr. Jane Edwards / president of Central College, and a number of professors at other state colleges organized a/program for area colleges. In the agreement each college made available to every other/college all of its software that was not under copyright, software that was in the public domain. This program helped/all the area colleges to expand their library of computer software.

The program is now being/extended to include all schools in the area. To enter the program, all you need do is fill out the/enclosed form and return it along with your registration fee of $50. Then you will have access to all/software that is available from the network. The only additional cost will be a monthly service fee/of $10, which is payable the first of each month. A copy of the current catalog is enclosed. An/updated catalog supplement of all software is mailed to all members monthly.

We hope you will consider/entering your school in the program, Mr. Morgan. We know you will find it a valuable educational/resource.
Sincerely, Enclosure (245)

	esl cosl sals co l n g:
	Rose n co s proud l anounc
	t opn g o ls acounlg srvc n
, date	Memphis, TN, on Mon, Mar 4.
, geographic	R n co, 1 o t fmosl orgs o ls
, extra	kind n ts prl o t na, now h
, series	ofcs n 25 cles n TN, NC, n GA.
, extra	n r nu M ofc, C s locald on
	Oak sl, e l ofr cmp acounlg n

DOCUMENT 26-2 continued

lx srvc f ndvduls s wl s f bot lrg n sml buss. r slf

, series

incls t gnrl mgr, 3 xprl acounlnls, n 2 asslnls.

, introductory

if u ned r asslnc, r xperencd slf l b gld l hlp u. pl cl r vsl

, introductory

r nu ofc. bgng Mar 4, e l b opn blwen 9 am n 6 pm ev wkda. a broSr tl lsls vrus srvcs s encd.

vsu

encr

DOCUMENT 26-2 — Speed Builder

East Coast Sales Company
Ladies and Gentlemen:

/Rose and Company is proud to announce the opening of its accounting service in Memphis, Tennessee, on/Monday, March 4.

Rose and Company, one of the foremost organizations of its kind in this part of the/ nation, now has offices in 25 cities in Tennessee, North Carolina, and Georgia.

In our new/Memphis office, which is located on Oak Street, we will offer complete accounting and tax service for individuals/as well as for both large and small businesses. Our staff includes the general manager, three expert/accountants, and two assistants.

If you need our assistance, our experienced staff will be glad to help you. Please call/or visit our new office. Beginning March 4, we will be open between 9 a.m. and 6 p.m. every/ weekday. A brochure that lists various services is enclosed. Very sincerely yours, Enclosure (153)

Mrs Marie Tuttle   d Mrs T:

t n&l ins co w v gld l rec u apl f hlt ins 3 mos ago. u l rmbr l tl lm u lk a fscl xmna& n tl u w found l b n gd hlt w t xcp& o a strand

, extra

msl n u bk. C w csd b an alo accdnl 2 mos prir l u apl.

u hlt ins w apruvd w t xclu& o lrelm f ny pr-xsl g

, extra

cnd& f a perod o 6 mos. ts, o cors, incld t strand msl n u bk.

lsl wk e recd u clam f lrelm o a bk njry. n od l pa ts

, introductory

clam, e msl h a slm fm u fs& sa g tl ts njry s nl rlald l

, introductory

t prvrs njry. wn e rec ts slm, e l rcns u crnl clam. encd s a fm n an nvlop f u cnv n hg u fsd rply.

vs

encr

DOCUMENT 26-3

Mrs. Marie Tuttle
Dear Mrs. Tuttle:

/The National Insurance Company was very glad to receive your application for health insurance three/months ago. You will remember at that time you took a physical examination and that you were found to/be in good health with the exception of a strained muscle in your back, which was caused by an auto accident two/months prior to your application.

Your health insurance was approved with the exclusion of treatment for any/pre-existing condition for a period of six months. This, of course, included the strained muscle in your back.

Last/week we received your claim for treatment of a back injury. In order to pay this claim, we must have a statement/from your physician saying that this injury is not related to the previous injury. When we/receive this statement, we will reconsider your current claim.

Enclosed is a form and an envelope for your convenience in/having your physician reply. Very sincerely, Enclosure (169)

Miss Natalie Nelson   d Miss N:

t Brady ins co h b n bus f mny yrs. Mary B prsdnt o t co h b a rsdnt o t area al hr life. r org s ddcald l srv g t neds o ndvduls n buss her n Princeton N J.

bcs t B ins co nos t locl ins bus nsid n ol e c srv u ins neds mC blr tn a co tl s locald n a dstnl cly. n ads e ma b ab l sav u hndrds o dlrs n prmums.

if t ins on u hous r cr l xpir n t cm g mos le / o r acount mgrs cm l u ofc sn l dscrib t plces tl e ofr. l l lak u onl a Srl perod n u l b gld u lkd w us.

encd s a broSr xplan g r xclnl plces. pl nol crfl hw u c lor u prmum sgnfcnll b sld g a hir ddclb aml. ts smpl mens tl u asum an inSl rsk eql l t *ddclb* u Cus.

also encd s a cnv *clndr* C incls r bus adrs n fon no. e hop u l njoy us g l durg t nxl yr.

s u

encrs

DOCUMENT 26-4   Punctuation Check

Keyboarding Goal: 18 minutes (14 words per minute)

Miss Natalie Nelson
Dear Miss Nelson:

/The Brady Insurance Company has been in business for many years. Mary Brady, president of the/company, *(extra)* has been a resident of the area all her life. Our organization is dedicated to/serving the needs of individuals and businesses here in Princeton, New Jersey. *(geographic)*

Because the Brady Insurance/Company knows the local insurance business inside and out, *(introductory)* we can serve your insurance needs much better/than a company that is located in a distant city. In addition, *(introductory)* we may be able to save you/hundreds of dollars in premiums.

If the insurance on your house or car will expire in the coming months, *(introductory)* let/one of our account managers come to your office soon to describe the policies that we offer. It will take/only a short period, and *(compound sentence)* you will be glad you talked with us.

Enclosed is a brochure explaining our excellent/policies. Please note carefully how you can lower your premium significantly by selecting a/higher deductible amount. This simply means that you assume an initial risk equal to the deductible/you choose.

Also enclosed is a convenient calendar, which includes our business address and phone number. *(extra)* We/hope you will enjoy using it during the next year.
Sincerely yours, Enclosures (231)

SUPPLEMENTARY ACTIVITY

A Word to the Wise

Making Corrections

/Correcting errors on documents is fairly easy today. If you have access to a word processor,/making corrections is extremely simple. If you make an error, you just backspace and hit the correct key. Corrections/can be made after the document is keyboarded. Even if an error is caught after a document/is printed, the document may be retrieved, the error corrected, and the page reprinted.

Correcting errors/made on typewriters is not as easy or as neat. On many electronic typewriters, a correction ribbon/may be used. Such corrections are usually quite neat. However, the sooner the error is caught, the better the/correction will be. In addition, you must correct the error before the paper is removed from the machine./If a letter is omitted, there may be a spacing problem. You should examine the paper carefully, and/if a correction is not neat, the paper should be typed again.

Correction fluid may be used with some types of/errors. It is very important to cover the error entirely, let the fluid dry, and make a very neat/correction. The fluid must be allowed to dry thoroughly before the correction is made. In some cases where/correction fluid has been used, a good photocopy will look better than the original document. You/must examine the paper critically, and if the correction is not neat, the paper should be typed again.

Erasers/are seldom used to correct typing errors today. In some cases, you may find it necessary to use one./If you do, be extremely careful not to damage the paper.

You and your company are often judged on how/neat your documents appear. Make sure that any corrections that you make are very neat. (317)

LESSON 27

SuperWrite REVIEW

Read the following words, referring to the key if necessary. Then copy the words in your own notebook.

Abbreviations

1. *pr prd prl pgm pgms pgmd*
2. *pvd pvds pvdd q qd q g*
3. *rec recd recg rgd rgdd rgd g*

Word Beginning En-

4. *ndvr nlir nlirl nlrnc nvy nlill*

Word Ending -ity

5. *cmun l abl rlib l oprlun l vri l vri ls*

Key

1. present; presented; presently; program; programs; programmed
2. provide; provides; provided; question; questioned; questioning
3. receive; received; receiving; regard; regarded; regarding
4. endeavor; entire; entirely; entrance; envy; entitle
5. community; ability; reliability; opportunity; variety; varieties

KEYBOARDING STYLE

Copy Notation

If you wish for the recipient of a letter to know that you are sending a copy to a third person, type **c** and the person's name at the left margin a double space under the last reference line.

```
lpj

Enc

c Mr. Alfredo Lopez
```

SPELLING

Here are additional spelling words. Pronounce and spell each word aloud; then copy it in your own notebook, being sure that you spell it correctly. When you read the Application section of the lesson, watch for these words.

affirmative
campaign
definitely
expertise
integrity
occupancy
prospective
reception
recommended
soliciting

VOCABULARY

Study the following words and definitions carefully, and notice how the words are used in the *SuperWrite* examples. Watch for these words in the Application section of the lesson.

expertise

Specialized knowledge or skill; the skill of an expert.

[SuperWrite script]

She has expertise in the subject.

integrity

Honesty; incorruptibility; adherence to strict standards.

[SuperWrite script]

He is a person of great integrity.

peers

Those of equal standing; those belonging to the same group.

[SuperWrite script]

She gets along well with her peers.

seminar

An advanced course featuring discussion.

[SuperWrite script]

We offer a seminar in accounting.

soliciting

Approaching with a request; trying to obtain.

[SuperWrite script]

We are soliciting funds for the charity.

APPLICATION

Time your reading speed with Document 1 before reading the remaining documents. Then write all four documents. Remember to insert the needed punctuation in Document 4 before typing it in the correct format. Be sure to note the length of the document and place it properly on the page.

Mr John J Edwards   d Mr E:

, introductory   dur g t nxl fu mos, a no o ledrs n r cmun l l b plng n orgg t unild fnd driv f t cm g yr. r gol s l pvd $1 m f wrty Crls n t area.

, extra   u h b hil rcmndd b mny o u frnds n asocals l Brown n co, hu sld tl u w a prsn o mlgr l n rlib l. e fel tl u r dfnll t prsn e wnl l hd t cmle ts yr.

, introductory   if u accpl t rspl o hdg t cmle, u l mng t nlir org f t yr n l b rsp f orgg n suprvisg t wk o abl l h pep hu l b slcl g fnds f t campan.

, introductory   if u h ny qs, pl le us no. e
, date   wd lik l no b Fri, June 1, if

u l b ab l accpl ts psS. e
hop l rec u afrmlv rply sn.
v c u

c: Mr Sam Nelson

DOCUMENT 27-1   **Timed Reading**

Goal: 1 minute, 33 seconds (120 words per minute)

Mr. John J. Edwards
Dear Mr. Edwards:

/During the next few months, a number of leaders in our community will be planning and organizing the/United Fund drive for the coming year. Our goal is to provide $1 million for worthy charities in/the area.

You have been highly recommended by many of your friends and associates at Brown and/Company, who stated that you were a person of integrity and reliability. We feel that you are/definitely the person we want to head the committee this year.

If you accept the responsibility/of heading the committee, you will manage the entire organization for the year and will be responsible/for organizing and supervising the work of about 100 people who will be soliciting/funds for the campaign.

If you have any questions, please let us know. We would like to know by Friday, June 1, if you/will be able to accept this position. We hope to receive your affirmative reply soon. Very cordially/yours,   c: Mr. Sam Nelson (185)

Ms Maria Sanchez   d Ms S:

, introductory

eC yr n June, t sci l o mgl l wstrn clg spnsrs a smnr n mgl. crnt studnts, grduts, n locl bus execs r nvitd t atnd. n t pst ts smnr h alrctd O 3h prtcpnts. ts yr t smnr l b hld June 4 n 5.

, series

bcs o u xprtes n t feld o prsnl mgl, e wd lik u t b t frst spekr ts yr. b accptg ts nvtaS, u l b abl t Sr u ideas w hndrds o crnt n prspctv mgrs.

, introductory

, introductory

t opn g adrs l b gvn on June 4 fm 5 pm t 6 pm n fclty hl on t clg cmpus. aft t adrs, a rcpS n bnqt l b hld n Jones hl, C s ajacnt t fclty hl. t

, introductory

, extra

, extra

lpc o u lk wd b nlirl up l u. e no tl ny area o mgl wd b o inl l r prlcpnls.

pl le us no if u l b ab l accpl ts nvlaS, Ms S. e lk fwrd l her g fm u.

v c

c: Dr Paul Martin

DOCUMENT 27-2   *Speed Builder*

Ms. Maria Sanchez
Dear Ms. Sanchez:

/Each year in June, the Society of Management at Western College sponsors a seminar in management./ Current students, graduates, and local business executives are invited to attend. In the past this/seminar has attracted over 300 participants. This year the seminar will be held June 4 and 5./

Because of your expertise in the field of personnel management, we would like you to be the first speaker this/year. By accepting this invitation, you will be able to share your ideas with hundreds of current and/prospective managers.

The opening address will be given on June 4 from 5 p.m. to 6 p.m. in/Faculty Hall on the college campus. After the address, a reception and banquet will be held in Jones Hall, which/is adjacent to Faculty Hall. The topic of your talk would be entirely up to you. We know that any/area of management would be of interest to our participants.

Please let us know if you will be able/to accept this invitation, Ms. Sanchez. We look forward to hearing from you. Very cordially,   c: Dr. Paul Martin (203)

Mr Kenneth Samuels   d Mr S:

   Miss Ann Scott rol l me rcntl

, geographic

llg me tl Se h muvd l Providence,
RI, n h apld f a psS w u co.
Se askd if I wd ril a lr o

, compound
sentence

rcmndaS f hr, n I m v hpy
l d so.

   I h non Miss S f a no o yrs.
Se bgn wkg f my co afl Se

, date

fnSd hi scul June 30, 1985. Se
w a clrk n t acounlg depl

, geographic

her l Mason sals co n Jackson,

, introductory

MS. afl onl a fu mos, Se bcam
a scrlry n t advrlisg depl.

   Miss S Nd nil scul l sout

, extra

cosl clg n 1986, wil Se cnlnud
l wk f my co. lsl yr Se rlrnd

, compound
sentence

l clg fl lm, n Se recd hr
dgre lsl mo.

, introductory

Miss S s a prsnb yng wmn n a v hrd wkr. Se s a prsn o dpndb l n nlgrl. Se s wl likd b hr pers s wl s b mbrs o mgl. I m hpy l gv hr my hisl rcmndas. if u hir hr, I m Sr tl Se l d an xclnl jb f u.

v s u

DOCUMENT 27-3

Mr. Kenneth Samuels
Dear Mr. Samuels:

/Miss Ann Scott wrote to me recently telling me that she has moved to Providence, Rhode Island, and has applied for/a position with your company. She asked if I would write a letter of recommendation for her, and I/am very happy to do so.

I have known Miss Scott for a number of years. She began working for my/company after she finished high school June 30, 1985. She was a clerk in the accounting department/here at Mason Sales Company in Jackson, Mississippi. After only a few months, she became a/ secretary in the advertising department.

Miss Scott entered night school at South Coast College in 1986,/while she continued to work for my company. Last year she returned to college full time, and she received her/ degree last month.

Miss Scott is a personable young woman and a very hard worker. She is a person of/ dependability and integrity. She is well liked by her peers as well as by members of management. I/am happy to give her my highest recommendation. If you hire her, I am sure that she will do an/excellent job for you. Very sincerely yours,   (205)

Miss Alice Murphy   d Miss M:

n t mal lda I recd svrl cpes o t pgm f t strn mgl asoca$ bus cnfrnc l b hld July 26 27 n 28 l t Baxter holl n Miami FL.

I h alndd ts cnfrnc n t psl n I dfnll rcmnd l f u mples. t cnfrnc ts yr C s dvold nlirl l info mgl prmss l b v gd. I blev tl svrl mbrs o u slf mil lik l h an oprlun l l alnd.

bcs u org s a mbr o t strn mgl asoca$ u r nlilld l snd s mny s 30 u mples fre o rgslra$ Crg. prlcpnls ma sla l ny o t holls lsld n t pgm f a ral o $75 pr da sngl ocupncy r $90 pr da db ocupncy. holl rsrva$s msl b mad sprll.

[handwritten shorthand notes]

encd s a cpy o t cmp pgm. pl fl
ol n rlrn t rgstra$ fm C s prnld
on t bk cv if ny o u pep w$ l alnd.
v s

c: Mrs May Brown
encr

DOCUMENT 27-4   Punctuation Check

Keyboarding Goal: 15 minutes (16 words per minute)

Miss Alice Murphy
Dear Miss Murphy:

/In the mail today I received several copies of the program for the Southern Management Association/business conference to be held July 26, 27, and 28 *(series)* at the Baxter Hotel/ in Miami, Florida *(geographic)*.

I have attended this conference in the past, and *(compound sentence)* I definitely rec-ommend/it for your employees. The conference this year, which is devoted entirely to information management, *(extra)*/promises to be very good. I believe that several members of your staff might like to have an/opportunity to attend.

Because your organization is a member of the Southern Management/Association, *(introductory)* you are entitled to send as many as three of your employees free of registration charge./ Participants may stay at any of the hotels listed in the program for a rate of $75 per day/single occupancy or $90 per day double occupancy. Hotel reservations must be made/ separately.

Enclosed is a copy of the complete program. Please fill out and return the registration form /which is printed on the back cover, *(extra)* if any of your people wish to attend.
Very sincerely,   c:/Mrs. May Brown   Enclosure (224)

SUPPLEMENTARY ACTIVITY

A Word to the Wise

Developing Speed and Accuracy

/As you gain skill in *SuperWrite,* you will write faster and more accurately. How can you ensure that you are/practicing correctly? Here are a few reminders for you to remember as you practice.

Your ability to/read quickly is the key to writing quickly. After you have read the entire document and you feel very/comfortable with the content, then write it in your notebook. Read a phrase or a sentence and write as much of it as/possible without referring to the text. If you should have a question about a word, refer to the/*SuperWrite* notes quickly. Spell the word aloud in *SuperWrite,* and write it once or twice on a piece of scratch paper. You will/likely not have trouble with it again.

When you are under pressure to build your writing speed, it is likely that/your notes may become a bit difficult to read. In order to build writing speed, you must push yourself to a speed/that is slightly higher than one at which you are comfortable. Your teacher will give you dictation that will push/you to write faster and faster.

When you are writing notes to use, you should drop back only a few words per minute/ to a comfortable writing speed. You will find that your notes improve, and you will be able to read them easily./

Correct reading and writing practice will ensure that you will develop expertise in *SuperWrite.* (239)

LESSON 28

SuperWrite REVIEW

Read the following words, referring to the key if necessary. Then write the words in your own notebook.

Abbreviations

1. *sl sls sld sg sgs sgd*
2. *tk tks tkf tkd t ty*
3. *lm lml lmd lmg v w*

Word Beginning Re-

4. *rlir rsum rprs rtnk rgrup rml*

Word Ending -tion

5. *cS acS frcS mnS lnS fS*

Key

1. state, street; states, streets; stated; suggest, suggestion; suggests, suggestions; suggested
2. thank; thanks; thankful; thanked; the; they
3. time; timely; timed; timing; very; was, were, with
4. retire; resume; repress; rethink; regroup; remit
5. caution; action; friction; mention; tension; fashion

KEYBOARDING STYLE

Subject Line

A subject line may be used in a business letter to help the reader and to assist both the writer and the recipient in filing.

The subject line is keyed in capitals a double space below the salutation. The first paragraph begins a double space below the subject line.

```
                         May 5, 20--



Miss Jane Massey
1401 University Court
Boston, MA 33388-5610

Dear Miss Massey

ADVERTISING CONFERENCE

The advertising conference that was originally scheduled to
be held in the Madison Hotel on January 21 will be held on
January 23.
```

SPELLING

Here are additional spelling words. Pronounce and spell each word aloud; then copy it in your own notebook, being sure that you spell it correctly. When you read the Application section of the lesson, watch for these words.

analyzing
appropriate
imperative
liability
management
mandatory
mentioned
retention
retirement
sensible

VOCABULARY

Study the following definitions carefully, and notice how the words are used in the *SuperWrite* examples. Watch for these words in the Application section of the lesson.

formal *According to custom, form, or rule.*

t fml ddcaß s tmro.

The formal dedication is tomorrow.

imperative *Necessary; not to be avoided; expressing a command.*

l s mprlv tl u tak acß.

It is imperative that you take action.

liability insurance *Insurance that provides financial protection from a claim by another person.*

libl ins prtcts u fm fnnßl los if u r sud.

Liability insurance protects you from financial loss if you are sued.

mandatory *Required; obligatory.*

ins s mndtory n ts st.

Insurance is mandatory in this state.

retention *The act of keeping or holding in possession.*

he s n Crg o t rtnß o r rcrds.

He is in charge of the retention of our records.

APPLICATION

Time your reading speed with Document 1 before reading the remaining documents. Then write all four documents. Remember to insert the needed punctuation in Document 4 before typing it in the correct format. Be sure to note the length of the document and place it properly on the page.

Mr Wallace Brice   d Mr B:

rcrds rln$ sslm

tks f t rpl on r rcrds rln$
sslm, C u rcnll cmpd. l arivd
l r ofcs lsl wk, n r mgl slded
l crfl. t oncluss tl u dru r al
v snsb, n e plm l us u sgs s
e rvis r rcrds rln$ pgm O
t nxl fu mos.

e ap t xclnl jb tl u dd
anlyz g r sslm, Mr B, n e lk
fwrd l wkg w u co m t fulr.

e l b hpy l ril a lr o
rcmnda$ f t Wells org if u
wd lik us l d so.

v s u

c: Mrs Ann Davis

, extra

, compound
sentence

, compound
sentence

, compound
sentence

, extra

Goal: 1 minute, 1 second (120 words per minute)

Mr. Wallace Brice:
Dear Mr. Brice:

RECORDS RETENTION SYSTEM

/Thanks for the report on our records retention system, which you recently completed. It arrived at our/offices last week, and our management studied it carefully. The conclusions that you drew are all very sensible,/and we plan to use your suggestions as we revise our records retention program over the next few months./

We appreciate the excellent job that you did analyzing our system, Mr. Brice, and we look forward/to working with your company in the future.

We will be happy to write a letter of recommendation/for The Wells Organization if you would like us to do so. Very sincerely yours, c: Mrs. Ann/Davis (121)

, extra

, date

, introductory

(continued)

, introductory

, introductory

if u r plng t h a rtirm prty f Miss F, I wd v mC lik t atnd. pl le me no if u blev ts wd b aprpral. n t menlm, I l lk f a sml gfl l pr l hr smlm bf hr fml rtirm.

s u

c: Mr H T Kent

Miss Natalie Mason
Dear Miss Mason:

RETIREMENT OF ANN FRY

/Last week I spoke with Mr. Anthony Davis, head of the advertising department of your company. He/mentioned that Miss Ann Fry will be retiring on Friday, July 28. As you will remember, Miss Fry worked/with my company a number of times over the past few years as we revised many of our company/publications.

If you are planning to have a retirement party for Miss Fry, I would very much like to attend./Please let me know if you believe this would be appropriate. In the meantime, I will look for a small gift to/present to her sometime before her formal retirement. Sincerely yours, c: Mr. H. T. Kent (113)

Mr Charles Clark   d Mr C:

cr ins xpra$

   2 mos ago e rol u tl t ins plcy on u cr wd sn xpir. e dd

, compound sentence

nl rec a rply, n e mald u a scnd lr 1 mo ago. wn e sll dd nl her fm u, e almpld l

, introductory

cnlcl u b llfon. e w, hwev,

, extra

uab l reC u.

   u plcy l xpir on Sept 1 if e

, introductory

d nl her fm u. s u no, alo lib l ins s mndlory n r sl. if u Sd b nvlvd n an accdnl n

, introductory

h no cvg, u cd b sbjcl l a lrg fin.

(continued)

, extra

[handwritten shorthand]

c: Mr Al Cole

encr

DOCUMENT 28-3

Mr. Charles Clark
Dear Mr. Clark:

CAR INSURANCE EXPIRATION

/Two months ago we wrote you that the insurance policy on your car would soon expire. We did not receive a/reply, and we mailed you a second letter one month ago. When we still did not hear from you, we attempted to/contact you by telephone. We were, however, unable to reach you.

Your policy will expire on September/1 if we do not hear from you. As you know, auto liability insurance is mandatory in/our state. If you should be involved in an accident and have no coverage, you could be subject to a large fine./

It is imperative that you take action now, Mr. Clark. Renew your policy by checking the appropriate/box on the enclosed card and returning it to us. You can pay later. Sincerely yours, c: Mr./Al Cole (143)

Dr Mary Alice Norton   d Dr N:

adrs Cang

on Apr 20 I l b muvg l Chicago IL wr I l N la scul. pl Cang my adrs on u rcrds n snd al mal l my cmpus adrs C s encd ull ftr nolfcas.

u l rmbr tl 3 wks ago I rqsld tl a cpy o my mdcl rcrds b snl l me. uflnll I h nl recd tes rcrds. if ty Sd b rlrnd l u ofc I wd ap u sndg tm l my C adrs.

tks f u asslnc Dr N.

v s u

encr

Keyboarding Goal: 7 minutes (16 words per minute)

Dr. Mary Alice Norton
Dear Dr. Norton:

ADDRESS CHANGE

/On April 20 I will be moving to Chicago, Illinois, (*geographic*) where I will enter law school. (*extra*) Please change my/address on your records, and (*compound sentence*) send all mail to my campus address, which is enclosed, (*extra*) until further notification./

You will remember that three weeks ago I requested that a copy of my medical records be sent to/me. Unfortunately, (*introductory*) I have not received these records. If they should be returned to your office, (*introductory*) I would/appreciate your sending them to my Chicago address.

Thanks for your assistance, Dr. Norton. (*extra*) Very sincerely yours,/Enclosure (101)

SUPPLEMENTARY ACTIVITY

A Word to the Wise

Retention

/While you are taking dictation, you will occasionally fall behind the speaker. If you do, make every effort/to retain the sentence in your mind until you have a moment to finish it.

Most employers will stop/for a moment while speaking. This will be your opportunity to catch up. Keep the material in your mind/and write quickly when you have a chance.

You should not interrupt the speaker during dictation unless it is/absolutely essential. An interruption will most likely break the speaker's concentration and can result in/an omission of vital information. If you ever fall too far behind and feel that you must ask the person/to wait, simply hold up your hand for a moment. This will usually cause the speaker to stop, and you will/not cause further distraction by speaking.

Be ready to read back the last sentence or two after a break. This will/enable the dictator to remember the line of thought.

Practice to increase your retention by reading an/entire sentence and then writing it in your notebook. (189)

LESSON 29

SuperWrite REVIEW

Read the following words, referring to the key if necessary. Then write the words in your own notebook.

Abbreviations

1. *cmp cmp& cnv cnvl cns cnss*
2. *cv cvs rcvd depl depls dv*
3. *dvd dvm d mpl mpld mplm*

Word Beginning Inter-

4. *Nn&l Nvu Nfer Nvl Nmlnl Nmlnll*

Word Endings -pal, -ple

5. *prncp prncpl pep amp ap xmp*

Key

1. complete; completion; convenience, convenient; conveniently; consider, consideration; considers, considerations

2. cover; covers; recovered; department; departments; develop

3. developed; development; do; employ; employed; employment

4. international; interview; interfere; interval; intermittent; intermittently

5. principal; principally; people; ample; apple; example

KEYBOARDING STYLE

Attention Line

An attention line may be included in a business letter to indicate that the letter concerns company business and that the writer wishes to route the letter to a particular person, position, or department. When an attention line is used, it is typed as the first line of both the inside address and the envelope address.

```
Attention Claims Manager
The Jefferson Company
9800 Main Line Drive
Missoula, MT 59888-1324

Ladies and Gentlemen
```

Notice that the salutation refers to the second line of the address rather than the attention line.

SPELLING

Here are additional spelling words. Pronounce and spell each word aloud; then copy it in your own notebook, being sure that you spell it correctly. When you read the Application section of the lesson, watch for these words.

break
copywriter
exceeding
invaluable
precede
principal
resumé
sustained
touch
vehicle

VOCABULARY

Study the following definitions carefully, and notice how the words are used in the *SuperWrite* examples. Watch for these words in the Application section of the lesson.

exceeding

Going beyond the limits; surpassing.

t drivr w rcedg t sped lml.

The driver was exceeding the speed limit.

precede

To come before in time or order; to be in a position in front.

t dnr l prced t speC.

The dinner will precede the speech.

principal

Main; first; highest.

my prncplgol s l wk n mgl.

My principal goal is to work in management.

resumé

A summary of one's history and experience.

pl snd a rsma w u lr.

Please send a resumé with your letter.

sustained

Endured; withstood.

e ssland a gral del o wlr dmg.

We sustained a great deal of water damage.

APPLICATION

Time your reading speed with Document 1 before reading the remaining documents. Then write all four documents. Remember to insert the needed punctuation in Document 4 before typing it in the correct format. Be sure to note the length of the document and place it properly on the page.

alns Miss Sandra Taylor
Nnsl pblsrs   l n g :

, extra

yslrda Dr Max Ray, my clg
advisr, mnsd tl n t nxl 6 mos
tr mil b an opn g f a cpyrilr
l Nnsl pblsrs. he rcmndd u
org hil n sgd tl I ril now
ask g f an Nvru.

, introductory

s u l nol on t encd rsma, I
h hd rado n nuspapr xperenc
tl sd b nvlub l me s a cpyrilr.

, introductory

f xmp, I h rln mny ads f
bot r locl nuspaprs.

n June I l grdual fm sl clg
w a dgre n jrnlsm. my prncp
inl now s n bcm g a cpyrilr
w a lrg co. my evnlul gol s
l bcm a mgr n a pblsg hous.

*I wd ap u scdul g an Nvu
f me l u cnv. I l b av blwen
t hrs o 9 am n 6 pm ny da
durg t wk o Apr 6.*

vcu

c: Dr M R

encr

DOCUMENT 29-1 | **Timed Reading**

Goal: 1 minute, 33 seconds (120 words per minute)

Attention Miss Sandra Taylor
International Publishers

Ladies and Gentlemen:

/Yesterday Dr. Max Ray, my college advisor, mentioned that in the next six months there might be an opening/for a copywriter at International Publishers. He recommended your organization highly/and suggested that I write now asking for an interview.

As you will note on the enclosed resumé, I have/had radio and newspaper experience that should be invaluable to me as a copywriter./For example, I have written many ads for both our local newspapers.

In June I will graduate from State/College with a degree in journalism. My principal interest now is in becoming a copywriter/with a large company. My eventual goal is to become a manager in a publishing house.

I would/appreciate your scheduling an interview for me at your convenience. I will be available between/the hours of 9 a.m. and 6 p.m. any day during the week of April 6. Very cordially yours,/c: Dr. Max Ray Enclosure (185)

Dr Darlene Taylor   d Dr T:

Madison clg h scduld an NnSl bus cnfrnc n Miami, FL, Feb 21, 22, n 23 nxt yr. e h snt anouncms t O it pep, n e r xpctg a v gd atndnc.

, geographic

, series

, compound sentence

e r nvitg NnSl ledrs n t feld o bus t b gst spekrs, n e wd lik t xtnd an nvtaS t u t join ts grup. bcs o u xprtes n mgt, e wd lik u t gv t prncp adrs t t cnfrnc.

, compound sentence

, introductory

t prncp adrs t b on t frst evn g, Feb 21, t 9 pm. a rcpS n dnr t prced t speC. if ts t nt Nfer w u v bsy scdul, e hop u t accpt r nvtaS. pl le us no sn if u t b ab t join us.

, extra

, introductory

c

c: Dr Kurt Krause

Dr. Darlene Taylor
Dear Dr. Taylor:

/Madison College has scheduled an international business conference in Miami, Florida,/ February 21, 22, and 23 next year. We have sent announcements to over 1,000 people,/and we are expecting a very good attendance.

We are inviting international leaders in the field/of business to be guest speakers, and we would like to extend an invitation to you to join this group. Because/of your expertise in management, we would like you to give the principal address at the conference.

The/principal address will be on the first evening, February 21, at 9 p.m. A reception and/dinner will precede the speech. If this will not interfere with your very busy schedule, we hope you will accept our/invitation. Please let us know soon if you will be able to join us. Cordially, c: Dr. Kurt Krouse/(160)

DOCUMENT 29-3

, extra

alns Mr C T Courtland
legl asocats   l n g:

I h b rfrd t u la co b Miss
Joan Kent, hu wkd f u org
svrl yrs ago. I ned t hlp o a
layr bcs o a lasut tl h b
fild agnsl me.

svrl wks ago I w nvlvd
n a majr alo accdnl t t Nscs
o Broad sl n Main ave. I w
strk b a trk tl hd jsl sld fm

(continued)

, compound
sentence

, extra

t Nsl hiwa. I w almpl q l lrn
lfl, n tr w amp lm l d so. t
lrk drivr, hu w aprnll xced g
t sped lml, hl my vehcl on
t psngr sid. t cl& csd m tn

, introductory

$5t n dmg l my cr. alto I w
nl hrl, t drivr o t lrk w
lakn l t hspll b ambulnc.

lda I recd a lr slg tl I w
bq sud f $1 m n cncS w t
accdnl. my libl ins s f onl

, compound
sentence

$2 h t, n I fel I Sd rlan a
layr l ts lm.

, compound
sentence

I dd nl brak my lrfc las,
n t otr drivr w nlirl l
blam. pl ask 1 o u pep l gl
n lC w me s sn s psb.
          v l u

c: Miss J K

Attention Mr. C. T. Courtland
Legal Associates

Ladies and Gentlemen:

/I have been referred to your law company by Miss Joan Kent, who worked for your organization several years/ago. I need the help of a lawyer because of a lawsuit that has been filed against me.

Several weeks/ago I was involved in a major auto accident at the intersection of Broad Street and Main Avenue./I was struck by a truck that had just exited from the interstate highway. I was attempting to turn left, and/there was ample time to do so. The truck driver, who was apparently exceeding the speed limit, hit my/vehicle on the passenger side. The collision caused more than $5,000 in damage to my car. Although/I was not hurt, the driver of the truck was taken to the hospital by ambulance.

Today I received a/letter stating that I was being sued for $1 million in connection with this accident. My/liability insurance is for only $200,000, and I feel I should retain a lawyer at/this time.

I did not break any traffic laws, and the other driver was entirely to blame. Please ask one of your/people to get in touch with me as soon as possible. Very truly yours, c: Miss Joan Kent (213)

DOCUMENT 29-4   Punctuation Check

Keyboarding Goal: 9 minutes (18 words per minute)

alns Miss Susan Marsh
gnrl ins co   l m g :

ins clam
     dur g t hvy rans e hd n ts area on Apr 5 6 n 7 my hous sfrd a gral del o dmg. t ruf C w onl 8 yrs old lekd n svrl placs n tr w dmg l t flor o t lvg rum n dn.

(continued)

(handwritten shorthand content)

I rpld t prblm l u ins co n I w advisd l go ahd w rprs. t ruf hd l b rplacd n I hd l d a gral del o Nor panl g. t csl o t rpr w $5 t. t ins ajslr finll cam l my hom m tn 2 wks lalr n qkl mad a lsl o onl a fu ilms. n t mal lda I recd a Ck f $5 h C s onl a frcS o t aml o t ls.

pl snd a prsn l rcns t clam. I fel tl $5 h s smpl nl an amp aml f t ls I ssland.

u l

c: Mr Barry White

Keyboarding Goal: 9 minutes (18 words per minute)

Attention Miss Susan Marsh
General Insurance Company

Ladies and Gentlemen:

INSURANCE CLAIM

/During the heavy rains we had in this area on April 5, 6, and 7, (*series-introductory*) my house suffered a great deal/of damage. The roof, which was only eight years old, (*extra*) leaked in several places, and (*compound sentence*) there was damage to the/interior of the living room and den.

I reported the problem to your insurance company, and (*compound sentence*) I was/ advised to go ahead with repairs. The roof had to be replaced, and (*compound sentence*) I had to do a great deal of interior/painting. The cost of the repair was $5,000. The insurance adjuster finally came to my home/more than two weeks later and quickly made a list of only a few items. In the mail today I received a/check for $500, which is only a fraction of the amount of the loss. (*extra*)

Please send a person to/reconsider the claim. I feel that $500 is simply not an ample amount for the loss I sustained./Yours truly, c: Mr. Barry White (146)

SUPPLEMENTARY ACTIVITY

A Word to the Wise

Concentrating on Content

/When you are taking dictation, concentrate on content and do not let your mind wander. You will be much more/likely to take the dictation correctly if you concentrate on what is being said, rather than only on/writing isolated words. Your principal job is to get the correct meaning.

Do not let outside interferences/distract you. Keep your mind strictly on the business at hand as you write.

Try to anticipate what will be said/in a document. In this way you will be able to take all the dictation correctly. Occasionally/you will be able to help the person dictating by supplying an appropriate word. However, you should/not interfere unless the person wishes to have assistance.

As you read your notes before you transcribe, you should/ask yourself such questions as Who? What? Where? When? If all relevant points are not covered in your notes, ask for/ clarification before transcribing. If you realize there has been an omission after you have typed your notes, the/missing information should be obtained and inserted, and the paper should be reprinted or retyped.

For/example, if you take a memo scheduling a meeting, you should determine if the following items are/included: Who is to be at the meeting? What is the meeting for? Where is it to be held? When is it scheduled?/Any other relevant information should also be included so that additional correspondence is/not required. (242)

LESSON 30

SuperWrite REVIEW

Read the following words, referring to the key if necessary. Then copy the words in your own notebook.

Abbreviations

1. *abt aft aftwrds m aml amlg*
2. *n ny apl apls ap ap8*
3. *r t av avl ave aves*

Word Beginning Over-

4. *Odu Ocm Otm Onil Osit Ol*

Word Endings -ious, -eous, -ous, -us

5. *crtus crtusl vrus vrusl famus stalus*

Key

1. about; after; afterwards; am, more; amount; amounting
2. and, in; any; application, apply; applications, applies; appreciate; appreciation
3. are, or, our; at, it, to; available; availability; avenue; avenues
4. overdue; overcome; overtime; overnight; oversight; overly
5. courteous, courteously; various; variously; famous; status

KEYBOARDING STYLE

Envelopes

Return Address. Many companies use preprinted letterhead envelopes, which include the company name and return address. The writer's name should be typed above the return address. If preprinted envelopes are not available, the complete return address must be entered.

Recipient's Name and Address. Type the name and address of the recipient near the center and begin about two inches from the top. The address should be single-spaced and typed in capital letters. No periods or commas should be included. Use the state abbreviations recommended by the United States Postal Service, as shown in the Appendix, and include the ZIP Code.

Notations. Mailing notations such as PERSONAL, which are intended for the recipient, should be typed in capital letters a double space below the return address. Mailing notations such as PRIORITY MAIL, which are intended for the Postal Service, should be typed in capital letters a double space below the stamp.

Envelope

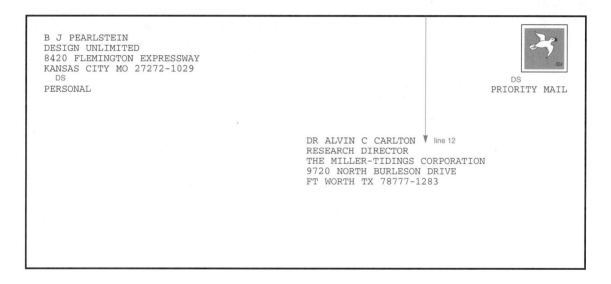

SPELLING

Here are additional spelling words. Pronounce and spell each word aloud; then copy it in your own notebook, being sure that you spell it correctly. When you read the Application section of the lesson, watch for these words.

arrangements
discourteous
evaluation
former
insolvent
oversight
personnel
simulator
techniques
viable

VOCABULARY

Study the following definitions carefully, and notice how the words are used in the *SuperWrite* examples. Watch for these words in the Application section of the lesson.

former   *Coming before in order; occurring earlier in time.*

he s a fmr mple o my co.

He is a former employee of my company.

insolvent   *Unable to pay debts; having liabilities greater than assets.*

e sspd tl u co ma b nslvnl.

We suspect that your company may be insolvent.

personnel   *People employed by an organization.*

Se s a mbr o r prsnl.

She is a member of our personnel.

VOCABULARY continued

simulator   *One that imitates; an apparatus that generates conditions similar to actual conditions.*

e prclcd wa llfon smulalr.

We practiced with a telephone simulator.

viable   *Capable of success; practicable.*

e ofr a vib pln.

We offer a viable plan.

APPLICATION

Time your reading speed with Document 1 before reading the remaining documents. Then write all four documents. Remember to insert the needed punctuation in Document 4 before typing it in the correct format. Be sure to note the length of the document and place it properly on the page.

DOCUMENT 30-1   *Timed Reading*

Goal: 1 minute, 47 seconds (120 words per minute)

Mr Oliver Van   d Mr V:
"Jones n co. hold on."
h u ev recd sC a dscrlus
, introductory *grel g O t llfon? if so, I'm Sr*
u dd nl ap l l al. u prbbl h
a pur opnn o t co u w clg.
, extra *bl, Mr V, d u on ofc wkrs*
grel clrs n a smlr mnr? if ty

(continued)

, introductory

d, u c esl imgn hw u cstmrs msl fel abl u bus.

cntrl cmuncaŝs s a sml co tl h b n bus jsl O 3 yrs. r onl bus s hlp g cos mpruv tr llfon lcneqs, n e lak tl bus v serusl.

, compound sentence

hw d e go abl hlp g cos mpruv t slalus o tr llfon mnrs? e snd 1 o r crlus nstrctrs l u ofc f 5 sŝs l wk w u ofc prsnl l mpruv tr llfon lcneqs. e us a llfon smulalr, a vdeolap rcrdr, n vrus otr dvrcs n r pgm. t csl o ts vlub srvc s v sml, bt t bnfls c b xlreml bg.

, series

, compound sentence

cl us lda. e l dmnstral l u O t llfon hw e apl wl e leC.

vsu

Goal: 1 minute, 47 seconds (120 words per minute)

Mr. Oliver Van
Dear Mr. Van:

/"Jones and Company. Hold on."

Have you ever received such a discourteous greeting over the telephone? If/so, I'm sure you did not appreciate it at all. You probably have a poor opinion of the company/you were calling.

But, Mr. Van, do your own office workers greet callers in a similar manner? If they do,/ you can easily imagine how your customers must feel about your business.

Central Communications is/a small company that has been in business just over three years. Our only business is helping companies/improve their telephone techniques, and we take that business very seriously.

How do we go about helping/companies improve the status of their telephone manners? We send one of our courteous instructors to your/office for five sessions to work with your office personnel to improve their telephone techniques. We use a telephone/simulator, a videotape recorder, and various other devices in our program. The cost/of this valuable service is very small, but the benefits can be extremely big.

Call us today. We/will demonstrate to you over the telephone how we apply what we teach. Very sincerely yours, (213)

DOCUMENT 30-2   *Speed Builder*

prirl mal

Ms Martha Fuentes   d Ms F:
evluas sslm

   tks f cl g ystrda l arang a lm l cm l r co l sldy r mple evluas pgm. tr r numrus serus prblms n r evluas pgm tl e msl Ocm n t ner fulr.

(continued)

, compound
sentence

, date

, compound
sentence

, extra

I h lkd t sluas O w vrus mbrs o t mgl o r co, n ty blev tt e Sd prced w t sldy s sn s psb. e l b av l wk w u al da Mon, June 4. s ts dal slsfclry w u?

I m gtr g al t info u rqsld, n l l b av wn u ariv. jsl cl if u h ny qs abl r evluas sslm r if u ned ny ftr info.

pl le me no if tes arangms r slsfclry w u, Ms F.

v s u

c: Mr Carlos Lopez

PRIORITY MAIL

Ms. Martha Fuentes
Dear Ms. Fuentes:

EVALUATION SYSTEM

/Thanks for calling yesterday to arrange a time to come to our company to study our employee/evaluation program. There are numerous serious problems in our evaluation program that we must/overcome in the near future. I have talked the situation over with various members of the management/of our company, and they believe that we should proceed with the study as soon as possible. We will be/available to work with you all day Monday, June 4. Is this date satisfactory with you?

I am gathering/all the information you requested, and it will be available when you arrive. Just call if you have/any questions about our evaluation system or if you need any further information.

Please let me/know if these arrangements are satisfactory with you, Ms. Fuentes. Very sincerely yours, c:/Mr. Carlos Lopez (163)

DOCUMENT 30-3

cnfdnSl

Ms Janet Gross   d Ms G:

rfrnc f Miss Alice Froy

, extra

lsl wk Miss Alice Froy, a fmr mple o u co, apld f a jb l my slor. I rqsld rfrncs fm 2 o hr

, extra

, introductory

fmr mplrs. du l an Osil, hwev, I dd nl ask f a rfrnc fm u. I prlculrl wnl l h u opnn o hr wk bcs u w hr lsl mplr n t prsn f hum Se wkd t lngsl perod o lm.

(continued)

, extra

, introductory

[shorthand handwriting]

DOCUMENT 30-3

CONFIDENTIAL

Ms. Janet Gross
Dear Ms. Gross:

REFERENCE FOR MISS ALICE TROY

/Last week Miss Alice Troy, a former employee of your company, applied for a job at my store. I requested/references from two of her former employers. Due to an oversight, however, I did not ask for/a reference from you. I particularly want to have your opinion of her work because you were her last/employer and the person for whom she worked the longest period of time.

I would appreciate it very/much, Ms. Gross, if you will fill out the enclosed form giving us information about Miss Troy. Please answer the/various questions and return the form in the envelope that is also enclosed.

If we may return the/favor in the future, we will be very glad to do so. Yours sincerely, Enclosure (130)

Keyboarding Goal: 10 minutes (18 words per minute)

prsnl

Mr Sumio Saga   d Mr S:

    on Thurs Oct 5 e rcl u a crlus lr slg tl t pam f u od o Aug 10 w Odu. e asumd tl u hd nl pd u bl bcs o an Osil. e sll dd nl her fm u n e rcl u agn on Nov 1. l tl lm e prposd a vrb pln tl incld an xlnS o 3 mos f u l pa t bl.

    now anotr mo h gn b. e h nl recd u pam nr h u ofrd ny xplnaS. e r qil cncrnd abl t prblm n e sspcl tl u co cd b nslvnl. e d nl wS l lrn u acounl O l a layr bl e ma h no otr Coic. if e d nl her fm u b Dec 15 e l b fcd l d so. lak slps now l prlcl u vlub crdl Mr S. snd us u Ck f $9 h lda.

                         u l

c: Mrs Mable Morris

Keyboarding Goal: 10 minutes (18 words per minute)

PERSONAL

Mr. Sumio Saga
Dear Mr. Saga

/On Thursday, October 5, *(date)* we wrote you a courteous letter stating that the payment for your order of/August 10 was overdue. We assumed that you had not paid your bill because of an oversight. We still did not hear/from you, and *(compound sentence)* we wrote you again on November 1. At that time we proposed a viable plan that included/an extension of three months for you to pay the bill.

Now another month has gone by. We have not received your/payment, nor *(compound sentence)* have you offered any explanation. We are quite concerned about the problem, and *(compound sentence)* we suspect that your/company could be insolvent. We do not wish to turn your account over to a lawyer, but *(compound sentence)* we may have no/ other choice. If we do not hear from you by December 15, *(introductory)* we will be forced to do so. Take steps now to/protect your valuable credit, Mr. Saga *(extra)*. Send us your check for $900 today. Yours truly, c: Mrs. Mable Morris (163)

SUPPLEMENTARY ACTIVITY

A Word to the Wise

Handling Special Instructions

/When you take a document, your employer may give special instructions. He or she may say, "Send this Express," "This/letter is confidential," or "This is a rush job." The special information may be for the Postal Service,/for the person receiving the letter, or for you.

When your employer gives special instructions, mark them in your/notebook at the beginning of the document. Even if the instructions are given after the document/has been dictated, you should mark the special notation at the beginning.

If your employer specifies/overnight delivery, you should write this at the top of your notes. Later you will type EXPRESS MAIL, or the name of/one of the various other delivery services, both on the letter and on the envelope. If you/are asked to mark a letter "personal," you should write this at the top of your notes. Later you will type PERSONAL/both on the letter and on the envelope. If your employer says, "Please type this letter now," you should write/"immediate" or "rush" at the top of your notes. Then you will remember to type the letter first.

Whatever special/instructions are given, mark them clearly at the beginning of your notes and then follow the instructions. (218)

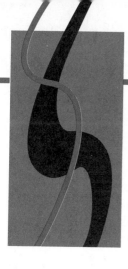

LESSON F

TOWARD PERSONAL SUCCESS

PRESENTING YOURSELF

In business you should be constantly aware of how you present yourself to others. This is not to say that you should be concerned about your appearance to the detriment of the other aspects of your work. You must be primarily concerned with your work, of course, but you must be aware of the impression you are making on others. Here are a number of things that you should consider.

Your Clothing

Your clothing must always be suitable for your work. If you work in a formal situation, you should likely wear a suit to work each day. If your business is less formal, then you should dress neatly in the style appropriate for your particular job. But your clothing must always be neat, fresh, and clean. Take a clue from your employer. If your employer wears a suit to work daily, then you might wish to do the same.

Many garments should be washed after each wearing. Garments such as coats and jackets do not have to be cleaned daily, but they should be brushed, freshened, and left hanging in the open air until they are thoroughly dry. Shoes must be kept in good repair and should be cleaned daily. It is not a good idea to wear the same clothing or shoes on two consecutive days.

Your Voice

A confident person speaks in a tone that is clear and audible to the intended audience. You should always enunciate clearly, whether you are addressing one person, a small group, or a large number of people.

Try to maintain a normal range. Do not speak in a tone that is either lower or higher than your regular voice; this sounds artificial in most cases. Speak at a pace that is easy to follow, not too slowly or too fast.

Speaking is easier, particularly with your employer or with those you do not know well, if you plan what you wish to say beforehand. Choose your words carefully so that you convey the exact meaning that you wish.

Try to use a good variety of words, and never resort to profanity. Do not repeat needless phrases, such as "You know." Do not try to carry on a conversation while eating or drinking, unless you are having a meal with the other person, and do not try to carry on a conversation while chewing gum.

Your Walk

In business you must often walk from one work area to another, from one office to another, or even from one building to another. When you walk from one place to another, people notice you, and they should have the impression that you are on your way to do something important.

You should not stroll leisurely; this could make people think you have little to do. Or they might assume that you are in no hurry to get back to your work. This is the wrong impression to give co-workers or employers.

On the other hand, you should not run at your work. Even if you feel this might give the appearance that you must hurry to get to an important job, it gives the opposite impression. Those who see you run often think that you are late, that you have not planned your time properly, and that you are behind schedule.

Your Bag

When you arrive at work, you should probably have a briefcase or a bag, which contains any work that you have taken from your job to complete. The bag is actually a part of your wardrobe, and it represents you to other people.

Your bag should be kept clean and in good repair. If it becomes worn or broken, it will detract from your appearance. If you must open it in front of others, be sure that the items inside are in proper order and are business-related.

It is not a good idea to carry two bags. If you arrive at work with more than one bag, you give the impression that you must take an excessive amount of work home with you in the evening. This may or may not be true, of course, but that is the impression that is left. If others think that you must take a great deal of work home, they may wonder if you are able to do your work in the allotted time.

Your bag should be of a size that is easy to carry, even in a crowd, and it should not be cumbersome. It should be large enough to hold several folders containing business documents as well as any personal items that you may need.

When you enter another person's office, do not place your bag on that person's desk. If you wish to put the bag down, place it on the floor out of the way, but in a place where you will not forget it when you leave.

It is appropriate to place a small identification tag on the outside of your bag so that you will be able to identify it quickly should you need to. However, you should not place large or colorful stickers on your bag. This would detract from your appearance.

Greeting People

In most businesses today, good eye contact is essential. When you address someone, look at the person confidently. A smile will almost always be welcome.

When you enter another person's office, do so with confidence and self-assurance. Complete the conversation and try to bring the visit to a pleasant close. It is always important not to overstay your welcome!

If you are confident and are always concerned about the way you present yourself, you are sure to make a good impression, which will contribute greatly to your success.

Discussion

1. Do you feel it is essential to be concerned about the way you present yourself at work? Why or why not?

2. What do you think are the most important things to consider in the way your present yourself at work?

3. Do you feel it is a good idea to wear a business suit to work daily? Why or why not?

4. Do you believe that your voice has much to do with your success at business? Why or why not?

Case Study—Presentation

Marty has worked as clerk in a local insurance office for the past ten years. He is a quiet, unassuming person, and he often works late to get everything finished before the next day. Everyone agrees he is an efficient worker.

When Marty began work, he told his associates that he really preferred to wear comfortable clothing, rather than a business suit each day. Several of his friends suggested that he would make a better impression if he wore a suit, but Marty insisted that his appearance really did not have anything to do with his work.

Cynthia works at the same company, and she is very popular with her co-workers. She spends a lot of time at the vending machine in the lobby chatting with her friends. Although she is away from her desk a great deal of the time, she always gets her work done on schedule. She feels that if her work is good she should be able to spend as much time as she likes talking with others.

Mark is a supervisor at the same company. He arrives at work early each day and is at his desk until everyone has gone home each evening. He wears a business suit daily, and it is clean and neat. Mark is always in a hurry; he never stops to chat and he often skips lunch to get a job finished. Yesterday Mark almost knocked one of his associates down as he rushed to get to a meeting on time. He just said "Sorry" over his shoulder.

Discussion Questions

1. Marty, Cynthia, and Mark all have problems with the way they present themselves at work. What are the problems as you see them?

2. What suggestions would you give to the three workers that might help them to improve the way they present themselves at work?

Activities

1. Choose a person that you like and admire. Then make a list of at least five things that this person does to present himself or herself well.

2. Take a trip to a local store and choose a bag that you might like to have to take to work.

3. Choose a partner and listen to each other for a few minutes. Make a note of both the good voice qualities and the areas where your voices need improvement.

4. Make a list of at lest ten things you can do to enhance the appearance you make.

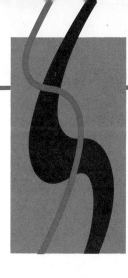

LESSON 31

SuperWrite REVIEW

Read the following words, referring to the key if necessary. Then write the words in your own notebook.

Abbreviations

1. *f fm h hr hrs hrl*
2. *enc encd encr ev exec execs*
3. *yr yrs yrl u us e*

Word Beginnings For-, Fore-, Fur-

4. *fwrd fc fml fclos fse fwrn*
5. *fnS fnSd fnlr ftr ftrm fnc*

Key

1. for; from; has, have; hour; hours; hourly
2. enclose; enclosed; enclosure; ever, every; executive; executives
3. year; years; yearly; you, your; yours; we
4. forward; force; formal; foreclose; foresee; forewarn
5. furnish; furnished; furniture; further; furthermore; furnace

KEYBOARDING STYLE

Memorandum Format

When a person in a business wishes to send a message to another person in the same organization, a memorandum is usually prepared. A memorandum is similar to a business letter with the following exceptions:

1. To, From, Date, and Subject lines are included at the top.

2. No salutation or complimentary close is used.

3. The writer may initial or sign the memorandum close to his or her typed name at the top.

Memos may be keyed on blank paper. In many businesses today, however, they are prepared using a word processing template in which the headings appear on the screen and information is supplied from the keyboard. Preprinted memo forms may also be used.

The person who types the memo must often supply an appropriate subject line.

Memorandum Format

TO: Ms. Myoko Ito, Administrative Services   line 10

FROM: Joe Billings, Personnel *JB*

DATE: February 23, 20—

SUBJECT: Approval of New Employee

The new line for hiring an additional employee in administrative services was approved yesterday afternoon by the personnel committee. The justification you provided was considered more than adequate for adding a new person in the information processing area. A copy of the minutes from the meeting is enclosed.

1"

Please gather the information needed in order for us to advertise the position and schedule interviews. As soon as I hear from you, I will proceed with the necessary paperwork in this department.

1"

rlm

Enc

c Ann Saunders

SPELLING

Here are additional spelling words. Pronounce and spell each word aloud; then copy it in your own notebook, being sure that you spell it correctly. When you read the Application section of the lesson, watch for these words.

bankruptcy
candidate
confidence
exemplary
financier
foreclose
oversee
recourse
unforeseen
vacated

VOCABULARY

Study the following definitions carefully, and notice how the words are used in the *SuperWrite* examples. Watch for these words in the Application section of the lesson.

bankruptcy
State in which one is legally declared incapable of paying debts; insolvency.

he askd t corl l estbls bnkrpcy.

He asked the court to establish
bankruptcy.

exemplary
Worthy of imitation; serving as a model.

Se dd hr wk n an xmplry mnr.

She did her work in an exemplary
manner.

financier
One who is expert in financial matters.

he srvd as fnncer f t co.

He served as financier for the company.   (continued)

VOCABULARY continued

foreclose   *To deprive a borrower of the right to mortgaged property, as when payments are not made.*

[shorthand]

When the borrower could not meet the payments,
the bank had to foreclose the property.

vacated   *Ceased to occupy.*

[shorthand]

The building was vacated last month.

APPLICATION

Time your reading speed with Document 1 before reading the remaining documents. Then write all four documents. Remember to insert the needed punctuation in Document 4 before typing it in the correct format. Be sure to note the length of the document and place it properly on the page.

DOCUMENT 31-1   *Timed Reading*

Goal: 34 seconds (130 words per minute)

[shorthand]

, extra

, geographic

, introductory

, introductory

bldg n Portland, ME. if Mrs J Sd ned ftr fnds f bldg r f ny ufsen crcmstncs, pl ask hr t cl us.

if e ma b o ftr asstnc t u r ny o t otr mbrs o u depl, pl le us no. e lk fwrd l wkg w u n t futr.

DOCUMENT 31-1   *Timed Reading*

Goal: 34 seconds (130 words per minute)

To: Mr. Elvin Grider, Marketing Department

From: Maria Sanchez, Finance Department

Date: —

Subject: Financing the Jefferson Building

/We were happy to have been able to serve as financier for Mrs. Jane Jefferson, your client, when she purchased/a new office building in Portland, Maine. If Mrs. Jefferson should need further funds for building or for any/unforeseen circumstances, please ask her to call us.

If we may be of further assistance to you or any of/the other members of your department, please let us know. We look forward to working with you in the future. (74)

l Mr Tom Granger　　fm Alice Simms
legl dept　　　　　　　　fnnc dept

, introductory

fcloSr o prprly l 8820 ndstral ave
s e dscsd ystrda, r bnk s
fcd l fclos t prprly locald l
8820 ndstral ave. t onr o t prprly,

, extra

Mr Ben Jones, h mad no pam

, introductory

on hs lon f m tn 6 mos. ftrm,
he vacald t stor lst July. lrs

, compound
sentence

l t bus h b rlrnd, n e h no
fwrd g adrs. e fer he ma sn
dclr bnkrpcy. r onl rcors l ts
lm s l prced w fml fcloSr.

, compound
sentence

pl lak wlev legl acS s ncsry,
n le me no t slalus o u wk.

To: Mr. Tom Granger, Legal Department

From: Alice Simms, Finance Department

Date: —

Subject: Foreclosure of Property at 8820 Industrial Avenue

/As we discussed yesterday, our bank is forced to foreclose the property located at 8820/ Industrial Avenue. The owner of the property, Mr. Ben Jones, has made no payment on his loan for more/than six months. Furthermore, he vacated the store last July. Letters to the business have been returned, and we have/no forwarding address. We fear he may soon declare bankruptcy. Our only recourse at this time is to proceed/with formal foreclosure.

Please take whatever legal action is necessary, and let me know the status of/your work. (101)

DOCUMENT 31-3

l Ms Grace Stern   fm Paul Moore

Parker co cntrcl

, introductory

encd s a cpy o a lr I recd fm Miss Mary Parker. s u l nol, Miss P h askd us l fnd hr nu ofc l 4 h Madison ave.

, compound
sentence

, introductory

ts reps a v lrg aml o bus f r org, n e msl d an mplry jb. s u no, t P co s l o t lrgsl prsnl agnces n ts area. mny

(continued)

, extra	*prspclv clints, inclg bus onrs,*
, series	*mgrs, n wkrs, N t ofc dal. l l*
	b qil gd f r bus l h fnSd ts
	imp ofc.
, extra	*I wd lik u l Ose ts jb, Ms*
	S. u h dn an xclnt jb n smlr
, compound sentence	*ofcs n t psl, n I no tl u l*
	onc agn d a jb tl l rep r org
	n an olstndg wa. I h gral
, compound sentence	*cnfdnc n u abl, n I lk fwrd*
	l hg u rply.
	encr

DOCUMENT 31-3

To: Ms. Grace Stern

From: Paul Moore

Date: —

Subject: Parker Company Contract

/Enclosed is a copy of a letter I received from Miss Mary Parker. As you will note, Miss Parker has asked/us to furnish her new office at 400 Madison Avenue.

This represents a very large amount/of business for our organization, and we must do an exemplary job. As you know, the Parker Company/is one of the largest personnel agencies in this area. Many prospective clients, including/business owners, managers, and workers, enter the office daily. It will be quite good for our business to have/furnished this important office.

I would like you to oversee this job, Ms. Stern. You have done an excellent job/in similar offices in the past, and I know that you will once again do a job that will represent our/ organization in an outstanding way. I have great confidence in your ability, and I look forward/ to having your reply. Enclosure (165)

DOCUMENT 31-4   *Punctuation Check*

Keyboarding Goal: 9 minutes (20 words per minute)

l Mrs May Edwards   fm Rosa Lopez

rfrnc f Gary Kent

    encd s a cpy o t prsnl rcrd o Mr Gary Kent. s u l se Mr K bgn wk f us July 8 1987 wn he fnSd hi scul. he bgn wk s an hrl mple n t mal rum bt he w prmotd on Feb 7 1988 l hd o t mal rum. Mr K recd no ftr prmoSs ull lsl yr wn he w Ifrd l t scur l dept. snc tn he h srvd s asslnl l t Cef scur l ofcr.

    Mr K recd v gd fml evluaSs n eC o t psSs he hld w r co. ftrm he s wl likd b hs suprvisrs n hs pers.

(continued)

I fel tl he s a gd cnddal f t nu psß s hd o scur l n t NnSl dvß. if u Sd ned ftr info pl le me no.

encr

DOCUMENT 31-4   *Punctuation Check*

Keyboarding Goal: 9 minutes (20 words per minute)

To: Mrs. May Edwards

From: Rosa Lopez

Date: —

Subject: Reference for Gary Kent

/Enclosed is a copy of the personnel record of Mr. Gary Kent. As you will see, *(introductory)* Mr. Kent began/work for us July 8, 1987, *(date)* when he finished high school. He began work as an hourly employee/in the mail room, but *(compound sentence)* he was promoted on February 7, 1988, *(date)* to head of the mail room./Mr. Kent received no further promotions until last year when he was transferred to the security department./Since then, *(introductory)* he has served as assistant to the chief security officer.

Mr. Kent received very good/formal evaluations in each of the positions he held with our company. Furthermore, *(introductory)* he is well liked/by his supervisors and his peers. I feel that he is a good candidate for the new position as head of/security in the international division. If you should need further information, *(introductory)* please let me know./Enclosure (162)

SUPPLEMENTARY ACTIVITY

A Word to the Wise

Your Desk

/In the office the principal item of furniture is the office desk. Chances are you will spend the major/part of every workday sitting at your desk. Your desk is your home while you are at work. It should be a comfortable/and attractive place to work. It should be orderly and neat, and there should be ample room for everything you/need during the workday. The drawers should not be stacked with items that you seldom use.

Many office desks have a large/drawer where pens, pencils, scissors, correction fluid, clips, and so on are kept. You should make a real effort to keep this drawer/in proper order. Items should be arranged so that they can be found quickly. When an item is used, it should be/ returned to the same area of the drawer. For example, such items as pencils should be kept at the front of/the drawer so that they can be reached quickly. Scissors may be placed a bit farther back in the drawer. Some office workers/find it helpful to place a number of small open boxes in the drawer. For example, one small box may contain/rubber bands while another contains postage stamps.

The stationery drawer should contain letterhead paper, memo/forms, and envelopes. It should also contain any form that you use on a daily basis. Stationery/items that are not used regularly should be kept in a supply closet. Any items that you seldom use should/not take space in your stationery drawer.

Many desks have one large file drawer. This drawer should not be used for the/general files in a large office. Most papers should be kept in some type of file cabinet or shelf file. Such a file is/often open to any worker who needs the information. Other workers should have no occasion to open/the file drawer of your desk. This drawer may be used to file items of a confidential or personal nature./

Work to manage your desk properly. You will find that your work will be much easier. (335)

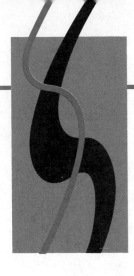

LESSON 32

SuperWrite REVIEW

Read the following words, referring to the key if necessary. Then write the words in your own notebook.

Abbreviations

1. *hw imp impl incl incld incls*
2. *o od ods odd org uorgd*
3. *ot pd upd pl pld plg*

Ou

4. *flour hous houss proud ounc trousrs*

Ow

5. *towr powr now cow down town*

Key

1. how; importance, important; importantly; include; included; includes
2. of; order; orders; ordered; organization, organize; unorganized
3. out; paid; unpaid; please; pleased; pleasing
4. flour; house; houses; proud; ounce; trousers
5. tower; power; now; cow; down; town

PUNCTUATION

Requests Phrased as Questions

In a business letter, requests may seem very blunt.

snd t rpl l me nxt wk.

    Send the report to me next week.

If you wish to soften the tone, a request may be written as a question. However, if compliance is expected, use a period rather than a question mark.

l u pl snd t rpl l me nxt wk.

    Will you please send the report to me next week.

If you wish to soften the tone still further, a question mark may be used. However, this may appear to give the person an option of whether or not to comply.

l u pl snd t rpl l me nxt wk?

    Will you please send the report to me next week?

In the Application, when a request is phrased as a question and is followed by a period, it will be noted in the margin as follows:

. request   *l u pl mal t paprs l me.*

    Will you please mail the papers to me.

SPELLING

Here are additional spelling words. Pronounce and spell each word aloud; then copy it in your own notebook, being sure that you spell it correctly. When you read the Application section of the lesson, watch for these words.

advisory   questionnaire
completing   rotated
coupon   tune-up
entrepreneurs
informal
innovative
lubrication

VOCABULARY

Study the following definitions carefully, and notice how the words are used in the *SuperWrite* examples. Watch for these words in the Application section of the lesson.

associate's degree

A degree conferred after two years of work, often at a community or junior college.

he recd an asocal's dgre.

He received an associate's degree.

entrepreneurs

Business persons; those who assume the duties and responsibilities of a business.

r org hlps nu nlrprnurs.

Our organization helps new entrepreneurs.

informal

Casual, ordinary, or familiar; marked by absence of ceremony.

e l h svrl nfml mel gs.

We will have several informal meetings.

innovative

Characterized by new ideas or methods.

e h an invalv ins pgm.

We have an innovative insurance program.

rotated

Revolved; exchanged in a set pattern.

u lirs Sd b rolald prodcl.

Your tires should be rotated periodically.

APPLICATION

Time your reading speed with Document 1 before reading the remaining documents. Then write all four documents. Remember to insert the needed punctuation in Document 4 before typing it in the correct format. Be sure to note the length of the document and place it properly on the page.

alnS Ms Christine Doran

org o rlird execs   l ng:

n a fu wks I l b opn g a nu clot g Sp n t downtown area, n I ned sm hlp n st g up my acount g sstm. I recd my asocal's dgre fm cntrl clg n June. I Ustnd t clot g bus v wl, bt I h hd no xperenc n acount g. I w told tl u org now pvds asstnc n advic l nu ntrprnurs fre o Crg.

l wd b a gral hlp l me l h an xperencd bus exec advis me on hw l hndl t acount g wk tl l b ncsry n my nu bus. I m prtculrl cncrnd

, compound
sentence

, compound
sentence

(continued)

, series

, introductory

. request

abl cmpg t rpls mndald b cly, st, n fdrl las. if u c sply ts typ o asstnc, l u pl cl me l 555-1809 nytm aft t hr o 9n t mrng. I sncerl ap u hlp. v c u

DOCUMENT 32-1 | Timed Reading

Goal: 1 minute, 15 seconds (130 words per minute)

Attention Ms. Christine Doran
Organization of Retired Executives

Ladies and Gentlemen:

/In a few weeks I will be opening a new clothing shop in the downtown area, and I need some help in/setting up my accounting system. I received my associate's degree from Central College in June. I/understand the clothing business very well, but I have had no experience in accounting. I was told that your/organization now provides assistance and advice to new entrepreneurs free of charge.

It would be a great/help to me to have an experienced business executive advise me on how to handle the accounting/work that will be necessary in my new business. I am particularly concerned about completing the/reports mandated by city, state, and federal laws. If you can supply this type of assistance, will you please/call me at 555-1809 anytime after the hour of nine in the morning. I sincerely/appreciate your help. Very cordially yours, (166)

l al mples   fm Joan Morrison

mple bnfts

rlirm pgm

, introductory

bgn g Jan 1, t Mason acount g co l pvd ls wkrs w an imp nu rlirm pgm. e r v proud

, compound sentence

o ts invalv pgm, n e blev tl ev mple l b qil hpy w t mny xtra bnfts av.

, introductory

n t nxt mo, eC mple l rec a prsnlizd bktt tl incls al t felrs o t nu pgm. wn t bktt

, introductory
. request
, introductory

arivs, l u pl rvu al t prvs crfl. if u h ny qs abt ny o tm, pl cl t prsnl ofc. e l b qld l hlp u.

, introductory

if l s nedd, e l scdul an nfml mel g l go O t prvs o t pgm smlm n t ner fulr.

To: All Employees

From: Joan Morrison, Employee Benefits

Date: —

Subject: Retirement Program

/Beginning January 1, the Mason Accounting Company will provide its workers with an important/new retirement program. We are very proud of this innovative program, and we believe that every employee/will be quite happy with the many extra benefits available.

In the next month, each employee will/receive a personalized booklet that includes all the features of the new program. When the booklet arrives, will/you please review all the provisions carefully. If you have any questions about any of them, please call the/personnel office. We will be glad to help you.

If it is needed, we will schedule an informal meeting to/go over the provisions of the program sometime in the near future. (130)

DOCUMENT 32-3

, geographic

, extra
, introductory

, series
. request

, introductory

dscount on my srvc on u frst vsl t r nu Sp.

also encd s a bklt o cupns tt u ma us durg t ntir mo o Aug. wn u us 10 tes cupns f t spcfid srvc, u l rec a dscount up t 30% of t rgulr pric. f xmp, cm n f a cmp lubrca& n oil Cang n sav 25% of t rgulr pric. if u w& l h u tirs rotatd n blncd, u l sav 30%. u l also sav 30% on t cst o a cmp tun-up. n ts s n ad& t t $20 dscount u l rec b mal.

e lk fwrd l recg u qnr n l se g u n r srvc cntr ofn.

s u

encrs

, introductory

, introductory

, introductory

DOCUMENT 32-3

Mr. J. T. Ball
Dear Mr. Ball:

/We are pleased to announce the opening of the new Central Auto Service Shop at 400 Main Street in/downtown Clarke, Mississippi. We want to offer exactly the type of service that you need, Mr. Ball. Therefore, we/have a very special request of you.

Will you please take a few moments now to fill out, sign, and return the enclosed/ questionnaire. When we receive the questionnaire, we will mail you a coupon that will allow you to take a/$20 discount on any service on your first visit to our new shop.

Also enclosed is a booklet of/coupons that you may use during the entire month of August. When you use one of these coupons for the specified/service, you will receive a discount up to 30 percent off the regular price. For example, come in for/a complete lubrication and oil change and save 25 percent off the regular price. If you wish to have/ your tires rotated and balanced, you will save 30 percent. You will also save 30 percent on the cost of/a complete tune-up. And this is in addition to the $20 discount you will receive by mail.

We look/forward to receiving your questionnaire and to seeing you in our service center often. Sincerely yours,/Enclosures (222)

DOCUMENT 32-4   *Punctuation Check*

Keyboarding Goal: 8 minutes (20 words per minute)

[Handwritten shorthand notes]

ı Mr Max Bloom   fm Lila Blake

prsnl advisry cmte apointm
ı t Mar 14 mel g t bord o drctrs
o t Black co vold ı st up an advisry
cmte ı asst t bord n ıs prsnl wk.
t bord mbrs fll tt u wd b t bst Coic
ı hd ts cmte.

[Shorthand/handwritten symbols corresponding to the letter text below]

DOCUMENT 32-4 **Punctuation Check**

Keyboarding Goal: 8 minutes (20 words per minute)

To: Mr. Max Bloom

From: Lila Blake

Date: —

Subject: Personnel Advisory Committee Appointment

/At the March 14 meeting, *(introductory)* the board of directors of the Black Company voted to set up an/advisory committee to assist the board in its personnel work. The board members felt that you would be the best choice to/head this committee.

The duties of the committee will be to review company personnel policy and/make recommendations concerning all personnel matters. The committee will be permanent and will consist/of five members. There will be one person from each of the major departments in the company. The members will/be appointed by the board for terms of two years.

We want you to know, Mr. Bloom, *(extra)* that we have great confidence in/your ability. Do you believe your duties will allow you time to accept this important/responsibility?

Will you please let me hear from you as soon as possible. *(request)* (149)

SUPPLEMENTARY ACTIVITY

A Word to the Wise

Managing Your Notebook

/Your notebook should be kept in a handy place so that you will be able to reach it easily. You may receive/a telephone call, someone may drop by and leave a message, or your employer may wish to dictate a memo./Your notebook should not be kept in a place where it can be seen easily by others or in a place where it could/be picked up accidentally and carried away by a visitor.

When you pick up your notebook, you should be/able to find a blank page quickly. In order to locate a blank page in your notebook, you may leave it open/to the page following the last document. Other ways are to mark the page with a paper clip or place a/rubber band around the used pages. A pen should be kept with your notebook.

Leave several blank lines after one document/before you begin writing another. Identify each document clearly at the beginning either/with a name or a subject. If you are using a notebook that is bound at the top, date each page at the bottom./If the notebook is bound at the left, date each page at the top. You will be glad that you have taken the time to/ identify documents by name or subject and date when you need to find your notes in a hurry.

While you are in/school, you may wish to keep two notebooks, one for classwork and one for homework. In this way you can locate your classwork/or your homework very easily. At work you may find having two notebooks is handy, particularly if/you work for two people. (264)

LESSON 33

SuperWrite REVIEW

Read the following words, referring to the key if necessary. Then write the words in your own notebook.

Abbreviations

1. *rpl rpld rpls rep repd urepd*
2. *rqr rqrd rqrm rsp rspl sn*

Word Beginning Im-

3. *mprs mprnt mport mprsnl mpct mpasl*

Word Beginning Enter-

4. *N Nd Npris Npriss Nlan Nlanm*

Word Beginning Under-

5. *U Unet Uground Upowrd Ucv Usld*

Key

1. report; reported; reports; represent, representative; represented; unrepresented
2. require; required; requirement; responsible; responsibility; soon
3. impress; imprint; import; impersonal; impact; impatient
4. enter; entered; enterprise; enterprises; entertain; entertainment
5. under; underneath; underground; underpowered; undercover; understood

PUNCTUATION

Semicolon with Independent Clauses and No Conjunction

Use a semicolon between two closely related independent clauses if there is no coordinating conjunction.

Mark dd nl fel wl; he wnl hom erl.

Mark did not feel well; he went home early.

If a transitional word, such as <u>therefore</u>, introduces the second independent clause, it is followed by a comma.

Mark dd nl fel wl; trf, he wnl hom erl.

Mark did not feel well; therefore, he went home early.

In the Application when two independent clauses are separated by a semicolon rather than by a conjunction, the following notation will appear in the margin:

; no conjunction

he slded f t xm; he mad a gd grad.

He studied for the exam; he made a
good grade.

SPELLING

Here are additional spelling words. Pronounce and spell each word aloud; then copy it in your own notebook, being sure that you spell it correctly. When you read the Application section of the lesson, watch for these words.

beneficiary
contingent
impatient
maximum
perturbed
projections
rejection
resolved
revision
tender

VOCABULARY

Study the following definitions carefully, and notice how the words are used in the *SuperWrite* examples. Watch for these words in the Application section of the lesson.

beneficiary
One who benefits; the designated person to receive monies from a trust or from insurance.

t bnfSary o t ins plcy
l rec a Ck.

The beneficiary of the insurance policy
will receive a check.

contingent
Depending upon; conditional; for use in circumstances not completely planned for.

hs rec g t pam s cnlngnl
on svrl fclrs.

His receiving the payment is contingent
on several factors.

perturbed
Disturbed greatly; made uneasy or anxious.

Se w prlrbd b t sluaS.

She was perturbed by the situation.

resolved
Settled; concluded; found a solution.

t cnflcl msl b rslvd sn.

The conflict must be resolved soon.

tender
A formal offer; a bid.

r lndr o $1m w accpld.

Our tender of $1 million was accepted.

APPLICATION

Time your reading speed with Document 1 before reading the remaining documents. Then write all four documents. Remember to insert the needed punctuation in Document 4 before typing it in the correct format. Be sure to note the length of the document and place it properly on the page.

DOCUMENT 33-1   *Timed Reading*

Goal: 1 minute, 50 seconds (130 words per minute)

l al mples   fm Amanda Cole
                        prsnl depl

rlirm pln
     encd s u prsnl cpy o t nu
NnSl Npriss rlirm pln. l u pl
lak sm lm s sn s psb l red t

. request   bkll trol u l nol tt t pln h
Ugn majr Cangs snc t lsl rvs
n 1995.

     pl nolc on pag 4 t prjcss o
u prsnl rlirm ncm. I msl mprs

; no conjunction   on u tl tes fqurs r onl eslmls;
ty r basd on u crnl anul slry
n cnlnud mplm. t aclul amls

; no conjunction   ma b mC hir; ty cd b lor.

, series

notc on pags 23, 24, n 25 t prv&s f cntnud ins f u n u fml aft rtirm. u l b abl cntnu

; no conjunction
, introductory

u hlt ins wol Nrp&, hwev, u l b rqrd l asum fl rspt f pam. u lif ins ma b cntnud,

, compound sentence

bt t mxmm amt l b hf tl o u finl yr o mplm. l u pt b &r tl t nam o t prsn lstd s

. request

primry bnf&ary s crct. l u also pt Ck t nam o u cntngnt

. request

bnf&ary.

if, aft u h hd a Cnc l rvu

, extra

at t prv&s, u h qs abt u

, introductory

prtculr sluas, pl cl t prsnl ofc.

encr

Goal: 1 minute, 50 seconds (130 words per minute)

To: All Employees

From: Amanda Cole, Personnel Department

Date: —

Subject: Retirement Plan

/Enclosed is your personal copy of the new International Enterprises retirement plan. Will you please/take some time as soon as possible to read the booklet thoroughly. You will note that the plan has undergone/major changes since the last revision in 1995.

Please notice on page 4 the projections of your/personal retirement income. I must impress on you that these figures are only estimates; they are based on your/current annual salary and continued employment. The actual amounts may be much higher; they could be/ lower.

Notice on pages 23, 24, and 25 the provisions for continued insurance/for you and your family after retirement. You will be able to continue your health insurance without/interruption; however, you will be required to assume full responsibility for payment. Your life/ insurance may be continued, but the maximum amount will be half that of your final year of employment. Will/you please be sure that the name of the person listed as primary beneficiary is correct. Will you/also please check the name of your contingent beneficiary.

If, after you have had a chance to review/all the provisions, you have questions about your particular situation, please call the personnel office./Enclosure (242)

, introductory

; no conjunction
, introductory

, introductory

; no conjunction

; no conjunction

[shorthand notes]

DOCUMENT 33-2   Speed Builder

To: All Company Employees

From: Harold Cox, President

Date: —

Subject: Acquisition of Moore Shipping Company

/On March 20 General Enterprises entered into an agreement to purchase Moore Shipping Company/for $1 billion. Our tender of $1,000 per share for 1 million shares of stock was accepted./

Under a requirement of the federal government, we must await approval of this purchase by federal/officials; however, we feel there is no reason for rejection.

(continued)

DOCUMENT 33-2 continued

When the purchase is formally approved,/there will be few changes in the operation of either company. I want to impress on each of you that/there will be no cutbacks in personnel and no layoffs. The transition will be a slow and gradual one; no/job is in jeopardy.

We extend a warm greeting to the members of Moore Shipping Company; welcome to our/family of workers. (143)

DOCUMENT 33-3

prir l mal
alns Mr Kenneth Taylor
Jenson, Taylor, and Cline l ng:

anul rpl
   rcnll I recd my anul slm
; no conjunction *fm u crdl co. I ap h q t slm;*
I us l l prpr my ncm lx fms.
tr r a fu ilms tl I d nl fll
, extra *Uslnd, hwev. l u pl ansr sm*
. request *qs n od l cler up a fu points*
   tr r 2 nos mprnld l t lp
; no conjunction *o t slm. / s my acounl no; wl*
s t otr?
   U t Dec hd q tr r 3 rfrncs

l n̲S̲l Npriss. I h no rcrd o bus w sC an org. l u pl ll me wy ts nam apers on my acounl smry.

. request

; no conjunction

my crdl lin s Son s $5t; l Sd b $3t.

. request

l u pl le me her fm u sn.

s u

DOCUMENT 33-3

PRIORITY MAIL

Attention Mr. Kenneth Taylor
Jenson, Taylor, and Cline
Ladies and Gentlemen:

ANNUAL REPORT

/Recently I received my annual statement from your credit company. I appreciate having the statement;/I use it to prepare my income tax forms. There are a few items that I do not fully understand, however./Will you please answer some questions in order to clear up a few points.

There are two numbers imprinted at the/top of the statement. One is my account number; what is the other?

Under the December heading there are three/references to National Enterprises. I have no record of business with such an organization./Will you tell me why this name appears on my account summary.

My credit line is shown as $5,000;/it should be $3,000.

Will you please let me hear from you soon. Sincerely yours, (131)

l Mr Carl Lindsey   fm Ann Murphy

Miss Janice Davis
     alCd s a lr I recd fm Miss J
D ı o r cslmrs n t sl o ME. s u l
nol Miss D s qil prlrbd w us. Se
prCsd a hom Nlanm cnlr n r Portland
ME slor lsl mo. uflnll l dd nl pvd t
ql l sound tl Se rpcld. wn Se almpld
l rlrn l Se w lold tl l cd nl b accpld
l r slor.
     Miss D sls tl t sals rep w mpasl
n lreld hr n a v mprsnl mnr. Se
rminds us tl Se h b a cslmr o r
slor f m tn 5 yrs.
     U tes cndss I blev tl u Sd cl hr
n ofr l h t Nlanm cnlr pkd up n
gv hr a fl rfnd. Se s a gd cslmr

trf e Sd try l kep hr gdl. l u pl le me no hw t prblm s rslvd.

encr

DOCUMENT 33-4   *Punctuation Check*

Keyboarding Goal: 8 minutes (22 words per minute)

To: Mr. Carl Lindsey

From: Ann Murphy

Date: —

Subject: Miss Janice Davis

/Attached is a letter I received from Miss Janice Davis, one of our customers in the state of Maine. *(extra)* As you/will note, *(introductory)* Miss Davis is quite perturbed with us. She purchased a home entertainment center in our Portland, Maine, *(geographic)* store/last month. Unfortunately, *(introductory)* it did not provide the quality sound that she expected. When she attempted to/return it, *(introductory)* she was told that it could not be accepted at our store.

Miss Davis states that the sales representative/was impatient and treated her in a very impersonal manner. She reminds us that she has been a/customer of our store for more than five years.

Under these conditions, *(introductory)* I believe that you should call her and offer/to have the entertainment center picked up and give her a full refund. She is a good customer; *(no conjunction)* therefore, *(introductory)* we/should try to keep her goodwill. Will you please let me know how the problem is resolved. *(request)* Enclosure (152)

SUPPLEMENTARY ACTIVITY

A Word to the Wise

Proofreading and Editing

/When you mail a letter, only the document in the envelope is available to represent you, your/employer, and your company. If the document is complete and accurate, the impression on the reader/will be good. If the document contains errors, the reader may not understand the contents; he or she may/even lose confidence in your company.

When you enter a document on the keyboard, it is your/responsibility to be sure that it is accurate. Proofreading or editing your work is an essential part of/your job; do not overlook this important function.

In business offices today there are many aids to help/you create accurate documents. There are spell-checkers with many word processors that can help you catch those/typographical and spelling errors. If you have such a device available, it is a good idea to use/it with each document that you prepare. Many times a spell-checker will point out an error that you may have missed,/even if you have proofread the paper several times.

However valuable electronic devices/may be, they cannot ensure that each sentence makes sense and contains the information that it should. They cannot ensure/that all details have been included and are in the correct order. They cannot verify that the dates/included in a document are the correct dates.

If there is time after you have completed a document, set/it aside briefly while you do another assignment. When you read the document later, you will see it in/a new light. Questions will occur to you, and you will be able to check to see if they are answered in the/document. You will be able to verify any information that may appear to be questionable. Read/for overall content, and then read for small details. Work carefully and do not rush as you proofread.

Proofreading/or editing your work is vital; take this important part of your work very seriously. (357)

LESSON 34

SuperWrite REVIEW

Read the following words, referring to the key if necessary. Then write
the words in your own notebook.

Abbreviations

1. *e wk wks wkl C l*
2. *lg ulg yr yrs yrl u*

Word Beginning Ex-

3. *xtra xmn xtrem xpnd xpns xpnss*

Word Beginning Pro-

4. *prtcl prduc prdcS prfl prtsl prfSl*

Word Beginning Un-

5. *ul uls ulold uncsry usold uab*

Key

1. we; week, work; weeks, works; weekly; which; will

2. willing; unwilling; year; years; yearly; you, your

3. extra; examine; extreme; expend; expense; expenses

4. protect; produce; production; profit; protest; professional

5. until; unless; untold; unnecessary; unsold; unable

PUNCTUATION

Coordinate Adjectives

Use a comma to separate two coordinate adjectives in a series if each independently modifies the following noun.

he s a dpndb, capb prsn.

    He is a dependable, capable person.

There are two ways to tell if the adjectives each independently modify the noun.

1. If the word <u>and</u> can be inserted between the adjectives.

    He is a dependable and capable person.
    (The word <u>and</u> can be inserted.)

2. If the two adjectives can be interchanged.

    He is a capable, dependable person.
    (The adjectives can be interchanged.)

Do not use a comma if the word <u>and</u> cannot be inserted between the adjectives.

Se wor a bulf blu sul.

    She wore a beautiful blue suit.
    (Not beautiful and blue)

Do not use a comma if the words cannot be interchanged.

    She wore a beautiful blue suit.
    (Not blue beautiful suit)

When coordinate adjectives appear in the Application, they will be marked as follows:

, coordinate
  adjectives

Se s a dlgnl, capb wkr.

    She is a diligent, capable worker.

SPELLING

Here are additional spelling words. Pronounce and spell each word aloud; then copy it in your own notebook, being sure that you spell it correctly. When you read the Application section of the lesson, watch for these words.

although	hinder	manual	recommended
excessive	incurring	professional	
exciting	lengthy	profitable	

VOCABULARY

Study the following definitions carefully, and notice how the words are used in the *SuperWrite* examples. Watch for these words in the Application section of the lesson.

excessive

More than what is proper or reasonable.

t rpnss h b xcsv.

The expenses have been excessive.

fiscal

Relating to financial matters.

fscl rspl s a ncsl.

Fiscal responsibility is a necessity.

incurring

Becoming subject to; bringing liability upon yourself.

e wnl l rduc csls wol ncr g prblms.

We want to reduce costs without incurring problems.

profit margin

Return on business investment after expenses are paid.

r prfl mrgn msl b ncresd.

Our profit margin must be increased.

(continued)

VOCABULARY continued

tax audit

An examination of tax records; a check of the accuracy of an account.

e r prpr g f a lx adl .

We are preparing for a tax audit.

APPLICATION

Time your reading speed with Document 1 before reading the remaining documents. Then write all four documents. Remember to insert the needed punctuation in Document 4 before typing it in the correct format. Be sure to note the length of the document and place it properly on the page.

DOCUMENT 34-1   Timed Reading

Goal: 1 minute, 26 seconds (130 words per minute)

, introductory

, introductory

, introductory

, coordinate adjectives

Mr Wayne Paul   d Mr P:
if u r msg fon cls wn u r awa fm u fon, u r likl msg bus. if u fon s lid up n clints cnl gl tru, u r prbl lus g prfls. if u r abl spek w onl l brus asocal l a lm, u ma b us g u lm mprprl.
l maks no sns l lry l cndcl brus lda w an oldald llfon sslm. brus lda dmnds mdrn, efsl cmunca$s.

, introductory	*wn u r awa fm u ofc, a gd sstm l alow u l fwrd u cls ull u rtrn. l l alrt u wn a scnd clr s try g l rec u. l l*
, series	*also alow u l spek w 2, 3, r evn m prsns l l tm.*
, introductory	*if u sstm s nt pvd g tes xtra fetrs, cl us tda. e l b gld l dmnstrat tes n mny*
, coordinate adjectives	*m intl g, xcit g fetrs tt c hlp u bus oprat m efctvl. e r*
; no conjunction	*opn fm 9 a m ull 6 p m wkdas; e r opn fm 9 a m ull 1 p m Sats.*
	u s

DOCUMENT 34-1   *Timed Reading*

Goal: 1 minute, 26 seconds (130 words per minute)

Mr. Wayne Paul
Dear Mr. Paul:

/If you are missing phone calls when you are away from your phone, you are likely missing business. If your phone is tied/up and clients cannot get through, you are probably losing profits. If you are able to speak with only one/business associate at a time, you may be using your time improperly.

(continued)

It makes no sense to try to/conduct business today with an outdated telephone system. Business today demands modern, efficient communications./

When you are away from your office, a good system will allow you to forward your calls until you/return. It will alert you when a second caller is trying to reach you. It will also allow you to speak/with two, three, or even more persons at one time.

If your system is not providing these extra features, call us/today. We will be glad to demonstrate these and many more interesting, exciting features that can help your/business operate more effectively. We are open from 9 a.m. until 6 p.m. weekdays; we are/open from 9 a.m. until 1 p.m. Saturdays. Yours sincerely, (189)

DOCUMENT 34-2   *Speed Builder*

, coordinate adjectives

, compound sentence

, coordinate adjectives

, extra

, introductory	nedls l sa, ts h lndd l dcres r prfl mrgn.
, introductory	l ts lm, l s ncsry l mak sgnfcnl Cangs n r mal q prcedrs n od l sav mny.
, introductory	frsl, onl ilms tl r cnsd
, introductory	urgnl l b snl xprs. scnd, locl dlvry srvc l b usd onl wn a cslmr fmll rqsls dlvry
, introductory	on t sam da. trd, al otr mal l b snl tru rqulr mal srvc.
; no conjunction	le me mfsiz tl I d nl wnl l hndr r opras; I smpl wS l rduc r xcsv mal csls. I fel tl e c acmplS a rdcS n xpnss wol ncrg majr prblms. if
, introductory	u wS l dscs ts w me, pl cl me l u cnv.

. request

l u pl dstrbut a cpy o t nu ruls t al mbrs o r stf pl ask tm t nsrt t ruls n tr prcedrs mnuls.

DOCUMENT 34-2   *Speed Builder*

To: Mr. Max Peters

From: Jackie Stevens

Date: —

Subject: Mailing Procedures

/Our business depends on prompt, timely delivery of mail. Our customers expect to receive their materials/quickly, and we have built our reputation on fast, dependable service.

During the past fiscal period,/however, we have experienced an extremely large increase in our mailing and delivery expenses. Our/costs have gone from $500 per week to well over $1,000 per week. Needless to say, this has/tended to decrease our profit margin.

At this time, it is necessary to make several significant/changes in our mailing procedures in order to save money.

First, only items that are considered urgent/will be sent Express. Second, local delivery service will be used only when a customer formally/requests delivery on the same day. Third, all other mail will be sent through regular mail service.

Let me emphasize/that I do not want to hinder our operation; I simply wish to reduce our excessive mail costs. I feel/that we can accomplish a reduction in expenses without incurring major problems. If you wish to/discuss this with me, please call me at your convenience.

Will you please distribute a copy of the new rules to all/members of our staff. Please ask them to insert the rules in their procedures manuals. (230)

Mr Louis Mattingly   d Mr M:

anul apoinlm

, introductory

lsl yr abl ts lm, u scduld an apoinlm w us l dscs u nvstms. u l rmbr tl e rcmndd tl u nvst n svrl

, coordinate adjectives

prflb, xcil g slks. e also sqd tl u rduc u nvstm n bnds.

, introductory

b flo g r advic, u w abl mpruv u prfls wrl prlcl g u rsorcs.

l s now lm l xmn u nvstms agn. r prfSl slf c rcmnd a no o imp slks n bnds tl e fel ma prduc evn gralr prfls f u ts yr.

e r lak g t lbrly o scdul g

, date

an apoinlm f u f Wed, June 3, l 4 pm. ts s t sam da n

(continued)

; no conjunction

lm u cam n lst yr; e hop l l b cnv f u agn. e l hold ts apoinlm f u ull June 1. l

. request

u pl cnfrm t lm n dal s sn s psb

u l

c: Miss Rose Lopez

DOCUMENT 34-3

Mr. Louis Mattingly
Dear Mr. Mattingly:

ANNUAL APPOINTMENT

/Last year about this time you scheduled an appointment with us to discuss your investments. You will remember that/we recommended that you invest in several profitable, exciting stocks. We also suggested that/you reduce your investment in bonds. By following our advice, you were able to improve your profits while/protecting your resources.

It is now time to examine your investments again. Our professional staff can/recommend a number of important stocks and bonds that we feel may produce even greater profits for you this year./

We are taking the liberty of scheduling an appointment for you for Wednesday, June 3, at 4 p.m. This/is the same day and time you came in last year; we hope it will be convenient for you again. We will hold this/appointment for you until June 1. Will you please confirm the time and date as soon as possible. Yours truly, c: Miss Rose Lopez (163)

Mr A B Peterson   d Mr P:

encd r u cmpd ncm lx paprs f t psl fscl yr. l u pl ril u sgntr n t dal l t blm o t scnd pag.

bcs tr w an Opam l l b uncsry f u l mak ny adSl pam l ts lm. s u l nol e h apld t fl aml o t Opam l u frsl eslmald pam f ts yr. trf u l nl h l mak an eslmald pam f ts yr ull June. rmbr l snd a Ck f $3 h on June 15 Sept 15 n Dec 15.

eC yr u msl fil a lngty dlald rpl on u prsnl rlirm pgm. ts rpl f t crnl yr s also encd. alto l s nl du ull July I sg tl u snd l now. t fm h b cmpd if al fgurs r crcl jsl sin dal n mal l.

t info on tes fms s basd on t info u gav us. l u pl rmn t fms

(continued)

crfl l b Sr tl tr r no errs. e sg tl u kep al t rcrds o bus xpnss f a mnmm o 7 yrs n cas tr Sd b a lx adl. if u h ny prblm Uslnd g ny o t fms pl cnld us.

s

encrs

DOCUMENT 34-4   Punctuation Check

Keyboarding Goal: 11 minutes (22 words per minute)

Mr. A. B. Peterson
Dear Mr. Peterson:

/Enclosed are your completed income tax papers for the past fiscal year. Will you please write your signature and the/date at the bottom of the second page. *(request)*

Because there was an overpayment, *(introductory)* it will be unnecessary for/you to make any additional payment at this time. As you will note, *(introductory)* we have applied the full amount of the/overpayment to your first estimated payment for this year. Therefore, *(introductory)* you will not have to make an/estimated payment for this year until June. Remember to send a check for $300 on June 15, September/15, and December 15. *(series)*

Each year you must file a lengthy, detailed *(coordinate adjectives)* report on your personal retirement/program. This report for the current year is also enclosed. Although it is not due until July, *(introductory)* I/suggest that you send it now. The form has been completed; *(no conjunction)* if all figures are correct, *(introductory)* just sign, date, and mail *(series)* it.

The/information on these forms is based on the information you gave us. Will you please examine the forms carefully/to be sure that there are no errors. *(request)* We suggest that you keep all records of business expenses for a minimum/of seven years in case there should be a tax audit. If you have any problem understanding any of/the forms, *(introductory)* please contact us. Sincerely, Enclosures (226)

SUPPLEMENTARY ACTIVITY

A Word to the Wise

Checking the Facts

/Before you type a document, you must determine if all the information included is accurate. The/words must be spelled correctly, of course, and the punctuation must be correct. But you must not overlook errors/in content. Verify all important facts by looking carefully at each sentence, assuming that it might/contain an error.

Dates and times often are sources of errors in business documents. For example, if your notes/read "The meeting will last until ten," determine if it is 10 a.m. or 10 p.m.

If your notes contain the/date "Tuesday, January 4," check your calendar to see if January 4 falls on a Tuesday.

If you/have written "The meeting will be in Portland," verify if the city is Portland, Oregon, or Portland, Maine./

If a document is to be sent to several people, be sure that the list of names is complete and accurate./An omitted name can cause a great deal of embarrassment.

The details in a business document are/extremely important. They affect goodwill as well as profits. Although both you and your employer are responsible/for producing accurate, complete documents, you must assume that you will be the person making the/final check. (222)

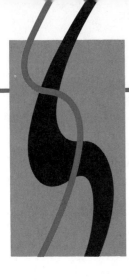

LESSON 35

SuperWrite REVIEW

Read the following words, referring to the key if necessary. Then write the words in your own notebook.

Word Beginning Be-

1. *blwen bcs bnet blev blra bgn g*

Word Beginning Trans-

2. *Tpir Tpos Tml Tcrib Tporl Tprla$*

Ow

3. *now flowr towr towl down town*

Ou

4. *hous ounc ouncs proud proudl dowl*

Qu

5. *ql qil qz aqir aqird nqir*

Key

1. between; because; beneath; believe; betray; beginning
2. transpire; transpose; transmit; transcribe; transport; transportation
3. now; flower; tower; towel; down; town
4. house; ounce; ounces; proud; proudly; doubt
5. quit; quite; quiz; acquire; acquired; inquire

PUNCTUATION

Compound Adjectives

When two or more words function as a single adjective <u>before</u> a noun, they are called a compound adjective.

Hyphenate a compound adjective before a noun.

l s a wl-non bld g.

It is a well-known building.

If the same words come <u>after</u> the noun, they are not a compound adjective. Do not use a hyphen.

t bld g s wl non.

The building is well known.

If the first word is an adverb ending in <u>ly</u>, do not use a hyphen whether the words come before or after the noun.

Se s a hil rgdd spekr.

She is a highly regarded speaker.

When a compound adjective appears in the Application, it will be marked as follows:

– compound
 adjective

l recd an up-l-t-mnl rpl.

We received an up-to-the-minute report.

SPELLING

Here are additional spelling words. Pronounce and spell each word aloud; then copy it in your own notebook, being sure that you spell it correctly. When you read the Application section of the lesson, watch for these words.

absence	employees
accommodate	expedite
acquiring	impede
compound interest	repeatedly
deliberation	transferred

VOCABULARY

Study the following definitions carefully, and notice how the words are used in the *SuperWrite* examples. Watch for these words in the Application section of the lesson.

certificate of deposit
: *A printed statement from a financial institution saying that a named person has a specified sum on deposit for a stated period.*

crlfcl o dpsl pd 9% inl.

certificate of deposit **paid 9 percent interest.**

compound interest
: *Interest computed on the accumulated interest as well as on the principal.*

e recd cmpnd inl on r dpsl.

We received compound interest **on our deposit.**

deliberation
: *Weighing in mind; thoughtful consideration for action.*

afl dlbra$, I dcidd l rlrn l scul.

After deliberation, **I decided to return to school.**

expedite
: *To carry out promptly; to accelerate.*

a gd cmunca$s sslm l hlp l rpdil u wk.

A good communications system will help to expedite **your work.**

impede
: *To slow progress; interfere with.*

a pur sslm l mped u wk.

A poor system will impede **your work.**

APPLICATION

Time your reading speed with Document 1 before reading the remaining documents. Then write all four documents. Remember to insert the needed punctuation in Document 4 before typing it in the correct format. Be sure to note the length of the document and place it properly on the page.

DOCUMENT 35-1 — Timed Reading

Goal: 1 minute, 4 seconds (130 words per minute)

Miss Beverley Medlin d Miss M:
her r sm tngs f u l tnk abl
cncrn q a llfon sslm.
(– compound adjective) a wl-dsind sslm alows
cslmrs l reC u wol b q Ifrd
rpeldl. l alows u mples l rdil
cls qkl b lCg 1 bln. l aclull
alows u l se t no o t clr bf u
ansr t fon.
ds ts sound lik u llfon sslm?
s u sslm mdrn n up l dal? r u
proud o u sslm? s l a hndy lul
(, compound sentence) tl hlps u xpdil u evda bus, r
ds l smlms sem l mped bus?

(continued)

, introductory

, coordinate adjectives

— compound adjective

if u sstm neds t b updatd, cl 1 o r reps tda n le us sho u r mdrn, up-t-dat fon sstms. u l prbbl b qit srprisd t hw rsnbl ty r pricd.

c u

DOCUMENT 35-1   *Timed Reading*

Goal: 1 minute, 4 seconds (130 words per minute)

Mrs. Beverley Medlin
Dear Mrs. Medlin:

/Here are some things for you to think about concerning a telephone system.

A well-designed system allows/customers to reach you without being transferred repeatedly. It allows your employees to redial calls quickly/by touching one button. It actually allows you to see the number of the caller before you answer the/phone.

Does this sound like your telephone system? Is your system modern and up to date? Are you proud of your system?/Is it a handy tool that helps you expedite your everyday business, or does it sometimes seem to impede /business?

If your system needs to be updated, call one of our representatives today and let us show you our/modern, up-to-date phone systems. You will probably be quite surprised at how reasonably they are priced./Cordially yours, (141)

DOCUMENT 35-2   *Speed Builder*

t Ms Maureen McGee   fm Nathan Cain

apointm t Iprtas dept
u mo ask g me if I wd accpt
an apointm t mng t Iprtas

depl arivd lda. I m v proud l
h b slcld l hd sC a lrg, imp
depl. uflnll, I cnl accpl.

   f sm lm I h b cns g rqsl g
a lev o absnc fm t co so tl I mil
cnlnu grdul wk n brus l sl clg
on a fl-lm bass. afl a gral del
o dlbraS, I h dcidd l prced w
ts cors o acS. trf, I l b uab l
accpl t asinm s mgr o t IprlaS
depl.

   I m v hpy l h wkd n sC a
wl-mngd org, n I l b rlrng l
wk her n abl a yr. I sncerl
hop tl t bord l cns alowg me
l srv n ts r sm smlr cpc l l
tl lm. l u pl xprs my apS l t
mbrs o t bord f tr cns.

, coordinate adjectives
, introductory
− compound adjective
, introductory
, introductory
− compound adjective
, compound sentence

To: Ms. Maureen McGee

From: Nathan Cain

Date: —

Subject: Appointment to Transportation Department

/Your memo asking me if I would accept an appointment to manage the transportation department arrived/today. I am very proud to have been selected to head such a large, important department. Unfortunately,/I cannot accept.

For some time I have been considering requesting a leave of absence from the/company so that I might continue graduate work in business at State College on a full-time basis. After a/great deal of deliberation, I have decided to proceed with this course of action. Therefore, I will be/unable to accept the assignment as manager of the transportation department.

I am very happy/to have worked in such a well-managed organization, and I will be returning to work here in about a/year. I sincerely hope that the board will consider allowing me to serve in this or some similar/capacity at that time. Will you please express my appreciation to the members of the board for their/consideration. (181)

DOCUMENT 35-3

---

l Mrs Nadine Short   fm Sam Wolfson

Ifr o fnds

lst evng t exec bord o t cntrl nvslm clb voLd l Ifr $5t fm r da-t-da savgs acounl l t NnSl bnk l a 6-mo crlfcl o dpsl l t sam bnk.

s u no, e now h abl $8t n r da-t-da savgs acounl. e d nl

– compound adjective

– compound adjective

, introductory

– compound adjective

; no conjunction

, introductory

pln l clos ts acount; e wnl l lev abl #3 t tr. hwev, e wnl l tak advntg o t hir int ral tl s now av fm a crtfd o dpsl. e l b abl l gt an int ral o 9% if e lev r mny on dpsl f 6 mos. n

, introductory

ad$, e l rec compound int rtr tn smp int. ts l mak gtt a dfrnc n t amt o int e ern; r pr acount

; no conjunction

pas onl 5%.

l u pl slp b t bnk s sn s

. request

psb n mak t Tfr tks f u hlp.

c: Mr Harold Jenkins

DOCUMENT 35-3

To: Mrs. Nadine Short

From: Sam Wolfson

Date: —

Subject: Transfer of Funds

/Last evening the executive board of the Central Investment Club voted to transfer $5,000 from/our day to day savings account at the International Bank to a six month certificate of deposit/at the same bank.

(continued)

As you know, we now have about $8,000 in our day-to-day savings account. We do/not plan to close this account; we want to leave about $3,000 there. However, we want to take advantage/of the higher interest rate that is now available from a certificate of deposit. We will be/able to get an interest rate of 9 percent if we leave our money on deposit for six months. In addition,/we will receive compound interest rather than simple interest. This will make quite a difference in the amount of/interest we earn; our present account pays only 5 percent.

Will you please stop by the bank as soon as possible and/make the transfer. Thanks for your help. c: Mr. Harold Jenkins (169)

DOCUMENT 35-4   Punctuation Check

Keyboarding Goal: 7 minutes (24 words per minute)

l Mr Mark Peters   fm J D Jones

Madison ofc towr
l t exec bord mel g on Fri May 4 e
dscsd aqir g t Madison ofc towr a wl
non bld g locald n downtown M. e ned
t xtra spac bcs r co h gron rpdl O t
psl 5 yrs.
t towr h 9 flors o ofc spac. t ofcs r
wl dsind n I h no doul tl t bld g wd
acmdal r neds f l lesl 20 yrs.
wn e ngird lsl yr t pr onrs w
ask g f $10 m f t towr. e fll tl t bld g
w smwl Opricd. l u pl gl n LC w tm

[handwritten shorthand notes]

agn l dlrmn tr ask g pric now. wn u
h ts info l u pl Iml l l Mr Doyle n
snd a cpy l me. e l tn dcid on r nxl
slp.

c: Mr D

DOCUMENT 35-4   *Punctuation Check*

Keyboarding Goal: 7 minutes (24 words per minute)

To: Mr. Mark Peters

From: J. D. Jones

Date: —

Subject: Madison Office Tower

/At the executive board meeting on Friday, May 4, *(date)* we discussed acquiring the Madison Office Tower, a/well-known *(compound adjective)* building located in downtown Madison. *(extra)* We need the extra space because our company has grown/rapidly over the past five years.

The tower has nine floors of office space. The offices are well designed, and *(compound sentence)* I have/no doubt that the building would accommodate our needs for at least 20 years.

When we inquired last year, *(introductory)* the present/owners were asking for $10 million for the tower. We felt that the building was somewhat overpriced. Will you/please get in touch with them again to determine their asking price now. *(request)* When you have this information, *(introductory)* will you please/transmit it to Mr. Doyle and send a copy to me. *(request)* We will then decide on our next step. c: Mr./Doyle (141)

SUPPLEMENTARY ACTIVITY

A Word to the Wise

Expediting Information in the Electronic Office

/You will find that your ability to use *SuperWrite* will help you to expedite the flow of information/in the electronic office.

Of course, you will use your ability to write quickly as you take dictation/of letters, memos, and reports. You will save your time and that of your employer because you can write notes quickly/and transcribe them later.

You will also use your *SuperWrite* ability to write instructions and messages./You will likely receive many telephone calls during the course of the day, and you will have to take messages/for one or more business associates. It is your responsibility to take a complete, accurate/telephone message, and you will be able to do so using *SuperWrite*. You will then type a well-organized/message and leave it for the person who was called.

You will also use your skill to make notes to yourself in the office./As you outline your work for the day, you will do so in *SuperWrite*. You will use your skill when you make lists of/needed supplies. Your employer may ask you to take care of three or four items. You will be able to jot down the/work easily in your notebook and then do the work in order of priority.

In the electronic/office of today, being able to make quick, legible notes is a great asset. You will find that you will use your/*SuperWrite* skills to help you expedite information throughout the day. (252)

LESSON G

TOWARD PERSONAL SUCCESS

TIME MANAGEMENT

Do you work hard every day but never seem to get your work completed? Do you spend hours on an assignment only to find that it is of little importance? Do you sometimes feel that you waste your time? If you answer yes to these questions, you should take a close look at the way you manage your time.

Setting Priorities

You have only a limited amount of time available, and you will likely never be able to do everything you would like to do. Therefore, you must decide which things are the most important and concentrate on them. This becomes a matter of placing a relative value on the things you need to do and taking care of the most important things first.

There may be jobs that you do not enjoy doing, and under ordinary circumstances, you might put them off and complete other work instead. However, the things that you put off may be the most important things that you should do. They should be given a high priority.

There may be jobs that you enjoy doing, but these jobs might be of little real value to you in your personal, business, or school life. These activities should receive a low priority.

When you decide which jobs to spend your time on, you should look at each one and determine its overall value in relation to the other jobs that you should do.

An easy method of setting priorities is to sit down every morning and make a list of the things that you should do during the day. Let's suppose that your list contains six jobs. When you have decided what should be done, you should rank the jobs in order of importance. The most important should be first, and the least important should be last.

You should then begin working at the top of the list. As you do each task, mark it off. Perhaps you will be able to mark off all the items, but you may complete only three or four. This is satisfactory, however, because you used your time on the items of most importance. If you do not complete one or two jobs at the bottom of the list, do not worry. They were the least important.

You will probably never complete every job you want to do. If you do the most important things every day, however, you will be successful. You will have set your priorities correctly, and you will have managed your time properly.

Using a Calendar

If you have ever missed an appointment or forgotten an interview, you know how important it is to keep an appointment calendar. It is a very good idea to keep a calendar so you will not miss important deadlines. A small calendar should be kept with you so that it will be handy whenever you need it.

You may prefer to use a daily calendar, a weekly calendar, or a monthly calendar. A daily calendar is often divided into hourly segments. A weekly calendar lets you see a full week at one time. A monthly calendar allows you to see a complete month. You should get a calendar that is large enough that you can jot down appointments in the proper place. Some businesses give away calendars as gifts. However, you can purchase a calendar in an office supply store for a few dollars.

Today, the use of electronic calendars is quite popular. If you have access to a computer on a regular basis, you can enter your appointments and manage your time by calling up the proper day on your electronic calendar. Many such calendars will remind you of daily appointments when you turn the computer on each day.

Some people try to keep several appointment calendars. They may have one at home, another at school, and a third in their briefcase. This is not a good idea. Whenever you fill in an appointment on one, you will have to fill it in on all the others if you are to be able to depend on them. Keep just one appointment calendar, and you will be able to rely on it.

When it is time to obtain a new calendar at the end of the year, you should file your old calendar. You will then be able to refer to it in later years to verify dates and other information.

Keeping a neat appointment calendar is a good idea for any student, but it will do little good if you do not use it every day. It is a very good idea to refer to it every morning to be sure that you remember any appointments for the day. Using an appointment calendar properly will help you to be at the proper place at the proper time, and it will be of assistance to you in meeting your deadlines. In addition, it can help you develop a reputation for dependability.

Discussion

Here are some questions for you to think about and discuss concerning time management.

1. Think about the work that you need to do today. What do you consider your top three priorities? Are you working on the jobs in this order? Why or why not?

2. Do you put in most of your time on the jobs that are of the most value to you? If not, why not?

3. Many people do not use a calendar to keep up with their daily events. Do you use a calendar? If you do not, why not? Have you found using a personal calendar a help in keeping up with your appointments and assignments? What hints could you give to someone for using a calendar effectively?

Case Study 1—It's All Important

Bill was recently hired to work as a management trainee for a major insurance company in Indianapolis. He is very conscientious and works extremely hard. He does not try to work on jobs in order of importance; he feels that every job at the company is important.

In the past few weeks, he has spent many extra hours at work, but he has not completed several projects on time. His employer asked him what the trouble was, and Bill said, "There are just not enough hours in the day."

Discussion Questions

1. In your opinion, what is Bill doing right? What is he doing wrong?

2. What corrective action would you suggest to help Bill get his important work done on time?

Case Study 2—It's a Date

In the past, Kathryn missed a number of appointments and was late to many others. She always made a note of the appointment, but she usually forgot to look at her notes.

In desperation, Kathryn decided to buy several appointment calendars. She placed a weekly calendar in her room at home. She placed a monthly calendar with her schoolbooks. She purchased a daily calendar and left it at the desk where she works two hours every afternoon. She even began using an electronic calendar on her computer at home. However, she did not buy a calendar to carry in her bag.

Kathryn tried to enter her appointments on the calendars, but she often forgot to make an entry. The result was that she missed her appointments just as she had before.

Discussion Questions

1. Kathryn made a number of errors. What were they?

2. Would you recommend that Kathryn keep a calendar in her bag?

3. Do you think it is a good idea to keep several calendars?

Activities

1. Write down a list of things that you should do today and rank them in order of importance.

2. Use the list you made in Activity 1 above. Work on the list in order of importance for the remainder of the day.

3. Obtain a calendar at a local store and enter your appointments and assignments for the remainder of the month. Then check the calendar every morning to be sure that you meet your deadlines and keep your appointments.

LESSON 36

SuperWrite REVIEW

Read the following words, referring to the key if necessary. Then write the words in your own notebook.

Short I Before a Vowel

1. *mleral mlerals ado folo rado vranc*

Word Beginning Pre-

2. *prpr prprd prdcl prdcld prvu prfr*

Word Ending -tion

3. *moS sluaS rlaS fuS nolaS snsaS*

Sh

4. *Se Sl Srl Sgr Sp Sap*
5. *cS brS crS clS plS iSu*

Key

1. material; materials; audio; folio; radio; variance
2. prepare; prepared; predict; predicted; preview; prefer
3. motion; situation; relation; fusion; notation; sensation
4. she; shall; shirt; sugar; ship; shape
5. cash; brush; crush; clash; plush; issue

KEYBOARDING STYLE

Report Format

In business, reports are often used to present information. There are many acceptable formats. Some styles allow for three levels of headings; others provide for four or more. In this text, we will use a style that allows for four—a title and three levels of subtitles.

Margins and Spacing. The report is printed using one-inch side margins and is double-spaced with indented paragraphs.

Title. The title is centered in capitals an inch and a half (10 lines) from the top of the paper.

Subtitles. A first-level subtitle is centered with the first letter of the first word and the first letter of all other main words capitalized.

A second-level subtitle (also called a side heading) is printed at the left margin and underlined. The first letter of the first word and the first letter of all other main words are capitalized. The second-level subtitle is underscored; however, it may appear in bold type for emphasis.

A third-level subtitle (also called a paragraph heading) is indented, underlined, and followed by a period. The first letter of the first word is capitalized. The text of the paragraph follows, beginning on the same line.

Subsequent pages. The second and subsequent pages are numbered in the top margin about a half inch from the top and right edges of the paper. If a word processor is used, automatic page numbering will usually place the number in this position, and the text will begin an inch from the top of the paper. If automatic page numbering is not used, a double space is left between the page number and the first line of the text.

An Example of Report Format

TITLE OF REPORT   line 10
DS

   In business, reports are often used to present information. The report is double-spaced, and paragraphs are indented. A business report is usually typed with one-inch side margins. The title begins an inch and a half from the top edge of the paper. Subsequent pages in the body of the report have a top margin of an inch. A bottom margin of about one inch is left on all pages.

1"

First-Level Subtitle

   A first-level subtitle is centered. The first letter of the first word and the first letter of other main words are capitalized.

<u>Second-Level Subtitle</u>

   Second-level subtitles are typed at the left margin and underlined. They may appear in bold type for emphasis. The first letter of the first word and the first letter of other main words are capitalized.

   <u>Third-level subtitle</u>. A third-level subtitle is indented, underlined, and followed by a period. Only the first letter of the first word is capitalized. The paragraph follows, beginning on the same line.

1"

SPELLING

Here are additional spelling words. Pronounce and spell each word aloud; then copy it in your own notebook, being sure that you spell it correctly. When you read the Application section of the lesson, watch for these words.

dispensed	physician
eligible	portfolio
generic	reimbursed
maintenance	spouse
pharmacy	underwritten

VOCABULARY

Study the following definitions carefully, and notice how the words are used in the *SuperWrite* examples. Watch for these words in the Application section of the lesson.

dispensed

Prepared and distributed, as in medication.

t drgs l b dspnsd tru u locl frmcy.

The drugs will be dispensed through your local pharmacy.

generic

General; not bearing a company name.

f sav gs, r frmcy uss gnrc drgs.

For savings, our pharmacy uses generic drugs.

reimbursed

Paid back; repaid an equal amount.

t co rmbrsd us f r xpnss.

The company reimbursed us for our expenses.

spouse

A wife or husband.

u spous s cvd b r ins.

Your spouse is covered by our insurance.

VOCABULARY continued

underwritten   *Assumed liability for; agreed to pay for.*

r ins s Urln b t co.

Our insurance is underwritten by the company.

APPLICATION

The Application contains an extended business report. First read it carefully. Then copy it in *SuperWrite* in your notebook, inserting the necessary punctuation. From your notes, type it in the business report format shown in this lesson.

NOTE: Business documents in the Application section of Lessons 36-40 are Punctuation Checks. Therefore, no reasons for using punctuation will appear in the *SuperWrite* documents. Punctuation marks and reasons for using the punctuation will continue to appear in the key for each document.

DOCUMENT 36
Extended Business Report   *Punctuation Check*

Keyboarding Goal: 24 minutes (24 words per minute)

t Pace co hlt ins pgm

al wkrs hu r mpld fl tm b t Pco r elgb f cvg U 1 o t co hlt ins plns. tr r 2 plns av. t frsl s t basc pln n t scnd s t hlt mantnc pln. U etr pln t fl tm wkr s cvd l no ol o pkl xpns. t spous n Cldrn o an mple ma b cvd U etr pgm f a sl mol fe.

(continued)

t basc pln

foSs n hsplls

U t basc pln u ma Cus ny foS r
hspll u wS. if t splir ds nl accpl
asinm o rpnss fm us u l b rsp f
cS pam f t srvc. u r rqrd l prpr a
fm n sbml l l us f pam. u l tn b
rmbrsd l r prscribd rals f rpnss
tl u ncr. if t splir Crgs m tn r
prscribd rals u r rsp f t dfrnc.

prscrpS drgs

prscrpS drgs ma b prCsd fm ny
frmcy. ty r cvd l a ral o 50% o tr
aclul csl. u ma us etr brnd nam r
gnrc drgs. hwev u msl prpr n mal
a fm l us n od l rec rmbrsm.

csl

t csl o t <u>basc</u> pln s Urln b t co f t fl lm wkr. t csl o inclg a spous s $25 pr mo. t csl f eC Cild s an adSl $25 pr mo. hwev a fml l nl b rqrd l pa m tn $1 h pr mo f cvg.

t hlt manlnnc pln

fs&s n hsplls

U t <u>hlt</u> manlnnc pln u u spous n u Cldrn msl us fs&s n hsplls lsld n t co porlfolo. tes r t co apruvd splirs. ny rxpnss ncrd l b pd n fl drcl l t fs& r hspll. u l nl b rsp f pa g c& f ny bls n u ned nl fl ol ny fms.

prscrp& drgs

prscrp& drgs r dspnsd tru t co frmcy.

(continued)

qnrc drgs. n od l ns̄r sav gs qnrc
drgs l b usd wnev psb.
    brnd nam drgs. brnd nam drgs
l b dspnsd onl n tos cass wr t
fs̄s̄ so drcls.

csl
    mple onl. t csl o t <u>hlt</u> manlnnc
pln s Urln b t co f t fl lm mple.
    fml mbrs. t csl o incl g al mbrs o
t imedal fml s $50 pr mo.

        slcs̄

    wn mples r hird on a fl lm bass
ty r gvn t ops̄ o slcl g 1 o t plns.
eC yr n Jan al fl lm mples ma elcl
l Cang fm 1 pln l anotr. afl Feb 1 no
Cangs otr tn t ads̄ r dles̄ o a fml
mbr ma b mad ull t flo g Jan.

adSl info

f adSl info n a co portfolo o ins cvg pl cl t prsnl ofc dur g rgulr wk g hrs. f ny otr mlerals pl slp b t prsnl ofc.

DOCUMENT 36
Extended Business Report
Punctuation Check

Keyboarding Goal: 24 minutes (24 words per minute)

THE PACE COMPANY HEALTH INSURANCE PROGRAM

/All workers who are employed full time by the Pace Company are eligible for coverage under one of/the company health insurance plans. There are two plans available. The first is the Basic Plan, and *(compound sentence)* the second/is the Health Maintenance Plan. Under either plan, *(introductory)* the full-time *(compound adjective)* worker is covered at no out-of-pocket *(compound adjective)* expense./The spouse and children of an employee may be covered under either program for a set monthly fee.

The/Basic Plan

Physicians and Hospitals

Under the Basic Plan, *(introductory)* you may choose any physician or hospital you/wish. If the supplier does not accept assignment of expenses from us, *(introductory)* you will be responsible for cash/payment for the service. You are required to prepare a form and submit it to us for payment. You will then be/reimbursed at our prescribed rates for expenses that you incur. If the supplier charges more than our prescribed/rates, *(introductory)* you are responsible for the difference.

Prescription Drugs

Prescription drugs may be purchased from any pharmacy./They are covered at a rate of 50 percent of their actual cost. You may use either brand-name *(compound adjective)* or/generic drugs. However, *(introductory)* you must prepare and mail a form to us in order to receive reimbursement.

(continued)

Cost

The cost/of the Basic Plan is underwritten by the company for the full-time *(compound adjective)* worker. The cost of including/a spouse is $25 per month. The cost for each child is an additional $25 per month./However, *(introductory)* a family will not be required to pay more than $100 per month for coverage.

The/Health Maintenance Plan

Physicians and Hospitals

Under the Health Maintenance Plan, *(introductory)* you, your spouse, and your children *(series)* must use/physicians and hospitals listed in the company portfolio. These are the company-approved *(compound adjective)* suppliers./Any expenses incurred will be paid in full direct to the physician or hospital. You will not be/responsible for paying cash for any bills, and *(compound sentence)* you need not fill out any forms.

Prescription Drugs

Prescription/drugs are dispensed through the company pharmacy.

Generic drugs.   In order to ensure savings, *(introductory)* generic drugs/will be used whenever possible.

Brand-name *(compound adjective)* drugs.   Brand-name *(compound adjective)* drugs will be dispensed only in those cases where the/physician so directs.

Cost

Employee only.   The cost of the Health Maintenance Plan is underwritten by the/company for the full-time *(compound adjective)* employee.

Family members.   The cost of including all members of the/immediate family is $50 per month.

Selection

When employees are hired on a full-time *(compound adjective)* basis, *(introductory)* they/are given the option of selecting one of the plans. Each year in January, *(introductory)* all full-time *(compound adjective)* employees may/elect to change from one plan to another. After February 1, *(introductory)* no changes other than the addition/or deletion of a family member may be made until the following January.

Additional/Information

For additional information and a company portfolio of insurance coverage,/*(introductory)* please call the personnel office during regular working hours. For any other materials, *(introductory)* please stop/by the personnel office. (564)

SUPPLEMENTARY ACTIVITY

A Word to the Wise

Body Position

/A lounge chair may be a good place to take a nap, but it is not a good place to work.

In an office you should be/constantly aware of your posture. If you lounge in your office chair, there will be two major consequences.

1. When/you do not sit erect with your feet on the floor, you will become tired fairly quickly. You put a strain on your/back muscles, and you develop back pain and become tired.
2. When you have poor posture, you present a very poor/image to those who see you. You project the image of someone who is not taking work very seriously/when you sit with your legs crossed or when you lean far back in your chair.

Choose a chair that is the right height for you. A tall/person needs a higher chair than someone who is short. It is a good idea to select an adjustable chair/so that you will be able to raise or lower the height to just the position that you prefer.

Find an adequate/surface when you take notes so that your notebook will lie flat. If you have to place your notebook on top of other materials/on the desk, you will prepare poor notes. Conditions should be ideal when you are at your desk, but you will often need/to take notes when you are away from your desk. If you have to take notes in the office of a business associate,/try to locate a proper writing surface. However, you should not write on the edge of another person's desk/without permission.

Sofas and large chairs are often found in executive offices. However, you should not/ choose these because they are quite often very low. It is difficult to write when sitting on a sofa or a low chair. You will probably have to place your notebook on your knee or on the arm of the chair, and neither choice is a/good one. If you must take notes while sitting on a low chair, sit erect near the front edge of the seat and keep your feet/close to the chair, not extended forward.

Proper body position not only makes your work easier, it also/helps you to project the right image. (365)

LESSON 37

SuperWrite REVIEW

Read the following words, referring to the key if necessary. Then write the words in your own notebook.

Oi

1. *oil soil soild boil boilr toil*

Oy

2. *boy boys loyl loylly royl njoym*

Ch

3. *Cef Cer Ck Cild Crm Cnc*
4. *reC teC teCrs aproC srC bnC*

Th

5. *tem tl bot pt rtr brtr*

Key

1. oil; soil; soiled; boil; boiler; toil
2. boy; boys; loyal; loyalty; royal; enjoyment
3. chief; cheer; check; child; charm; chance
4. reach; teach; teachers; approach; search; bench
5. theme; that; both; path; rather; brother

PUNCTUATION

Titles of Publications

Enclose the title of a part of a published work in quotation marks.

t lill o t Cpdr s "glg ahd."

The title of the chapter is "Getting Ahead."

t arlcl w nlilld "wkg f uslf."

The article was entitled "Working for Yourself."

Underscore or key in all capitals the titles of books, magazines, newspapers, or other separately published works.

e l red t lxl, wrld hslry.

We will read the text, World History.

t arlcl aperd n lim.

The article appeared in Time.

r locl nuspapr s t dal rprlr.

Our local newspaper is The Daily Reporter.

SPELLING

Here are additional spelling words. Pronounce and spell each word aloud; then copy it in your own notebook, being sure that you spell it correctly. When you read the Application section of the lesson, watch for these words.

abandon
already
choose
function key
initiate
opening menu
prompt
screen
scrolling
stacks

VOCABULARY

Study the following definitions carefully, and notice how the words are used in the *SuperWrite* examples. Watch for these words in the Application section of the lesson.

function key
A key on a computer keyboard that when struck causes the computer to perform a series of predetermined steps.

t fnc& ky css t cmpulr l prnl a dcum.

The function key causes the computer to print a document.

initiate
To cause to begin.

strik g / ky l in&al a srC o t dalabas.

Striking one key will initiate a search of the database.

opening menu
The beginning section of a computer program that allows the user to choose a desired application.

u ma slcl an apl fm t opn g mnu.

You may select an application from the opening menu.

prompt
A symbol on the computer screen that reminds the user to take some type of action.

strik t prpr ky wn t prmpl apers on t scren.

Strike the proper key when the prompt appears on the screen.

VOCABULARY continued

stacks

The area in a library in which reading matter is shelved.

u msl find t bk n t slks.

You must find the book in the stacks.

APPLICATION

The Application contains an extended business report. First read it carefully. Then copy it in *SuperWrite* in your notebook, inserting the necessary punctuation. From your notes, type it in a business report format.

DOCUMENT 37
Extended Business Report   Punctuation Check

Keyboarding Goal: 30 minutes (26 words per minute)

hw l us t librry cmpulr cllg

blwen Jan 5 1998 n Aug 25 1999 t sl unvrs l librry Ifrd t crd cllg rfrnc sslm l a cmpulr basd rfrnc sslm. t flo g info l hlp u n find g mleral n t librry.

find g a bk

t nu sslm s smlr l t old sslm. l local a bk n t librry u l lk f a lill

(continued)

a sbjcl r an atr. hwev u l insal a
srC tru t cmpulr dala bas rtr tn
tru crds.

frsl local a cmpulr lrmnl tl s nl
n us. swC l on if l s nl alrdy on. t
swC s locald l t bk o t lrmnl on t
lfl sid. an opn g mnu l aper on t
scren.

u l nolc tl tr s a fl alfblc kybord
tr r also a no o spSl kys l t lp o t
kybord. eC o tes kys h a spSl fncS
n s cld a fncS ky. t kys r clerl labld
n u Sd b abl l us tm esl afl u h rd ts
info.

local g a bk b lill

wn u no t lill o a bk hl fncS ky
no 1. wal f t prmpl on t scren lyp t
lill n hl t N ky. t dala bas l b srCd
n t fl bblogrfc rfrnc l aper on t
scren. jl down t rfrnc n us l l local

t bk n t stks us g t mps locald on eC flor.

f rmp if u wS l find t bk nlilld rcis g f njoym lyp t lill n fl. t cmpulr l rspnd w t fl bblogrfc rfrnc incl g t atr nam t pblSr n t plac n dal o pblcaS s wl s t rfrnc no.

local g a bk b sbjcl

if u wd lik l local a bk on a crln sbjcl slrik fncS ky no 2. wal f t prmpl lyp t sbjcl n slrik t N ky.

if t cmpulr rspnds tl no bk w found Ck t sbjcl w t rfrnc lxl nlilld sbjcl hd gs. a cpy s locald ner eC bnk o cmpulr lrmnls. if t wrd u Cos s nl a lsld sbjcl tr l b a crs-rfrnc tl l sg a no o smlr wrds l us l srC t dala bas.

(continued)

wn u h typd an apruvd sbjct nam t cmputr l lst a no o bks tt cntan ts sbjct mtr. jt down t rfrnc nos n local t bks n t stks.

f xmp if u ws l find a bk on t sbjct o xplor g f oil t rfrnc ttl l gv a no o sbjct hd gs tt u ma us. u ma find a ttl w a Cptr ntilld drlg f oil r anotr ntilld local g oil. etr Sd cntan t info u wnt.

local g a bk b atr

if u no t atr o a bk u ws l local strik fncS ky no 3. wat f t prmpt typ t lst nam o t atr n strik t N ky. if t lst nam s frl cmn typ t frst nam also.

t cmputr l rspnd w al t bks b tt prtculr atr. jt down t rfrnc nos n find t bk u wnt n t stks.

adSl fncSs

tr r a no o adSl fncSs tl u ma us s u srC f a lxl.

scrol g
if u h Cosn a sbjcl tl incls a gral mny rfrncs u ma ned l slp t rfrncs fm scrol g of t scren so tl u ma cpy tm.

slpg a scrol. red t mleral fm t vrus rfrncs s l apers on t scren. wn u se a rfrnc u wS l cpy slrik fncS ky no 4. ts l slp t scren fm scrol g.

rsum g a scrol. wn u h cped t mleral fm t scren n wS l se otr rfrncs slrik fncS ky no 4 onc agn. ts l cs t cmpulr l rsum scrol g.

(continued)

slp g

if u ws l abndn t fncs u r now
us g strik fncs ky no 5. ts l cs t
fncs l slp n t opn g mnu l aper
agn. u ma tn Cus anotr fncs.

ql g

wn u h fnsd us g t trmnl n ws
l ql strik fncs ky no 5 C l cs t
cmputr l slp t crnl fncs. u ma lev t
trmnl on r u ma swC l of.

ql g adSl hlp

ny mbr o t librry stf l b qld l
hlp u n local g mteral. if u h ny
trb find g wl u ned jst ask. e r her
l hlp u.

Keyboarding Goal: 30 minutes (26 words per minute)

HOW TO USE THE LIBRARY COMPUTER CATALOG

/Between January 5, 1998, and August 25, 1999, *(dates)* the State University/library transferred the card catalog reference system to a computer-based *(compound adjective)* reference system./The following information will help you in finding material in the library.

Finding a Book

The/new system is similar to the old system. To locate a book in the library, *(introductory)* you will look for a/title, a subject, or an author. *(series)* However, *(introductory)* you will initiate a search through the computer data base/rather than through cards.

First, *(introductory)* locate a computer terminal that is not in use. Switch it on if it is not already/on. The switch is located at the back of the terminal on the left side. An opening menu will/appear on the screen.

You will notice that there is a full alphabetic keyboard; *(no conjunction)* there are also a number of/special keys at the top of the keyboard. Each of these keys has a special function and is called a function key. The keys/are clearly labeled, and *(compound sentence)* you should be able to use them easily after you have read/this information.

Locating a Book by Title

When you know the title of a book, *(introductory)* hit function key number 1. Wait for the prompt on/the screen, type the title, and hit the enter key. *(series)* The data base will be searched, and *(compound sentence)* the full bibliographic/reference will appear on the screen. Jot down the reference, and *(compound sentence)* use it to locate the book in the stacks, using the/maps located on each floor. *(extra)*

For example, *(introductory)* if you wish to find the book entitled Exercising for Enjoyment,/*(underscore book title-extra)* type the title in full. The computer will respond with the full bibliographic reference, including/the author name, the publisher, and the place and date of publication *(extra-series)*, as well as the reference number./*(extra)*

Locating a Book by Subject

If you would like to locate a book on a certain subject, *(introductory)* strike function key number/2. Wait for the prompt, type the subject, and strike the enter key. *(series)*

If the computer responds that no book was found, *(introductory)* check/the subject with the reference text entitled Subject Headings. *(underscore book title)* A copy is located near each bank of/computer terminals. If the word you chose is not a listed subject, *(introductory)* there will be a cross-reference that will/suggest a number of similar words to use to search the data base.

(continued)

When you have typed an approved subject name, *(introductory)* the/computer will list a number of books that contain this subject matter. Jot down the reference numbers, and *(compound sentence)*/locate the books in the stacks.

For example, *(introductory)* if you wish to find a book on the subject of exploring for oil, *(extra)* the/reference text will give a number of subject headings that you may use. You may find a text with a chapter/entitled "Drilling for Oil" *(quote chapter title)* or another entitled "Locating Oil." *(quote chapter title)* Either should contain the information you want./

Locating a Book by Author

If you know the author of the book you wish to locate, *(introductory)* strike function key/number 3. Wait for the prompt, type the last name of the author, and strike the enter key. *(series)* If the last name is fairly/common, *(introductory)* type the first name also.

The computer will respond with all the books by that particular author. Jot/down the reference numbers, and *(compound sentence)* find the book you want in the stacks.

Additional Functions

There are a number of/additional functions that you may use as you search for a text.

Scrolling

If you have chosen a subject that/includes a great many references, *(introductory)* you may need to stop the references from scrolling off the screen so that you/may copy them.

Stopping a scroll.   Read the material from the various references as it appears on the/ screen. When you see a reference you wish to copy, *(introductory)* strike function key number 4. This will stop the screen from scrolling./

Resuming a scroll.   When you have copied the material from the screen and wish to see other references,/*(introductory)* strike function key number 4 once again. This will cause the computer to resume scrolling.

Stopping

If you wish to/abandon the function you are now using, *(introductory)* strike function key number 5. This will cause the function to stop, and *(compound sentence)* the/opening menu will appear again. You may then choose another function.

Quitting

When you have finished using/the terminal and wish to quit, *(introductory)* strike function key number 5, which will cause the computer to stop the current/function. *(extra)* You may leave the terminal on, or *(compound sentence)* you may switch it off.

Getting Additional Help

Any member of the/library staff will be glad to help you in locating material. If you have any trouble finding what you/need, *(introductory)* just ask. We are here to help you. (785)

SUPPLEMENTARY ACTIVITY

A Word to the Wise

Confidential Material

/It is very important to keep confidential material confidential. In an office you will have/ access to information of such a nature.

When a business is negotiating to purchase property,/for example, the figures should not be made available to the public. Matters of a legal nature should/be kept strictly confidential. Payroll and tax records are generally not public knowledge.

When you deal with/confidential material, you should be very careful. If you are working on a confidential/document and someone stops at your desk, take steps to ensure that the person does not read the material. If you are/working on a word processor, the screen may be visible to visitors. Should someone stop at your desk, quietly/turn off the monitor. It is important, of course, to do this in an inoffensive way. If you rush to/cover up documents or shove papers into a drawer, the person will feel that you doubt his or her loyalty. One way/to direct a person's attention away from materials you are working on is to rise and greet the/caller and direct him or her politely to a chair away from your desk.

If you must leave your desk while you are/working on a confidential document on a word processor, you should not leave the computer on. Transfer the/document to a memory device and switch the computer off before leaving the desk. You will be able/to retrieve the document quickly when you return. If you leave the monitor on, anyone who comes into/ your office will be able to read the material. If you simply turn the monitor off, another/ person may switch it back on and read the material. If you store your document but leave the computer on, a/dishonest visitor could view your directory and retrieve a confidential item.

Whenever you leave your/desk, it is a good idea to lock it. In addition, file cabinets containing sensitive documents should/be kept locked.

You are responsible for many items that are of a confidential nature. Take this/respon-sibility very seriously. (387)

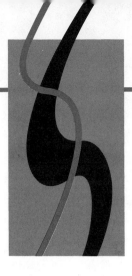

LESSON 38

SuperWrite REVIEW

Read the following words, referring to the key if necessary. Then copy the words in your own notebook.

Mem

1. *mbr mbrs mriz mrzas rmbr rmbrs*
2. *rmbrd mry mrb cmral cmrald cmras*

Word Ending -ment

3. *jgm murm nvlvm asinm gvrnm lrelm*

Word Ending -ble

4. *rlib rlibl slab slbl ralb snsb*

Word Ending -ity

5. *cmdl cmdls sulbl psbl psbls vrils*

Key

1. member; members; memorize; memorization; remember; remembers
2. remembered; memory; memorable; commemorate; commemorated; commemoration
3. judgment; movement; involvement; assignment; government; treatment
4. reliable; reliability; stable; stability; ratable; sensible
5. commodity; commodities; suitability; possibility; possibilities; varieties

KEYBOARDING STYLE

Citations

In business reports, you may wish to refer to information from a published source such as a textbook, a reference book, or a journal article. In many business documents today, citations are used instead of footnotes. A citation is a direct reference to the bibliography or list of references.

A citation is typed in parentheses following the information for which the reference is supplied. The author's last name is included, followed by the year of publication and the page number(s) where the information was found. For example, if the material in this paragraph were from page 92 of a text by Gerald A. Smith, the citation would look like this: (Smith, 1987, 92). Note that the last name of the author is used, followed by a comma, the year of publication, followed by a comma, and the page reference.

A list of all references, including complete bibliographic information, will be typed at the end of the report.

SPELLING

Here are additional spelling words. Pronounce and spell each word aloud; then copy it in your own notebook, being sure that you spell it correctly. When you read the Application section of the lesson, watch for these words.

charities
eventuality
indefinitely
intestate
jurisdiction
levied
livelihood
nonprofit
possessions
priority

VOCABULARY

Study the following definitions carefully, and notice how the words are used in the *SuperWrite* examples. Watch for these words in the Application section of the lesson.

eventuality — *A possible occurrence; outcome.*

t evnlull s tll u l lv
f mny yrs.

The eventuality is that you will live
for many years.

inheritance tax — *An assessment imposed on property willed to another; a tax on an estate.*

t la rqrs tl t nhrlnc lx
b pd frsl.

The law requires that the inheritance tax
be paid first.

intestate — *Having no legal will.*

if u di nlslal, otrs l
dlrmn hw u prprly l
b dslrbuld.

If you die intestate, others will
determine how your property will
be distributed.

jurisdiction — *Authority or control; the right or power to govern and apply the law.*

t mlr s U t jrsdc$ o t
corl.

The matter is under the jurisdiction of the
court.

levied *Collected a tax or assessment.*

t sl lved t lx on t prprly.

The state levied the tax on the property.

APPLICATION

The Application contains an extended business report. First read it carefully. Then copy it in *SuperWrite* in your notebook, inserting the necessary punctuation. From your notes, type it in a business report format.

DOCUMENT 38
Extended Business Report   *Punctuation Check*

Keyboarding Goal: 29 minutes (26 words per minute)

pln g u eslal

no 1 liks l spek o sC tngs bl evon msl pln f dt. t evnlull s tl l l ocr n t dslnl fulr tr s also a psbl tl l ma ocr sn. t wis prsn maks crf cmp plns abl hw hs r hr psSs l b dslrbuld afl dt. if tr r tos hu dpnd on u f tr livlhd u l wnl l b Sr tl ty r prlcld agnsl fnnSl ls. if u wSl lev mny l crln pep r orgs u Sd mak u wSs non legll n t fm o a l. if u di nlslal otrs nl u l dlrmn hw u

(continued)

prprty l b dstrbuld. (Jones, 1989, 34)
her r sm tngs u Sd kep n mind
wn u r plng u estat.

u imedat fml

u frst cncrn s prbbl u imedat fml.
if u r lik most otr pep u spous n u
Cldrn r u frst prir l. u spous Sd b
ab l cntnu t crnt styl o lif wol b g
fcd l mak Cangs. Cldrn hu r n scul
Sd b ab l cntnu n t sam sculs wol
NrpS. tr Sd b adql ncm l cr f al
mbrs o u imedat fml. u ma wnt l
pvd f u spous ndfntt n f u Cldrn
utl ty r slf-sport g.

lif ins
t mjrt o yng slf sport g pep mst
sply tes neds w lif ins. tr r a no o

typs o ins eC ofr g spsl felrs. t idea
s l gl enf ins l lak cr o basc neds
l t mosl rsnb csl. a gd lif ins plcy
s a basc elm n mosl eslals.

otr ilms o vlu
    otr ilms C u msl cns r u hous u
cr n ny otr prprly o majr vlu s l
s prsnl prprly. tes ilms usull r
lfl l mbrs o t imedal fml.

        u xlndd fml

    u ma wS l lev prprly l mbrs o u
xlndd fml. u xlndd fml mil incl
grndprnls anls uncls csns n otr rllvs.
    n mosl cass sply g ncs ls s nl rqrd
f t xlndd fml. if sC a prsn s a mbr
o u houshold hwev u mil ned l cns
ts prsn wn u prCs lif ins. n sm cass

(continued)

majr ilms r prsnl prprly ma b lfl l
a mbr o t xlndd fml.

Crls n nnprfl nsllus

most pep h l r m Crls l C ty gv
sm typ o sporl. mny pep ws l gv
mny l a rlgus r sosl org. wn pln g
an eslal a prsn sd cns wl ilms r hw
mC mny sd b lfl l sC an org.

ncm prprly
n sm cass a pec o prprly tl
prducs ncm s an xclnl Coic l gv l
a Crl r nnprfl org. a rnll hous s a
gd xmp. hwev sC a dcs sd b dscsd
w an ofcr o t nsllus l C u ws l mak
t gfl. t ofcr l b ab l ll u if t gfl s
aprpral. (Brown, 1988, 92)

otr ilms o vlu

sm pep wS l gv otr arlcls o vlu
l Crls r nnprfl agnces. ts mil incl
arlwk a rr bk r a pec o julry.

otr cnss

tr r mny otr ilms tl u Sd kep
n mind wn u r plng u eslal. her
r 2 o tm.

lxs

a majr cns wn plng an eslal s
an nhrlnc lx. lxs r lved l vry g
rals fm 1 lxg jrsdcS l anotr. mosl
pep wS l kep al nhrlnc lxs s lo s
psb. gd plng c hlp a prsn aSr tl
prprly s dslrbuld prprl n tl tr s
adql cS l pa al ncsry lxs.

(continued)

pln erl

most cnss l b o an ndvdul natr n no 2 estats r likl l b xcll t sam. t cmn elm hwev s tl plng Sd b dn erl. l c esl b lu lat l pln l c nvr b lu erl. tr s no sbstltul f wl mad plns.

DOCUMENT 38
Extended Business Report   *Punctuation Check*

Keyboarding Goal: 29 minutes (26 words per minute)

PLANNING YOUR ESTATE

/No one likes to speak of such things, but *(compound sentence)* everyone must plan for death. The eventuality is that it will/occur in the distant future; *(no conjunction)* there is also a possibility that it may occur soon. The wise person makes/careful, complete *(coordinate adjectives)* plans about how his or her possessions will be distributed after death. If there are those who/depend on you for their livelihood, *(introductory)* you will want to be sure that they are protected against financial loss. If/you wish to leave money to certain people or organizations, *(introductory)* you should make your wishes known legally in/the form of a will. If you die intestate, *(introductory)* others, not you, *(extra)* will determine how your property will be/distributed. (Jones, 1989, 34)

Here are some things you should keep in mind when you are planning your estate./

Your Immediate Family

Your first concern is probably your immediate family. If you are like/most other people, *(introductory)* your spouse and your children are your first priority. Your spouse should be able to continue/the current style of life without being forced to make changes. Children who are in school should be able to continue/in the same schools without interruption. There should be adequate income to care for all members of your/immediate family. You may want to provide for your spouse indefinitely and for your children until/they are self-supporting.

Life Insurance

The majority of young, self-supporting *(coordinate and compound adjectives)* people must supply these needs/with life insurance. There are a number of types of insurance, each offering special features. *(extra)* The idea/is to get enough insurance to take care of basic needs at the most reasonable cost. A good life insurance/policy is a basic element in most estates.

Other Items of Value

Other items which you/must consider are your house, your car, and any other property of major value, *(series-extra)* as well as personal/property. These items usually are left to members of the immediate family.

Your Extended/Family

You may wish to leave property to members of your extended family. Your extended family/might include grandparents, aunts, uncles, cousins, and other relatives. *(series)*

In most cases, *(introductory)* supplying necessities/is not required for the extended family. If such a person is a member of your household, *(introductory)* however,/*(extra)* you might need to consider this person when you purchase life insurance. In some cases major items or/personal property may be left to a member of the extended family.

Charities and Nonprofit/Institutions

Most people have one or more charities to which they give some type of support. Many people wish/to give money to a religious or social organization. When planning an estate, *(introductory)* a person should/consider what items or how much money should be left to such an organization.

Income Property

In some/cases, *(introductory)* a piece of property that produces income is an excellent choice to give to a charity/or nonprofit organization. A rental house is a good example. However, *(introductory)* such a decision should/be discussed with an officer of the institution to which you wish to make the gift. The officer will be/able to tell you if the gift is appropriate. (Brown, 1988, 92)

Other Items of Value/

Some people wish to give other articles of value to charities or nonprofit agencies. This might/include artwork, a rare book, or a piece of jewelry. *(series)*

Other Considerations

There are many other items/that you should keep in mind when you are planning your estate. Here are two of them.

(continued)

Taxes

A major consideration/when planning an estate is an inheritance tax. Taxes are levied at varying rates from one taxing/jurisdiction to another. Most people wish to keep all inheritance taxes as low as possible. Good/planning can help a person assure that property is distributed properly and that there is adequate/cash to pay all necessary taxes.

Plan Early

Most considerations will be of an individual/nature, and *(compound sentence)* no two estates are likely to be exactly the same. The common element, however, *(extra)* is that/ planning should be done early. It can easily be too late to plan; *(no conjunction)* it can never be too early. There is no/substitute for well-made *(compound adjective)* plans. (765)

SUPPLEMENTARY ACTIVITY

A Word to the Wise

Responsibility

/When your employer gives you a job to do, it is your responsibility to complete it. If you do not/finish the work, you have not met your responsibility. If you do not do the work accurately, you have/not met your responsibility. If you do not do the work in the allotted time, you have not met your/responsibility. Occasionally almost everyone will have trouble meeting a goal, but if it happens/repeatedly, you may well be looking for employment elsewhere.

If your employer gives you an assignment and/for any reason you do not complete it, it is very likely that your employer will have to do the job./No employer wants to have to complete work that was delegated to an employee.

Responsibility/does not include only those jobs that your employer assigns to you; it also includes those jobs that you assign/yourself. When you see a job that needs to be done, you should take the responsibility of doing it before/someone points it out to you.

Accept responsibility willingly. Remember to do the jobs that are/assigned to you completely and in a timely fashion. Look for other jobs that need to be done and complete them on/your own. Soon you will develop the reputation that you are indeed a responsible person. (238)

LESSON 39

SuperWrite REVIEW

Read the following words, referring to the key if necessary. Then write the words in your own notebook.

Word Beginning Under-

1. *Ulak Ulo Udvd Uslm Uslnd Usld*

Word Endings -ious, -eous, -ous, -us

2. *famus slalus crlus crlusl vrus vrusl*

Word Ending -ly

3. *onsll soll lrmndusl cAull panslak gl Srl*

4. *hrdl brl grall opnl crfl rdl*

Word Beginning De-

5. *dvol dvold dlil dlild dlilf dplel*

Key

1. undertake; undertow; underdeveloped; understatement; understand; understood

2. famous; status; courteous; courteously; various; variously

3. honestly; solely; tremendously; casually; painstakingly; surely

4. hardly; barely; greatly; openly; carefully; readily

5. devote; devoted; delight; delighted; delightful; deplete

KEYBOARDING STYLE

References

A list of references is a complete listing of all sources used in a report. The list is keyed on the last page of the body of the report if it can be completed on the page. Otherwise, it should begin on a new page.

The heading REFERENCES is keyed in capital letters a double space below the last line of the body of the report.

The sources are alphabetized according to the last name of the author. The first line of each reference begins at the left margin, and subsequent lines are indented five spaces. Each reference is single-spaced, and there is a double space between references.

Here is an example of a list of references keyed below the last line of a report.

```
                              REFERENCES    line 10
                                  DS
        Brown, William Carl.  "Insuring Your Family."  Insurance Today.
             September 1997, 34-46.

        Green, Miller C. Your Future.  Denver: Mountain State Publishers,
             1995.

        Jones, Anna S. "Excavation in America."  Exploring the World,
             May 1998, 24.

        Menendez, Rafaella.  Oil Exploration in New Mexico.  Santa Fe:
             The Western Press, 1997.

        Smith, Gerald A. Exploring for Gold. Boston: National Publishing
             Company, 1996.
```

SPELLING

Here are additional spelling words. Pronounce and spell each word aloud; then copy it in your own notebook, being sure that you spell it correctly. When you read the Application section of the lesson, watch for these words.

burden	impractical	rectify	tremendously
duration	incumbent	severity	
expedient	queue	time-consuming	

VOCABULARY

Study the following definitions carefully, and notice how the words are used in the *SuperWrite* examples. Watch for these words in the Application section of the lesson.

duration
: *A period of time; until the end.*

t wal w 1 mnl n duraS.

The wait was one minute in duration.

expedient
: *Appropriate for achieving a goal quickly.*

e msl find an xpedent sluS.

We must find an expedient solution.

incumbent
: *Taken as an obligation or duty.*

l s ncmbnl on us l rduc csls.

It is incumbent on us to reduce costs.

queue
: *A system whereby those in line are accommodated in order; a waiting line.*

tr s no qu f olgo g cls.

There is no queue for outgoing calls.

rectify
: *To correct; adjust.*

e msl rclfy t sluaS.

We must rectify the situation.

APPLICATION

The Application contains an extended business report. First read it carefully. Then copy it in *SuperWrite* in your notebook, inserting the necessary punctuation. From your notes, type it in a business report format.

DOCUMENT 39
Extended Business Report   Punctuation Check

Keyboarding Goal: 21 minutes (28 words per minute)

rpt on t Smith tlfon sstm

t S tlfon sstm w nstlld n t vrus ofcs o t cntrl sals co bgn g Jan 2 1980. (Carson, 1980, 42) t flog s a rvu o t status o t sstm s wl s rcmnda&s f t futr.

cntrl swCbord

al ncmg cls n eC ofc r rould tru a cntrl swCbord. l s nt ucmn f a clr t h t wal f an xtndd perod bf t cl s ansrd. t lngt o t wal dpnds on t tm o t cl. t most trblsm hrs r fm 9 a m ull 11 a m n fm 4 pm ull 5 pm.

Ifrd cls

bcs al cls r ansrd b an opratr eC cl msl b Ifrd ts also rqrs xtra tm. O a 2 wk perod t avrg ncmg cl tk almost 2 mnts bf t clr reCd t crct prsn. t locl ndstry stndrd s ls tn 1 mnt. (Williams, 1998, 3)

olsid lins

alto olsid cls c b mad wol t ncs t o dil g t opratr olgo g cls d go tru t cntrl sstm. r pep ofn h t wal f an olsid lin t bcm av. ocaSll t wal s m tn a mnt n duraS. tr s no qu sstm n t prsn smpl msl pk up t fon wn a lin s av. ts c b an anoy g xperenc n t c b trmndusl tm-
cnsum g.

(continued)

lng-dstnc cls

al lng-dstnc cls r placd O t rgulr lng-dstnc ntwk l t pr lm. evn cls l r otr ofcs msl b hndld n ts mnr. r lng-dstnc tlfon bls r n rcs o $1 t pr mo n eC o r ofcs. ts csl cnl b jslfid now n l apers tl l l ncres n t fulr uls a Cang s mad.

fwrd g cls

wn 1 o r pep s awa fm hs r hr dsk t opralr h no wa l fwrd cls almtcll. n ad& l s mprctcl f eC o r pep l cl t opralr n rqsl tl cls b fwrdd. l wd creal an xtra brdn on t opralr s wl. an xpedent altrntv msl b found.

lm usd n dil g

mC o r bus dpnds on llfon sals n r slf msl spnd a gral del o lm dil g cls n rdil g cls wn a lin s bsy. r pr sslm h no sped dil g r rdil g fclr.

rcmnda$

t $ sslm w a dpndb ef$l sslm wn l w nslld bl l s hrdl capb o gv g us t lyp o srvc e ned lda. l s ncmbnl on us l rclfy t prblms e r now facg.

t cntrl sals co $d cntcl a no o splirs n oblan bds on rplac g t nlir llfon sslm. bcs o t svr l o t pr sluas ts $d b dn w al du hasl.

(continued)

rfrncs

Carson, Forrest R. hstry o t cnlrl sals
co. Milwaukee: globl pblsg co, 1980.
Williams, Reba A. ndstry slndrds n
Medford. Chicago: cnlrl prs, 1998.

DOCUMENT 39
Extended Business Report   Punctuation Check

Keyboarding Goal: 21 minutes (28 words per minute)

REPORT ON THE SMITH TELEPHONE SYSTEM

/The Smith telephone system was installed in the various offices of the Central Sales Company beginning/January 2, 1980. *(date)* (Carson, 1980, 42) The following is a review/ of the/status of the system as well as recommendations for the future.

Central Switchboard

All incoming/calls in each office are routed through a central switchboard. It is not uncommon for a caller to have to wait/for an extended period before the call is answered. The length of the wait depends on the time of the call./The most troublesome hours are from 9 a.m. until 11 a.m. and from 4 p.m. until 5 p.m./

Transferred Calls

Because all calls are answered by an operator, *(introductory)* each call must be transferred; *(no conjunction)* this also requires/extra time. Over a two-week *(compound adjective)* period, *(introductory)* the average incoming call took almost two minutes before the/caller reached the correct person. The local industry standard is less than one minute. (Williams, 1998, 3)/

Outside Lines

Although outside calls can be made without the necessity of dialing the operator,/*(introductory)* outgoing calls do go through the central system. Our people often have to wait for an outside line to become/available. Occasionally, *(introductory)* the wait is more than a minute in duration. There is no queue system, and *(compound sentence)* the/person simply must pick up the phone when a line is available. This can be an annoying experience,/and *(compound sentence)* it can be tremendously time-consuming

Long-Distance Calls

All long-distance calls are placed over the regular/long-distance network at the present time. Even calls to our other offices must be handled in this/manner. Our long-distance telephone bills are in excess of $1,000 per month in each of our offices./This cost cannot be justified now, and *(compound sentence)* it appears that it will increase in the future unless a change is made./

Forwarding Calls

When one of our people is away from his or her desk, *(introductory)* the operator has no way to forward/calls automatically. In addition, *(introductory)* it is impractical for each of our people to call the/operator and request that calls be forwarded. It would create an extra burden on the operator as well./An expedient alternative must be found.

Time Used in Dialing

Much of our business depends on telephone/sales, and *(compound sentence)* our staff must spend a great deal of time dialing calls and redialing calls when a line is busy. Our present/system has no speed dialing or redialing feature.

Recommendation

The Smith system was a dependable,/efficient *(coordinate adjectives)* system when it was installed, but *(compound sentence)* it is hardly capable of giving us the type of service we/need today. It is incumbent on us to rectify the problems we are now facing.

The Central Sales Company/should contact a number of suppliers and obtain bids on replacing the entire telephone system./Because of the severity of the present situation, *(introductory)* this should be done with all due haste.

REFERENCES

Carson,/Forrest R. History of the Central Sales Company. Milwaukee: Global Publishing Company, 1980./

Williams, Reba A. Industry Standards in Medford. Chicago: Central Press, 1998. (578)

SUPPLEMENTARY ACTIVITY

A Word to the Wise

Office Talk

/"Have you heard . . . ?" "Did you know that . . . ?" "Wait till you hear what I just heard."
Do these words sound familiar? They are all too often/heard in business today.

When you work in an office, you will hear many things that may be of interest to you/
and your friends. However, information that is heard in an office is often of a confidential
nature./In addition, information that may not be classified as confidential is sometimes of a
sensitive/nature. Even business that would not be considered sensitive is often considered
private. You should not/discuss the business that goes on in your office with outsiders or
with others who work in the same company. It/is a serious mistake to do so.

If you discuss all the previous day's business, no matter how sensitive,/with your friends,
you will soon become known as someone who may not be trustworthy. A person who
develops this/kind of reputation in business will seldom be promoted into a position of
greater responsibility./

How do you keep your friends from questioning you about office matters that should be
kept confidential?/When a question is asked, simply reply, "I'm sorry, I cannot discuss that."
Just one time is usually/enough to stop that type of questioning. When your friends understand that you will not discuss business transacted in your/office, they will respect you. In
addition, your employer will respect you, and you will position yourself as/a person who is
responsible—one who can be trusted with even more responsibility. (278)

LESSON 40

SuperWrite REVIEW

Read the following words, referring to the key if necessary. Then copy the words in your own notebook.

Word Beginning Trans-

1. *Tporl Tprtas TS TSl Tml Tmld*

Word Beginning Pro-

2. *prduc prtcl prtc$ prced prcedr prcs*

Word Beginning Pre-

3. *prdcl prclud prcludd prsum prrgslr prlmnry*

Oi

4. *nois noisy join soil boil void*

Oy

5. *loyl royl boy boys toy njoy*

1. transport; transportation; transition; transitional; transmit; transmitted
2. produce; protect; protection; proceed; procedure; process
3. predict; preclude; precluded; presume; preregister; preliminary
4. noise; noisy; join; soil; boil; void
5. loyal; royal; boy; boys; toy; enjoy

SPELLING

Here are additional spelling words. Pronounce and spell each word aloud; then copy it in your own notebook, being sure that you spell it correctly. When you read the Application section of the lesson, watch for these words.

adequate
adjacent
amenable
conform
integral
plain
preclude
site
transmitted
zoning

VOCABULARY

Study the following definitions carefully, and notice how the words are used in the *SuperWrite* examples. Watch for these words in the Application section of the lesson.

adjacent

Close to; lying near; next to.

t lnd s ajacnl l a prk.

The land is adjacent to a park.

amenable

Willing to follow advice or suggestion.

e r amenb l u prposls.

We are amenable to your proposals.

flood plain

An area bordering a body of water, subject to flooding.

t lnd s nl n a fld plan.

The land is not in a flood plain.

VOCABULARY continued

integral

Necessary for completeness.

*lndscapg s an nlgrl prl o
r plns.*

Landscaping is an integral part of
our plans.

preclude

*To make impossible by previous action;
to prevent.*

*gd plng Sd prclud majr
prblms.*

Good planning should preclude major
problems.

APPLICATION

The Application contains an extended business report. First read it carefully. Then copy it
in *SuperWrite* in your notebook, inserting the necessary punctuation. From your notes, type
it in a business report format.

prposl f Spg cntr
8t fft ave
Lexington, PA

t Gilbreth co locald l 121 Baker st
n L PA prposs l bld a Spg cntr l
8t fft ave C s l t Nsc& o fft ave n
Green st n sbrbn L. t prlmnry plns
C wr mad b Yale asocals r cmpd n
h b Imld sprll l t zong bord.

siz o cntr

t insl plns r f a toll o 30 stors.
t cntr wd incl a grocry stor a lrg
dscount cntr n 28 otr Sps. t cntr wd
cntan l h t sqr fel o flor spac n
3 h t sqr fel o prkg spac.

crclr o cnlr

a Spg vlg

   t cnlr s dsind s a Spg vlg w
Nnl brk wkwas. l wd nl b a slrp
Spg cnlr w prk g onl n frnl o t
ndvdul slors. al Sps wd b sluald
l lesl 2 h fel fm t sl n adql of sl
prkg wd b pvdd.

cmun l slndrds

   t bld gs wd cnfm l cmun l slndrds
o slyl n slrclr n prfSl lndscap g wd
b an nlgrl prl o t cnlr. l wd b dsind
f t cnv n njoym o t rsdnls o t
cmun l.

         drang

   t drang n t area s cnsd abv avrg.
l crnr o t prposd cnlr s wn lt fel

(continued)

o a crnl fld plan. (cly o L, 1985, 842) hwev nn o t area h ev hd ny serus wlr dmg.

lrfc n Iprla$ pln

erler tr w sm g s l wtr t cnlr wd creal a lrfc prblm f t nabrhd. bcs nlrncs l t cnlr wd b alowd onl l loca$s spcfid b t sl gvrnm tr $d b no lrfc prblms.
tr s no Iprla$ lrmnl n t vcnl bl 2 bus rouls srv t nabrhd.
t dvrs r amenb l t $rg o cnslrc$ csls o al ncsry sl mpruvms n t imedal area.

nois

bcs no slor wd b locald wn 2 h fel o ny rsl g bldg tr $d b no nois prblm. n ad$ a 10 fl brk fnc wd spral t bk o t cntr fm ajacnl prprly.

    tr wd b no rcreasl fcl ls n t cntr l wd b cmposd o rlal Sps n rstrnls onl.

csl

    t csl o t cntr incl g lnd sil mpruvms n al cnstrc8 wd b n rcs o $50 m. t fnncg wd b tru estrn nSl bnk.

lm fram

sil prpra8

    prpr g t sil C incls cler g t lnd n nsil g wlr gs n drang pips wd lak aprxmll 6 mos.

cnstrc8

    t aclul cnstrc8 wd lak abl 1 yr if no ufsen prblms dv.

(continued)

les g

les g wd bgn wn aclul cnslrc&
cmncs. t pln s l h t cnlr l lesl 75%
lesd wn t frsl bld g s rdy l opn.

cnclu&

if t cnlr s apruvd l l b a majr
ad& l t cly. dur g cnslrc& l l pvd mny
jbs f locl rsdnls. wn t cnlr s cmpd
l l pvd prmnl mplm f m tn 3 h
wkrs. n ad& l l pvd mC nedd srvcs
l t rsdnls o t area. tr r no smlr
fcl ls wn 5 mils.

e h dn evtng n r powr l prlcl t
nabrhd nvirnm. e fel r ac&s l
prclud ny majr prblms tl mil ocr.

if t plns r apruvd s Tmld e l
prced w r plns l cler t lnd n bgn
cnslrc& imedall.

rfrnc

cty o L. cty rgstr. L, PA: main prs, 1985.

DOCUMENT 40
Extended Business Report   **Punctuation Check**

Keyboarding Goal: 25 minutes (28 words per minute)

PROPOSAL FOR SHOPPING CENTER
8000 FIFTH AVENUE
LEXINGTON, PENNSYLVANIA

/The Gilbreth Company, located at 121 Baker Street in Lexington, Pennsylvania, *(extra-geographic)* proposes/to build a shopping center at 8000 Fifth Avenue, which is at the intersection of Fifth Avenue/and Green Street in suburban Lexington. *(extra)* The preliminary plans, which were made by Yale and Associates, *(extra)* are/completed and have been transmitted separately to the zoning board.

Size of Center

The initial plans are/for a total of 30 stores. The center would include a grocery store, a large discount center, and 28/other shops. *(series)* The center would contain 100,000 square feet of floor space and 300,000 square feet/of parking space.

Character of Center

A Shopping Village

The center is designed as a shopping village with/internal brick walkways. It would not be a strip shopping center with parking only in front of the individual/stores. All shops would be situated at least 200 feet from the street, and *(compound sentence)* adequate off-street *(compound adjective)* parking/would be provided.

Community Standards

The buildings would conform to community standards of style and/structure, and *(compound sentence)* professional landscaping would be an integral part of the center. It would be designed for the/convenience and enjoyment of the residents of the community.

Drainage

The drainage in the area is/considered above average. One corner of the proposed center is within 1,000 feet of a current flood/plain. (City of Lexington, 1985, 842) However, *(introductory)* none of the area/has ever had any serious water damage.   (continued)

Traffic and Transportation Plan

Earlier there was some/question as to whether the center would create a traffic problem for the neighborhood. Because entrances to the/center would be allowed only at locations specified by the state government, *(introductory)* there should be no traffic/problems.

There is no transportation terminal in the vicinity, but *(compound sentence)* two bus routes serve the neighborhood.

The/developers are amenable to the sharing of construction costs of all necessary street improvements in the/immediate area.

Noise

Because no store would be located within 200 feet of any/existing building, *(introductory)* there should be no noise problem. In addition, *(introductory)* a ten-foot *(compound adjective)* brick fence would separate the back of/the center from adjacent property.

There would be no recreational facilities in the center; *(no conjunction)* it/would be composed of retail shops and restaurants only.

Cost

The cost of the center, including land, site improvements,/and all construction, *(extra-series)* would be in excess of $50 million. The financing would be through the Eastern/National Bank.

Time Frame

Site Preparation

Preparing the site, which includes clearing the land and installing/water, gas, and drainage pipes, *(extra-series)* would take approximately six months.

Construction

The actual construction would take/about one year if no unforeseen problems develop.

Leasing

Leasing would begin when actual construction/commences. The plan is to have the center at least 75 percent leased when the first building is ready to/open.

Conclusion

If the center is approved, *(introductory)* it will be a major addition to the city. During/construction, *(introductory)* it will provide many jobs for local residents. When the center is completed, *(introductory)* it will provide/permanent employment for more than 300 workers. In addition, *(introductory)* it will provide much-needed *(compound adjective)* services to/the residents of the area. There are no similar facilities within five miles.

We have done everything/in our power to protect the neighborhood environment. We feel our actions will preclude any major/problems that might occur.

If the plans are approved as transmitted, *(introductory)* we will proceed with our plans to clear the land and/begin construction immediately.

REFERENCE

City of Lexington. City Register. Lexington, Pennsylvania:/Main Press, 1985. (706)

SUPPLEMENTARY ACTIVITY

A Word to the Wise

Getting Ready for an Interview

/You will probably be planning for an interview sometime in the near future. When you find a company where/you really want to work, you will want the interview to be excellent. There are a number of things you can do/to prepare for that all-important job interview.

You will have sent your letter of application and personal/data sheet to the company several weeks earlier. If the company does not call you, you may wish/to send a follow-up letter, one in which you give updated or additional information. When you are/called, be ready to go.

Have your clothing cleaned and ready for the interview. Wear clothing that is appropriate/for office wear. Choose neutral colors and a conservative style. Your shoes should be unsoiled. Your hair should be neat and/styled in a becoming way. Do not wear excessive jewelry. A good rule to follow is, "If you have a doubt/about a piece of jewelry, don't wear it."

Be prepared to answer questions concerning your professional goals, both your/immediate goals and your long-term goals. Be ready to handle a question such as "How much money do you wish/to make here?" A noncommittal answer such as, "That is open to discussion" is probably the best type of/response. Be able to present your education, your particular skills, and your experience in a/positive light.

Be able to ask intelligent questions about the company where you are interviewing./ Interviewers often ask, "Is there anything you would like to ask?" No is a very poor answer. There are probably/a number of items about which you would like to have information. Have a few good, thoughtful questions/ready.

In addition, you should practice interviewing. Ask a friend to play the role of the interviewer and go/through a practice interview several times. This will help you to feel more comfortable when the actual/interview takes place.

Give yourself every possible chance. When you find the company where you want to work, make the interview/pay off. (363)

LESSON H

TOWARD PERSONAL SUCCESS

INVESTING FOR THE FUTURE

Over the years you will make many investments for your future. It is important that you plan well and invest properly. There are many types of investments that you can make. Some involve investing money; others involve an investment of time and energy.

You might put money in a savings account, you might purchase stocks, or you might invest in real estate. You might invest in a business of your own, or you might make an investment of time, energy, and money in your education. Think about the different ways you can invest that will pay off for you in the future.

A Savings Account

A savings account at a local bank is one place to invest your money. In the United States most savings accounts are insured by an agency of the federal government up to a stated amount; therefore, this investment is considered safe. You can open a savings account at most banks with a small initial deposit. However, there will probably be a monthly fee if your balance is below a certain level.

The account will not pay much interest, but this is usually satisfactory for a small investment. The amount of interest paid to depositors on regular savings accounts varies from bank to bank; therefore, it is a good idea to shop for the bank that offers the best service and the highest interest.

Savings accounts allow you immediate access to your money, and they do pay interest. Therefore, for small savings, they are often recommended.

Time Deposits

A time deposit or a certificate of deposit at a bank will pay a higher rate of interest than a regular savings account, but you will be obligated to leave your money on deposit for a stated amount of time. Time deposits are also generally considered a safe investment.

The amount of interest paid on time deposits depends on how much money you leave on deposit and how long you leave it there. In general, the more money you deposit and the longer you leave it on deposit, the higher the interest rate. If you should withdraw funds before the stated time, you will usually lose the interest for the period and suffer a penalty as well.

Time deposits are a good way to invest for the future, but you should be sure that you will not need the funds until the stated time.

Investing in the Stock Market

If you wish to invest your money where there is a chance to make an even higher return, you may want to purchase stocks.

When you purchase common stock in a company, you become a part owner of the business. You are actually providing money to help make the company successful. If the company succeeds, the value of your stock will increase. However, if the business suffers a loss, the value of your stock will decrease.

It is essential to remember that there are no guarantees. There is no way to avoid taking a risk when you buy stock. With large, established companies, the risk may be less than with smaller businesses or those that are just getting started. Before you invest in stock, it is a very good idea to know the company very well.

Many people would like to invest in stocks, but they feel that they do not have appropriate information about the various companies to make a good selection. They would prefer to invest a small amount of money in each of many companies. However, the cost of purchasing only a few stocks in many companies could be quite high.

There are companies, however, which will do this work for you. They are investing companies called mutual funds. The manager of a mutual fund will sell shares of the company to a large number of investors. The manager of the fund will then use the money to buy a large number of shares of stock in many different companies. When investors buy stock in a mutual fund, therefore, they are actually investing in a large number of companies.

Mutual funds are extremely popular, of course. They give the investor the ability to buy stock in many companies without making too large an investment and without involving the risk of placing all funds in one company.

The fee to purchase stock in mutual funds varies from fund to fund. Some mutual funds charge a fee when you buy stock. Others charge a fee when you sell. Before investing, anyone should know exactly what fees are charged and when they are collected.

Investing in mutual funds can be a good way for the small investor to purchase stock. However, risk is involved in any investment, including mutual funds. Because the risk is spread over a number of companies, however, mutual funds are considered a relatively safe investment.

A Home

Most people want to own their own home. A house can be a very good investment, and most houses appreciate in value over the years. However, a home usually should be purchased for its value as a place to live rather than as an investment for the future.

However, if you purchase a home as a way of investing for the future, you should be sure that it is of the type of construction that will make it attractive to buyers in the future. In addition, the location of the property is extremely important as a factor is determining whether it will be easy to sell in the future.

Before making a large investment, it is a good idea to find out just what expenses will be involved over the years. In this way, you will be able to determine if your investment is a good one.

A Business of Your Own

Owning a business is a dream shared by many throughout the world. Indeed, it can be a very good investment for the future. However, starting a new business usually requires a large financial investment, and it may take years before it will make enough profit to be considered a sound investment. In addition, running your own business takes a great investment in time and energy.

Being your own boss and working for yourself is a dream many of us share. You can be a successful businessperson if you are willing to make an investment of money, time, and energy.

Your Education

One of the best investments you will ever make is in your education. The cost of going to college, business school, or other type of educational institution can be very high. However, the knowledge and skill you gain will likely repay your investment in a matter of a few years.

Many students who would like to enter specific job fields may not be able to finance their education personally. There are a number of sources of free information concerning scholarships, grants, and loans. The financial-aid office or the guidance counselor at a school will be able to supply you with this invaluable information.

You may be able to get a stipend from a nonprofit agency, which grants scholarships and low-interest loans. You may be able to get a loan through the federal government. You may be successful in getting a grant from a company that gives funds to students who plan to enter specific fields of work. However, it is your own investment of time and energy that will pay off in increased earnings over the years.

Conclusion

Your future will be what you make it. An investment of money, effort, and time will help you to have the things you want and to do the things you want to do in future years.

Discussion

1. What steps have you taken at this time to invest for your future? What steps do you plan to take in the near future?

2. Do you plan to have a savings account in a bank? Why or why not?

3. Do you plan to purchase stocks in individual companies or in mutual funds? Why or why not?

4. Do you consider purchasing a home an investment? Why?

5. Do you think that investing in your education is a good idea? Why?

6. Are you planning to own your own business? What are the advantages and disadvantages as you see them?

Case Study 1—It's in the Bank

Lynda Smith has worked for five years as an administrative assistant, and she has saved money regularly since she began working. She puts a set part of her salary in a savings account each month. Because she began investing with her first check, she never seems to miss the money. At this time, Lynda has more than $10,000 in the bank, and she is very happy. However, she wonders if her money is making enough interest. She has an account that pays 5 percent interest. She believes she might get a better return by investing at least a part of her money in mutual funds. However, she is not willing to take much risk.

Discussion Questions

1. Do you think Lynda should change her investment plan?

2. Where do you believe she should put her money?

3. If she invests in mutual funds, do you think she is taking too great a risk?

4. What recommendations would you give to Lynda at this time?

Case Study 2—Investing in Education

Joe Diaz completed high school two years ago and began work as an assistant manager at a local restaurant. Although he likes his work, he feels that he would rather work as an office manager. He has, therefore, decided to return to a local community college for two years and study management. He knows that he will have to use the funds he has saved in order to finance the two years in which he will be working only a few hours a day. In addition, he is planning to seek scholarship funds and a grant from the government.

Joe's friends at the restaurant do not understand why he would want to go back to school. They feel he will quickly use up the money he has saved, and it will take him a long time to get those funds accumulated again. They also feel that he has no guarantee that he will get an office management job, and even if he does, they do not think it will pay much more than he is making now. But Joe is still planning to further his education.

Discussion Questions

1. Do you feel Joe is doing the right thing to invest in his education at this time?

2. Do you agree with his friends who say he should stay at his current job?

3. What advice would you give Joe? What would you do in this situation?

Activities

1. Go to a local bank and find out what the current interest rate is on savings accounts and certificates of deposit.

2. Get a local newspaper each day for a week and find the financial page. Follow the price of one stock during the week to determine if it is worth more or less at the end of the week.

3. Select a house that is for sale in your city and ask what the selling price is. Determine if you think that an investment of this size would be a good idea for you.

APPENDIX

ADDRESSES FOR TRANSCRIPTION

SuperWrite, VOLUME ONE
PART 2 (LESSONS 21-35)

The addresses for all documents in *Volume One,* Part 2, are included in this list. In addition, addresses are included for all related documents, which appear in the Teacher's Manual.

Lesson 21

Document 21-1

Miss Angela Brown
Brown Office Systems
4200 Broadway
Albuquerque, NM 87503-1324

Related to Document 21-1

Mr. Charles Casey
Casey and Company
500 Main Street
Albuquerque, NM 87509-1442

Document 21-2

Mr. William Beatty
1609 Hancock Avenue
Macon, GA 35667-2312

Related to Document 21-2

Mr. Ronald Casey
Central Cable TV
100 Fourth Avenue
Macon, GA 35669-1102

Document 21-3

Mrs. Emma Bentley
803 - 21st Avenue
Salem, MA 01924-3214

Related to Document 21-3

Mrs. Emma Bentley
803 - 21st Avenue
Salem, MA 01924-3214

Document 21-4

Mr. Lee Lopez
402 North 62nd Street
Detroit, MI 48205-4422

Related to Document 21-4

Mr. Lee Lopez
402 North 62nd Street
Detroit, MI 48205-4422

Lesson 22

Document 22-1

Ms. Maxine Graves
1802 Tenth Avenue
Trenton, NJ 08622-1234

Related to Document 22-1

Mrs. Olga Jones
Eastern Sales Company
900 Elm Park Drive
Columbia, SC 29216-2341

Document 22-2

Micro Supply Company
4200 Central Expressway
Dallas, TX 75205-3342

Related to Document 22-2

Miss Lydia Jenkins
820 First Avenue
Dayton, OH 45355-4182

Document 22-3

Mrs. Carla Hastings
231 Kent Road
Lincoln, NE 68117-4323

Related to Document 22-3

Miss Evelyn Warren
800 - 35th Street
Birmingham, AL 36355-1233

Document 22-4

Mr. N. L. Maxwell
Western Jewelry Corporation
102 Main Street
Seattle, WA 98105-2251

Related to Document 22-4

Mr. Paul D. Henry
Ohio Jewelry Company
3300 Beltway Drive
Cleveland, OH 45266-2233

Lesson 23

Document 23-1

Dr. A. B. Ellis
809 State Boulevard
Portland, OR 97256-1255

Related to Document 23-1

Dr. A. B. Ellis
809 State Boulevard
Portland, OR 97256-1255

Document 23-2

Ms. Olivia Joyce
Bennington Industries
2828 Wellington Drive
Carson, WV 26005-1233

Related to Document 23-2

Mr. Robert D. Anderson
Anderson and Associates
898 Blair Avenue
Carson, WV 26005-1244

Document 23-3

Ms. Martha Strong
Cranford City Council
400 Main Street
Cranford, MO 66123-4213

Related to Document 23-3

Mrs. Virginia Stern
Stern Clothing Shop
82 Broad Street
Cranford, MO 66123-4122

Document 23-4

Central Airlines
826 Central Expressway
Dallas, TX 75226-1255

Related to Document 23-4

Mr. Warren Davidson
809 Third Avenue
Garland, TX 75222-3422

Lesson 24

Document 24-1

Mrs. Madeline Melton
Melton and Associates
9700 Lake Drive
Chicago, IL 62973-4532

Related to Document 24-1

Mrs. Madeline Melton
Melton and Associates
9700 Lake Drive
Chicago, IL 62973-4532

Document 24-2

Mr. Harold Moore
Electronic Publishers, Inc.
5700 Ocean Parkway
Orlando, FL 32822-1254

Related to Document 24-2

Mr. Milton Jenkins
Southern Sales Corporation
2100 South Main
Alexandria, LA 71446-1234

Document 24-3

Mr. James R. Potter
Attorney at Law
200 North Bell Avenue
Wheeling, WV 26303-4321

Related to Document 24-3

Ms. Elizabeth Randall
330 Ridge Drive
Covington, KY 41007-2323

Document 24-4

Miss Rita Jones
583 Central Avenue
Bangor, ME 04422-1277

Related to Document 24-4

Mr. Dwight Green
908 Oak Street
Bangor, ME 04423-1233

Lesson 25

Document 25-1

Mr. Lawrence Leith
1402 Steadman Drive
Tulsa, OK 74202-1124

Related to Document 25-1

Mr. Lawrence Leith
1402 Steadman Drive
Tulsa, OK 74202-1124

Document 25-2

Mrs. Dorothy Ray
1809 Capitol Drive
St. Paul, MN 55123-4223

Related to Document 25-2

Mrs. Melanie Mason
24 Butler Avenue
Newton, MN 54335-1123

Document 25-3

Principal
Central High School
Carson, CO 82331-1232

Related to Document 25-3

Principal
Central High School
Carson, CO 82331-1232

Document 25-4

Ms. Yoko Nozaki
Nozaki Furniture Company
889 Division Street
Little Rock, AR 72330-1432

Related to Document 25-4

Miss Amelia Warren
2399 Brentwood Boulevard
Little Rock, AR 73220-1234

Lesson 26

Document 26-1

Mr. Milton Morgan
Seabrook High School
100 Ocean Drive
Seabrook, FL 32344-1255

Related to Document 26-1

Dr. M. L. Pratt
Central College
4242 Southern Parkway
Lakeland, FL 34523-1234

Document 26-2

East Coast Sales Company
590 Second Street
Memphis, TN 38013-1998

Related to Document 26-2

Ms. Ann North
560 Madison Street
Memphis, TN 38010-1022

Document 26-3

Mrs. Marie Tuttle
41 Baylor Road
Hartford, CT 06124-1442

Related to Document 26-3

Mrs. Marie Tuttle
41 Baylor Road
Hartford, CT 06124-1442

Document 26-4

Miss Natalie Nelson
79 Mercer Road
Princeton, NJ 08622-1431

Related to Document 26-4

Miss Natalie Nelson
79 Mercer Road
Princeton, NJ 08622-1431

Lesson 27

Document 27-1

Mr. John J. Edwards
C. W. Burns Company
5000 Plymouth Way
Chester, MA 01870-1124

Related to Document 27-1

Miss Elizabeth Doyle
East Coast Associates
8001 Bradenton Parkway
Chester, MA 01877-1220

Document 27-2

Ms. Maria Sanchez
Sanchez Enterprises
5050 West 27th Street
Seattle, WA 98202-1144

Related to Document 27-2

Dr. Cynthia Morse
Professor of Business
Western State College
100 Pacific Boulevard
Seattle, WA 98100-1445

Document 27-3

Mr. Kenneth Samuels
The R. J. Jennings Company
234 Broadway
Providence, RI 02887-2114

Related to Document 27-3

Mr. Benjamin Stern, President
Mason Sales Company
Jackson, MS 38802-2131

Document 27-4

Miss Alice Murphy
3200 Commerce Street
Nashville, TN 39133-2121

Related to Document 27-4

Mr. Michael Tyler
400 Main Street
Nashville, TN 39122-1223

Lesson 28

Document 28-1

Mr. Wallace Brice
The Wells Organization
679 Third Avenue
Scranton, PA 18605-2312

Related to Document 28-1

Mr. George Casey, President
Casey and Company
800 Beaumont Street
Scranton, PA 18605-1213

Document 28-2

Miss Natalie Mason
General Manager
Starr Enterprises
200 Elm Street
Los Angeles, CA 90030-2448

Related to Document 28-2

Miss Clara Bennett
Western Sales Corporation
3389 Carter Street
Los Angeles, CA 90330-1289

Document 28-3

Mr. Charles Clark
1093 West Franklin Avenue
Trenton, NJ 08664-1244

Related to Document 28-3

Mr. Charles Clark
1093 West Franklin Avenue
Trenton, NJ 08664-1244

Document 28-4

Dr. Mary Alice Norton
Central Medical Plaza
889 Fifth Avenue
Racine, WI 53340-3349

Related to Document 28-4

Miss Alexandria Pace
Central Medical College
225 Michigan Avenue
Chicago, IL 60680-1234

Lesson 29

Document 29-1

Attention Miss Sandra Taylor
International Publishers
45 Lexington Avenue
Milwaukee, WI 53822-2131

Related to Document 29-1

Attention Mr. James Benson
Western Publishing Company
3397 Lakeside Drive
Spokane, WA 98223-3223

Document 29-2

Dr. Darlene Taylor
Pacific Management Consultants
77 Haven Boulevard
Honolulu, HI 96778-3332

Related to Document 29-2

Attention Dr. Art Hale
Madison College
6600 Shore Drive
Miami, FL 33802-3321

Document 29-3

Attention Mr. C. T. Courtland
Legal Associates
777 Taylor Street
Cedar Rapids, IA 52767-2288

Related to Document 29-3

Attention Mr. Martin Simms
National Insurance Company
339 - 42nd Street
Harrisburg, PA 17669-8778

Document 29-4

Attention Miss Susan Marsh
General Insurance Company
55007 North Keystone Drive
Detroit, MI 48277-3322

Related to Document 29-4

Attention Miss Susan March
General Insurance Company
55007 North Keystone Drive
Detroit, MI 48277-3322

Lesson 30

Document 30-1

Mr. Oliver Van
210 North Beltline Avenue
Baltimore, MD 21103-3322

Related to Document 30-1

Mr. Oliver Van
210 North Beltline Avenue
Baltimore, MD 21103-3322

Document 30-2

Ms. Martha Fuentes
Personnel Consultants, Inc.
505 Trinity Avenue
San Antonio, TX 78790-2211

Related to Document 30-2

Mrs. Stephanie Abbott
Personnel Manager
Southern Industries
1611 Highland Street
San Antonio, TX 78789-1021

Document 30-3

Ms. Janet Gross, Manager
Verybest Industries
887 Southern State Parkway
Knoxville, TN 38212-1243

Related to Document 30-3

Ms. Edyth Moon
Capital Industries
300 Mountain View Road
Santa Fe, NM 87552-1128

Document 30-4

Mr. Sumio Saga
9200 Park Avenue
New York, NY 10092-2231

Related to Document 30-4

Mr. Sumio Saga
9200 Park Avenue
New York, NY 10092-2231

Lesson 31

Document 31-1

To: Mr. Elvin Grider,
    Marketing Department
From: Maria Sanchez,
    Finance Department

Related to Document 31-1

To: Miss Maria Sanchez,
       Finance Department
From: Elvin Grider,
         Marketing Department

Document 31-2

To: Mr. Tom Granger,
       Legal Department
From: Alice Simms,
         Finance Department

Related to Document 31-2

To: Mrs. Alice Simms,
       Finance Department
From: Tom Granger,
         Legal Department

Document 31-3

To: Ms. Grace Stern
From: Paul Moore

Related to Document 31-3

To: Mr. Paul Moore
From: Grace Stern

Document 31-4

To: Mrs. May Edwards
From: Rosa Lopez

Related to Document 31-4

To: Mr. Gary Kent
From: May Edwards

Lesson 32

Document 32-1

Attention Ms. Christine Doran
Organization of Retired Executives
4920 West 42nd Street
Las Vegas, NV 89337-2289

Related to Document 32-1

Mr. George Flynn
345 Main Street
Las Vegas, NV 89336-1212

Document 32-2

To: All Employees
From: Joan Morrison,
         Employee Benefits

Related to Document 32-2

To: Mrs. Joan Morrison,
       Employee Benefits
From: Mildred Carson, Marketing

Document 32-3

Mr. J. T. Ball
239 Macon Court
Clarke, MS 39224-4345

Related to Document 32-3

Attention Mr. C. M. Green
Major Auto Service Center
400 North Main Street
Clarke, MS 39228-2311

Document 32-4

To: Mr. Max Bloom
From: Lila Blake

Related to Document 32-4

To: Miss Lila Blake
From: Max Bloom

Lesson 33

Document 33-1

To: All Employees
From: Amanda Cole,
         Personnel Department

Related to Document 33-1

To: Miss Amanda Cole,
         Personnel Department
From: Mark Green,
         Advertising Department

Document 33-2

To: All Company Employees
From: Harold Cox, President

Related to Document 33-2

To: Mr. William Curtis,
         Personnel Department
From: Mary Bentley,
         Shipping Department

Document 33-3

Attention Mr. Kenneth Taylor
Jenson, Taylor, and Cline
341 Central Avenue
Boise, ID 83707-1234

Related to Document 33-3

Miss Hilda Swenson
890 Mountain View Drive
Missoula, MT 59231-3322

Document 33-4

To: Mr. Carl Lindsey
From: Ann Murphy

Related to Document 33-4

To: Ms. Ann Murphy
From: Carl Lindsey

Lesson 34

Document 34-1

Mr. Wayne Paul
Southern Employment Agency
500 South Main Boulevard
Houston, TX 77000-9988

Related to Document 34-1

To: All Employees
From: Betty Henderson

Document 34-2

To: Mr. Max Peters
From: Jackie Stevens

Related to Document 34-2

To: All Employees
From: Max Peters

Document 34-3

Mr. Louis Mattingly
4992 Bennett Road
Cleveland, OH 44582-8901

Related to Document 34-3

Ms. Maxine Morton
341 Tatum Avenue
Cleveland, OH 44533-1255

Document 34-4

Mr. A. B. Peterson
1400 Riverside Drive
Chicago, IL 63772-8004

Related to Document 34-4

Mr. Clement Johnson
Johnson Tax Services
4309 State Street
Chicago, IL 63889-8991

Lesson 35

Document 35-1

Mrs. Beverley Medlin
3976 Lone Star Drive
Arlington, TX 75799-2321

Related to Document 35-1

To: Mr. Roberto Rodriguez
From: Ethyl Glynn

Document 35-2

To: Ms. Maureen McGee
From: Nathan Cain

Related to Document 35-2

To: Mr. Nathan Cain
From: Maureen McGee

Document 35-3

To: Mrs. Nadine Short
From: Sam Wolfson

Related to Document 35-3

To: Mr. Sam Wolfson
From: Nadine Short

Document 35-4

To: Mr. Mark Peters
From: J. D. Jones

Related to Document 35-4

To: Mr. Nathan Doyle
From: Mark Peters

SPELLING WORDS

Numbers refer to Lesson numbers.

abandon	37	calendar	26
absence	35	campaign	27
accept	25	candidate	31
access	26	catalog	22
accommodate	35	charities	38
accumulate	25	choose	37
acquiring	35	clients	22
adequate	40	community	27
adjacent	40	completing	32
advisory	32	compound interest	35
affirmative	27	confidence	31
already	37	conform	40
although	34	congratulations	24
amenable	40	contingent	33
analyzing	28	copyright	26
appeared	24	copywriter	29
appropriate	28	coupon	32
arrangements	30		
assigned	25	deductible	26
assistance	26	definitely	27
assistants	26	deliberation	35
associates	22	deposit	25
assured	23	discourteous	30
atmosphere	23	dispensed	36
attempt	22	disrepair	23
attorney	24	duration	39
bankruptcy	31	easement	24
banquet	23	eligible	36
beneficiary	33	embarrassing	25
break	29	employees	35
buffet	23	entrepreneurs	32
bulletin	24	equipment	24
burden	39	evaluation	30

Spelling Words by Lesson

Lesson 22
associates
attempt
catalog
clients
excellent
inheritance
liquidate
microcomputer
probate
received

Lesson 23
assured
atmosphere
banquet
buffet
disrepair
interruption
occasionally
peace
postponed
separate

Lesson 24
appeared
attorney
bulletin
congratulations
easement
equipment
library
piece
replacement
retract

Lesson 25
accept
accumulate
assigned
deposit

embarrassing
explanation
financial
percentage
restaurant
specified

Lesson 26
access
assistance
assistants
calendar
copyright
deductible
registration
software
sponsored
useful

Lesson 27
affirmative
campaign
community
definitely
expertise
integrity
occupancy
prospective
reception
soliciting

Lesson 28
analyzing
appropriate
imperative
liability
management
mandatory
mentioned
retention
retirement
sensible

Lesson 29
break
copywriter
exceeding
invaluable
precede
principal
resumé
sustained
touch
vehicle

Lesson 30
arrangements
discourteous
evaluation
former
insolvent
oversight
personnel
simulator
techniques
viable

Lesson 31
bankruptcy
candidate
confidence
exemplary
financier
foreclose
oversee
recourse
unforeseen
vacated

Lesson 32
advisory
completing
coupon
entrepreneurs
informal
innovative

lubrication
questionnaire
rotated
tune-up

Lesson 33
beneficiary
contingent
impatient
maximum
perturbed
projections
rejection
resolved
revision
tender

Lesson 34
although
excessive
exciting
hinder
incurring
lengthy
manual
professional
profitable
recommended

Lesson 35
absence
accommodate
acquiring
compound interest
deliberation
employees
expedite
impede
repeatedly
transferred

Lesson 36
dispensed
eligible
generic
maintenance
pharmacy
physician
portfolio
reimbursed
spouse
underwritten

Lesson 37
abandon
already
choose
function key
initiate
opening menu
prompt
screen
scrolling
stacks

Lesson 38
charities
eventuality
indefinitely
intestate
jurisdiction

levied
livelihood
nonprofit
possessions
priority

Lesson 39
burden
duration
expedient
impractical
incumbent
queue
rectify
severity
time-consuming
tremendously

Lesson 40
adequate
adjacent
amenable
conform
integral
plain
preclude
site
transmitted
zoning

VOCABULARY WORDS

Numbers refer to Lesson numbers.

Vocabulary Words by Lesson

Lesson 26
access
deductible
pre-existing
prior
public domain

Lesson 27
expertise
integrity
peers
seminar
soliciting

Lesson 28
formal
imperative
liability insurance
mandatory
retention

Lesson 29
exceeding
precede
principal
resumé
sustained

Lesson 30
former
insolvent
personnel
simulator
viable

Lesson 31
bankruptcy
exemplary
financier
foreclose
vacated

Lesson 32
associate's degree
entrepreneurs
informal
innovative
rotated

Lesson 33
beneficiary
contingent
perturbed
resolved
tender

Lesson 34
excessive
fiscal
incurring
profit margin
tax audit

Lesson 35
certificate of deposit
compound interest
deliberation
expedite
impede

Lesson 36
dispensed
generic
reimbursed
spouse
underwritten

Lesson 37
function key
initiate
opening menu
prompt
stacks

Lesson 38
eventuality
inheritance tax
intestate
jurisdiction
levied

Lesson 39
duration
expedient
incumbent

queue
rectify

Lesson 40
adjacent
amenable
flood plain
integral
preclude

ABBREVIATIONS

STATE, DISTRICT, AND TERRITORY ABBREVIATIONS

Alabama	*AL*	Indiana	*IN*
Alaska	*AK*	Iowa	*IA*
Arizona	*AZ*	Kansas	*KS*
Arkansas	*AR*	Kentucky	*KY*
California	*CA*	Louisiana	*LA*
Colorado	*CO*	Maine	*ME*
Connecticut	*CT*	Maryland	*MD*
Delaware	*DE*	Massachusetts	*MA*
District of Columbia	*DC*	Michigan	*MI*
Florida	*FL*	Minnesota	*MN*
Georgia	*GA*	Mississippi	*MS*
Guam	*GU*	Missouri	*MO*
Hawaii	*HI*	Montana	*MT*
Idaho	*ID*	Nebraska	*NE*
Illinois	*IL*	Nevada	*NV*

New Hampshire	*NH*	South Carolina	*SC*
New Jersey	*NJ*	South Dakota	*SD*
New Mexico	*NM*	Tennessee	*TN*
New York	*NY*	Texas	*TX*
North Carolina	*NC*	Utah	*UT*
North Dakota	*ND*	Vermont	*VT*
Ohio	*OH*	Virgin Islands	*VI*
Oklahoma	*OK*	Virginia	*VA*
Oregon	*OR*	Washington	*WA*
Pennsylvania	*PA*	West Virginia	*WV*
Puerto Rico	*PR*	Wisconsin	*WI*
Rhode Island	*RI*	Wyoming	*WY*

SuperWrite ABBREVIATIONS BY LESSON

Lesson 1

you, your	*u*
will	*l*
as, is	*s*

Lesson 2

are, or, our	*r*
can	*c*
for	*f*

Lesson 3

at, it, to	*t*
has, have	*h*
very	*v*
do	*d*

Lesson 4

we	*e*
which	*C*
soon	*sn*

Lesson 5

the	*t*
and, in	*n*

Lesson 6

am, more	*m*
be, been, by	*b*
month	*mo*

Lesson 7

from	*fm*
of	*o*
year	*yr*
let	*le*

Lesson 8

after	*aft*
business	*bus*
company	*co*
responsible	*rsp*

Lesson 9

was, were, with	*w*
importance, important	*imp*
department	*dept*
week, work	*wk*
employ	*mpl*

Lesson 10

how	*hw*
out	*ot*
require	*rqr*
they	*ty*

Lesson 11

appreciate	*ap*
please	*pl*
enclose	*enc*
thank	*tk*
provide	*pvd*

Lesson 12

ever, every	*ev*
about	*abt*
complete	*cmp*
interest	*int*

Lesson 13

include	*incl*
information	*info*
program	*pgm*
consider, consideration	*cns*

Lesson 14

any	*ny*
executive	*exec*
insurance	*ins*
hour	*hr*
present	*pr*
time	*tm*

Lesson 15

suggest, suggestion	*sg*
manager	*mgr*
management	*mgl*
report	*rpl*

Lesson 16

order	*od*
amount	*aml*
state, street	*sl*
receive	*rec*
number	*no*
letter	*lr*

Lesson 17

| available | *av* |

[Lesson 17 continued]

organization, organize	*org*
paid	*pd*
represent, representative	*rep*

Lesson 18

question	*q*
regard	*rgd*
cover	*cv*

Lesson 19

| avenue | *ave* |
| convenience, convenient | *cnv* |

Lesson 20

| application, apply | *apl* |
| develop | *dv* |

SuperWrite ABBREVIATIONS ALPHABETICAL LIST

Numbers refer to Lesson numbers.

about	12	for	2
after	8	from	7
am, more	6		
amount	16	has, have	3
and, in	5	have, has	3
any	14	hour	14
application, apply	20	how	10
apply, application	20		
appreciate	11	importance, important	9
are, or, our	2	important, importance	9
as, is	1	in, and	5
at, it, to	3	include	13
available	17	information	13
avenue	19	insurance	14
		interest	12
be, been, by	6	is, as	1
been, be, by	6	it, at, to	3
business	8		
by, be, been	6	let	7
		letter	16
can	2	management	15
company	8	manager	15
complete	12	month	6
convenience, convenient	19	more, am	6
convenient, convenience	19		
consider, consideration	13	number	16
consideration, consider	13		
cover	18	of	7
		or, are, our	2
department	9	order	16
develop	20	organization, organize	17
do	3	organize, organization	17
		our, are, or	2
employ	9	out	10
enclose	11		
ever, every	12	paid	17
every, ever	12	please	11
executive	14	present	14

program	13	time	14
provide	11	to, at, it	3
question	18	very	3
receive	16	was, were, with	9
regard	18	we	4
report	15	week, work	9
represent, representative	17	were, was, with	9
representative, represent	17	which	4
require	10	will	1
responsible	8	with, was, were	9
		work, week	9
soon	4		
state, street	16	year	7
street, state	16	you, your	1
suggest, suggestion	15	your, you	1
suggestion, suggest	15		
thank	11		
the	5		
they	10		

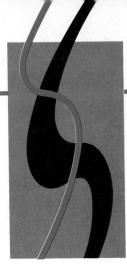

THEORY

ALPHABETICAL LIST

Principle	Lesson	Abbreviation
be-	6	b
-ble	8	b
ch	4	C
de-	6	d
em-	9	m
en-	6	n
enter-	12	N
-eous	19	us
ex-	14	x
for-	11	f
fore-	11	f
-ful	12	f
fur-	11	f
im-	9	m
in-	6	n
inter-	12	N
-ing	4	disjoined g
-ious	19	us
-ity	10	disjoined t
-ly	7	l
mem	19	m
-ment	8	m
oi	9	oi
ou	7	ou
-ous	19	us
over-	15	O
ow	7	ow
oy	9	oy
-pal	17	p
-ple	17	p
pre-	13	pr
pro-	13	pr

qu	10	q
re-	6	r
-s	4	s
sb	4	S
t	2	uncrossed t
tb	5	crossed t
-tion	7	S
trans-	15	T
un-	13	u
under-	16	U
-us	19	us

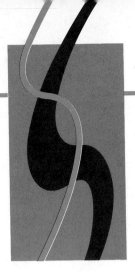

INDEX OF SuperWrite PRINCIPLES

Numbers refer to Lesson numbers

Word Endings

TRANSCRIPTION INDEX

Numbers refer to Lesson numbers.

Keyboarding Style

Punctuation